Praise for
The Heretics of Finance
Conversations with Leading Practitioners of Technical Analysis
by Andrew W. Lo and Jasmina Hasanhodzic

"*The Heretics of Finance* is a fascinating view of the art and craft of technical analysis. For finance professionals and academics alike, this book is an excellent introduction to what technical analysts do and why it may make sense in modern markets. An enjoyable and very enlightening book."

> —Maureen O'Hara
> Robert W. Purcell Professor of Finance
> The Johnson School, Cornell University

"Technical trading is ubiquitous in financial markets, which might explain some major financial-market anomalies and makes it an important topic for research. Like good scientists, Lo and Hasanhodzic explore this territory by gathering first-hand observations, with fascinating results."

> —Carol Osler
> Program Director, Lemberg Masters in
> International Economics and Finance
> Brandeis International Business School, Brandeis University

"In the last twenty years, academics have piled up evidence on the puzzling success of technical analysis, yet few researchers are very familiar with the thinking of technicians. Lo's and Hasanhodzic's interviews with well-known technicians illuminate their thinking on the markets and their profession. *The Heretics of Finance* is a must-read for economists studying technical analysis, behavioral finance, or related market anomalies. I recommend it highly."

> —Christopher J. Neely, PhD

THE
HERETICS
OF FINANCE

Related titles also available from Bloomberg Press

Breakthroughs in Technical Analysis
edited by David Keller

New Insights on Covered Call Writing
by Richard Lehman and Lawrence G. McMillan

New Thinking in Technical Analysis
edited by Rick Bensignor

Option Spread Strategies
by Anthony J. Saliba with Joseph C. Corona and Karen E. Johnson

Option Strategies for Directionless Markets
by Anthony J. Saliba with Joseph C. Corona and Karen E. Johnson

Technical Analysis Tools
by Mark Tinghino

Trading ETFs
by Deron Wagner

Trading Option Greeks
by Dan Passarelli

A complete list of our titles is available
at **www.bloomberg.com/books**.

THE HERETICS OF FINANCE

Conversations with Leading Practitioners of Technical Analysis

Andrew W. Lo

and

Jasmina Hasanhodzic

BLOOMBERG PRESS
NEW YORK

BLOOMBERG, BLOOMBERG ANYWHERE, BLOOMBERG.COM, BLOOMBERG MARKET ESSENTIALS, *Bloomberg Markets,* BLOOMBERG NEWS, BLOOMBERG PRESS, BLOOMBERG PROFESSIONAL, BLOOMBERG RADIO, BLOOMBERG TELEVISION, and BLOOMBERG TRADEBOOK are trademarks and service marks of Bloomberg Finance L.P. ("BFLP"), a Delaware limited partnership, or its subsidiaries. The BLOOMBERG PROFESSIONAL service (the "BPS") is owned and distributed locally by BFLP and its subsidiaries in all jurisdictions other than Argentina, Bermuda, China, India, Japan, and Korea (the "BLP Countries"). BFLP is a wholly-owned subsidiary of Bloomberg L.P. ("BLP"). BLP provides BFLP with all global marketing and operational support and service for these products and distributes the BPS either directly or through a non-BFLP subsidiary in the BLP Countries. All rights reserved.

This publication contains the authors' opinions and is designed to provide accurate and authoritative information. It is sold with the understanding that the authors, publisher, and Bloomberg L.P. are not engaged in rendering legal, accounting, investment-planning, or other professional advice. The reader should seek the services of a qualified professional for such advice; the authors, publisher, and Bloomberg L.P. cannot be held responsible for any loss incurred as a result of specific investments or planning decisions made by the reader.

First edition published 2009

3 5 7 9 10 8 6 4 2

Library of Congress Cataloging-in-Publication Data

Lo, Andrew W. (Andrew Wen-Chuan)
   The heretics of finance : conversations with leading practitioners of technical analysis / Andrew W. Lo and Jasmina Hasanhodzic.--1st ed.
      p. cm.
   Includes bibliographical references and index.
   Summary: "An exploration of the evolution and practice of technical analysis with thirteen of the industry's top practitioners"--Provided by publisher.
ISBN 978-1-57660-316-1 (alk. paper)
1. Investment advisors. 2. Investment analysis. I. Hasanhodzic, Jasmina. II. Title.

HG4621.L52 2009
332.63'2042--dc22

2008041629

Edited by Mary Ann McGuigan

*To Mike Epstein, a tireless and eloquent champion
of technical analysis, who gave this project life
and supported us every step of the way*

Contents

Acknowledgments

This book is the culmination of countless discussions and debates between us and with various colleagues over the years regarding the pros and cons of technical analysis in theory and in practice. Therefore, we have accumulated a long list of intellectual debts that may never be repaid but which we would like to acknowledge.

First and foremost, we thank Mike Epstein for his boundless energy and enthusiasm for technical analysis and for making this project possible. A number of the technicians interviewed in this volume would probably not have agreed to speak with us if it weren't for introductions from Mike. All the faculty, students, and staff at the MIT Laboratory for Financial Engineering have benefited tremendously from Mike's willingness to share his remarkable store of knowledge with us over the years, and we treasure not only his expertise but also his kindness and positive outlook on the markets and, more generally, on life. This book is dedicated to him.

We also thank the interview subjects: Ralph Acampora, Laszlo Birinyi, Walter Deemer, Paul Desmond, Gail Dudack, Robert Farrell, Ian McAvity, John Murphy, Bob Prechter, Linda Raschke, Alan Shaw, Tony Tabell, and Stan Weinstein. They are the main attraction of this volume and were extraordinarily generous with their time and knowledge. In addition, many of them opened their homes and their hearts to us, and we are humbled by their gracious hospitality. We hope we have captured in these interviews at least a portion of the creativity and genius with which they practice their craft.

The Market Technicians Association (MTA) has also been very supportive of our various initiatives, and a number of its founders and senior officers have become friends as well as professional colleagues over the years. We hope that this collection of interviews

Acknowledgments

will further the MTA's mission of making technical analysis more accessible to the broader financial community.

We also wish to acknowledge a small but growing number of academic colleagues who share our fascination with technical analysis, despite the potentially negative consequences that such unseemly interests might yield from the academic community. In particular, we thank Buzz Brock, David Brown, Kevin Chang, Bob Dittmar, Bob Ferguson, Bob Jennings, Blake LeBaron, Harry Mamaysky, Chris Neely, Carol Osler, Stephen Pruitt, Jack Treynor, Jiang Wang, Paul Weller, and Richard White for their open-mindedness and inspirational research on technical analysis in the face of enormous academic skepticism.

Finally, we wish to thank a number of individuals for making this book a reality: Seth Ditchik for introducing us to Bloomberg Press, Sophia Efthimiatou and Jared Kieling for signing us with Bloomberg Press, Mary Ann McGuigan and the rest of the staff at Bloomberg Press for terrific editorial support, and Svetlana Sussman for general administrative and moral support. The high production quality of this book is a direct reflection of their hard work and dedication to this project.

Introduction

How did two technical-analysis dilettantes—steeped in the theory of efficient markets, the random walk hypothesis, and all the other tenets of quantitative finance—end up interviewing fourteen leading technical analysts about their trade? To answer that, we must begin with a disclaimer: we are not practicing technical analysts, or "technicians," as professionals prefer to be called. To those who are familiar either with our research or with technical analysis, this will come as no surprise. But our fascination with the craft and culture of technical analysis, especially as it contrasts with quantitative analysis, has led us down a path of discovery and delight. We have had the pleasure and privilege of meeting with some of the most talented, and the most gracious and decent, individuals in the business.[1] And we have learned a great deal indeed about technical analysis, as it is practiced by the pros.

But how did our paths with these professionals finally cross? After all, technicians do not frequent the halls of academia, nor do they usually consort with finance professors or their students. This separation is understandable, given the disdain and disrespect most academics have for charting, which has been characterized by more than one academic with the following analogy: technical analysis is to financial analysis as astrology is to astronomy. Technicians have, on occasion, made use of astrological signs (see, for example, Weingarten, 1996), a practice which does not help their case.

Despite these misgivings, a number of intrepid academics have studied technical analysis in earnest, some because of prurient curiosity, and others because they realized that the random walk hypothesis is not always consistent with financial data. These studies have come to several interesting conclusions regarding the benefits and pitfalls of technical analysis.[2]

◈ The Death of the Random Walk

Our own initiation into this nether world of practical prognostication began two decades ago when one of us coauthored a paper in which the random walk hypothesis—the notion that past prices cannot be used to forecast future price changes—was resoundingly rejected for weekly U.S. stock returns (see Lo and MacKinlay, 1988). The significance of the random walk hypothesis for technical analysis cannot be overemphasized—the former implies the irrelevance of the latter. If prices follow random walks, then past prices cannot be used to forecast future prices, hence geometric patterns in historical prices contain no useful information for the future. And in 1985, when the research program for that paper began, the random walk hypothesis was still considered gospel truth by the high priests of academic finance. In fact, a number of well-known empirical studies had long since established that markets were "weak-form efficient," in Roberts's (1967) terminology, implying that past prices could not be used to forecast future price changes.[3] And although some of these studies did find evidence against the random walk, for example, Cowles and Jones (1937), they were largely dismissed as statistical anomalies or not economically meaningful after accounting for transactions costs, for example, Cowles (1960). For example, after conducting an extensive empirical analysis of the "runs" of U.S. stock returns from 1956 to 1962, Fama (1965) concluded that ". . . there is no evidence of important dependence from either an investment or a statistical point of view."

It was in this milieu that we (Lo and MacKinlay) decided to revisit the random walk hypothesis. Previous studies had been unable to reject the random walk, hence we surmised that perhaps a more sensitive statistical test was needed, one capable of detecting small but significant departures from pure randomness. In the jargon of statistical inference, we hoped to develop a more "powerful" test, a test that had a higher probability of rejecting the random walk hypothesis if it was indeed false. In retrospect, our more stringent test was quite unnecessary. The overwhelming rejections of the random walk hypothesis obtained for weekly U.S. stock returns from 1962 to 1985 implied that a more powerful test was not needed—the random walk could have been rejected on the basis of the first-order autocorrelation coefficient, which we estimated to be 30 percent for the equal-weighted weekly returns index! Taken completely by surprise, we carefully rechecked our programs several times for coding errors before debuting these results in a November 1986 conference. How could such compelling evidence against the random walk be overlooked by the vast literature that all finance graduate students are fed?

This puzzling state of affairs caused us (Lo and MacKinlay) to launch a series of investigations to reconcile what we, and many other academics, viewed as a sharp contradiction between our statistical inferences and the voluminous literature that came before us. These follow-on studies are contained in Lo and MacKinlay (1999), and at the end of this long sequence of painstaking investigations— including checking the accuracy of our statistical methods, quantifying the potential biases introduced by nonsynchronous prices, investigating the sources of the rejections of the random walk and tracing them to large positive cross-autocorrelations and lead/lag effects, and considering statistical fractals as an alternative to the random walk—we concluded that "Despite our best efforts, we were unable to explain away the evidence against the random walk hypothesis."

These scientific findings provided the impetus for a more systematic investigation of the efficacy of technical analysis and cleared the path that led to this collection of interviews.

◈ Cultural Biases

Apart from opening the door for technical analysis and other price-based forecasting models, the findings in Lo and MacKinlay (1999) had as much to say about the kinds of cultural biases that academics suffer from: "With the benefit of hindsight and a more thorough review of the literature, we have come to the conclusion that the apparent inconsistency between the broad support for the random walk hypothesis and our empirical findings is largely due to the common misconception that the random walk hypothesis is equivalent to the efficient markets hypothesis, and the near religious devotion of economists to the latter . . . Once we saw that we, and our colleagues, had been trained to study the data through the filtered lenses of classical market efficiency, it became clear that the problem lay not with our empirical analysis, but with the economic implications that others incorrectly attributed to our results—unbounded profit opportunities, irrational investors, and the like . . . We were all in a collective fog regarding the validity of the random walk hypothesis, but as we confronted the empirical evidence from every angle and began to rule out other explanations, slowly the fog lifted for us."

But we were not the first to comment on the cultural bias of finance academics. *The Education of a Speculator,* Victor Niederhoffer's entertaining and irreverent autobiography, sheds some light on the kinds of forces at work in creating such biases. In describing the random walk hypothesis as it developed at the University of Chicago in the 1960s, he writes (see Niederhoffer, 1997, p. 270):

> This theory and the attitude of its adherents found classic expression in one incident I personally observed that deserves memorialization. A team of four of the most respected graduate students in finance had joined forces with two professors, now considered venerable enough to have won or to have been considered for a Nobel Prize, but at that time feisty as hades and insecure as a kid on his first date. This elite group was studying the possible impact of volume on stock price movements, a subject I had researched. As I was coming down the steps from the library on the third floor of Haskell Hall, the main business building, I could see this group of six gathered together on a stairway landing, examining some computer output. Their voices wafted up to me, echoing off the stone walls of the building. One of the students was pointing to some output while querying the professors, "Well, what if we really do find something? We'll be up the creek. It won't be consistent with the random walk model." The younger professor replied, "Don't worry, we'll cross that bridge in the unlikely event we come to it."
>
> I could hardly believe my ears—here were six scientists openly hoping to find no departures from ignorance. I couldn't hold my tongue, and blurted out, "I sure am glad you are all keeping an open mind about your research." I could hardly refrain from grinning as I walked past them. I heard muttered imprecations in response.

The same kind of cultural bias can explain the current opposition to and skepticism about technical analysis, but with a key difference. There is a fairly wide *linguistic* gap between technicians and the rest of the world. To say that technical analysts are misunderstood is an understatement—many are not understood at all because they speak in a foreign tongue. To appreciate this communications

Introduction

barrier, consider the following statement that might be found in a typical technician's newsletter:

> The presence of clearly identified support and resistance levels, coupled with a one-third retracement parameter when prices lie between them, suggests the presence of strong buying and selling opportunities in the near term.

For most quantitatively trained academics and investment professionals, this statement carries little meaning and may be mildly entertaining to such an audience because it is so alien. Contrast the above with the following statement which might be found in an academic finance journal publication:

> The magnitudes and decay pattern of the first twelve autocorrelations and the statistical significance of the Box-Pierce Q-statistic suggest the presence of a high-frequency predictable component in stock returns.

Both statements are, in fact, saying the same thing: using historical prices, one can predict future prices to some extent in the short run. But because the two statements are so laden with jargon, the type of response they elicit depends very much on the individual reading them. To be sure, implicit in both statements are procedures for exploiting predictability that do differ considerably. However, because the semantic differences are so great, the authors of the two statements will probably never see how they might both have benefited from each other's insights.

These two hypothetical statements are, of course, oversimplifications of the kinds of tools and logics used by both academics and technicians, but they do illustrate what we consider to be the primary challenge in bringing technical analysts and academics together: finding a common language to exchange ideas. This is the second motivation for these interviews: we hope that allowing leading technical analysts to speak for themselves, but within the structure of interview questions designed by two outsiders with an admittedly strong quantitative bias, might catalyze the interactions between academics and technicians to the benefit of both communities. For example, the technical analyst might find that recent advances in statistical inference can help to identify spurious patterns in the data that occur simply by chance, reducing the number of "false positives" he falls prey to and increasing the overall accuracy of his forecasts. Similarly, the financial economist might find that technical trading rules contain good approximations of statistical inference for highly complex nonlinear systems and that relatively simple geometric patterns in historical prices can parsimoniously mimic otherwise intractable models of economic equilibrium.

❖ Automating Technical Analysis

The final motivator that led us to this volume is the academic study (Lo, Mamaysky, and Wang, 2000) that provided a detailed statistical analysis of the content in ten technical patterns ranging from head and shoulders to double bottoms, using a large collection of individual U.S. stock returns over a thirty-year period. In formulating the experimental design, we (Lo, Mamaysky, and Wang) acknowledged that we were not practicing technicians and did not have ready access to a team of technical analysts who could identify patterns in the historical record for the purposes of our academic study. Therefore, we proposed a novel method for "automating" technical analysis—developing a simple mathematical description for each type of pattern that can then be encoded in software and applied to large amounts of data. For example, a head-and-shoulders formation can be defined as a sequence of prices with three local maxima separated by two local minima, where the maxima are approximately the same height, the minima are also approximately the same height, and where the height of the maxima exceeds the height of the minima (so that the "neckline" is properly defined).

Armed with these definitions and a particularly flexible method for estimating nonlinear curves (nonparametric kernel regression), we were able to automate the otherwise tedious and time-consuming process of identifying every occurrence of each of the ten patterns for one hundred stocks over a thirty-five-year period. Then we proceeded to ask the following simple statistical question: do postpattern stock returns behave any differently from stock returns drawn randomly? If so, then patterns like the head-and-shoulders formation do provide incremental information about future stock returns; if not, then such patterns are merely random noise that tells us nothing about the future.

The findings were striking. NYSE stocks exhibited mixed results, with some statistically significant patterns among the ten, but a number of insignificant ones as well. However, the Nasdaq stocks told a different story: every one of the ten patterns was statistically significant, implying that all ten technical indicators contained incremental information about future returns. While "incremental information" does not necessarily imply that technical analysis can be used to generate profitable trading strategies—as most technicians would argue—these findings do raise the possibility that technical indicators can add value to the investment process. We concluded by raising an intriguing possibility:

> . . . [O]ur methods suggest that technical analysis can be improved by using automated algorithms such as ours, and that traditional patterns such as head and shoulders and rectangles, while sometimes effective, need not be optimal. In particular, it may be possible to determine "optimal patterns" for detecting certain types of phenomena in financial time series, for example, an optimal shape for detecting stochastic volatility or changes in regime. Moreover, patterns that are optimal for detecting statistical anomalies need not be optimal for trading profits, and vice versa. Such considerations may lead to an entirely new branch of technical analysis, one based on selecting pattern recognition algorithms to optimize specific objective functions.

To understand how this new branch of technical analysis might emerge, we must go back to the ultimate sources of inspiration, motivation, and innovation. This is why we undertook the challenge of interviewing leading technicians about their craft.

◈ What Did We Learn from the Interviews?

All the technicians we interviewed came across as highly intelligent, rational, and open-minded individuals, with a deep understanding of the markets. Highlighting the unconventional is hardly the best way for technicians to have their voices heard in the markets, although many of the most successful of them are well aware that much of the prejudice against them can be countered by careful communication of their ideas and avoidance of the technical jargon.

Most of the technicians we interviewed agree that their practice of technical analysis is based on intuition 10 to 50 percent of the

Introduction

time. Though Laszlo Birinyi, for one, argues that his decision making is for the most part automated, with intuition playing a minimal role, their practice of the craft seems largely intuitive. Judgment plays a role in deciding how exactly to design one's models and which ingredients to use. In John Murphy's words, "It's not so much a particular indicator, it's how you put it all together that matters," and the most successful at this synthesis are those who, through experience, have gained perceptive insight into how the economy and the markets function.

Several of the technicians argue that the ability to successfully integrate all the pieces of information that go into price analysis cannot easily be taught. As Murphy puts it, "I'm not sure I could explain to you how I do what I do. I look at many things in a short interval of time and come to a conclusion." That elusive skill may explain why these practitioners do not have a problem with sharing their knowledge, the tools they develop, or the strategies they pioneer. There is no single right way to put it all together. Everyone does it in slightly and sometimes widely different ways. In fact, some technicians operate best in complete isolation from the outside world—Linda Raschke, who does not watch television or read the *Wall Street Journal*, is a prime example. Others prefer to complement their technical perspectives with fundamental, economic, and political ones. Certainly, each of them starts from a very different place, and the differences in personality types among successful traders (Raschke, Weinstein), educators (Murphy, Acampora), long-term investors (Desmond, Deemer), artist technicians (McAvity), highly eclectic technicians (Dudack), historians (Shaw, Acampora), long-term market theme writers (Farrell), and those who insist on being labeled market analysts rather than technical analysts (Farrell, Birinyi) are striking, and emerge clearly from the substance and tone of the interviews.

These observations illustrate the striking heterogeneity among leading technicians, and also yield a potential explanation for the lack of impact that technical analysis has had on the broader financial community. Without a unified, standardized, and broadly recognized body of knowledge in which every practicing technician must be conversant, it is difficult to see how technical analysis can spread. The advent of the Chartered Market Technician (CMT) Program by the Market Technicians Association (MTA) is a step in

Introduction

the right direction, but as our interview subjects underscore, there is still a considerable amount of art and subjectivity in the practice of technical analysis. For example, their responses to the question "Does the lack of hard-and-fast rules in technical analysis ever bother you?" varied from "That's exactly what bothers me" to "But there *are* hard-and-fast rules in technical analysis." On this particular issue, the answer we got depended on how the individual interpreted the question—although certain rules can indeed be taught, the synthesis of rules and the interpretation of the results are based on practitioners' own experiences and perceptions, and hence are not hard-and-fast. Consequently, if technical analysis continues to be practiced the way it is practiced today, it will be a long time before quantitative algorithms become sophisticated enough to replace a human technical analyst. "This is still a human game," says Farrell.

As Alan Shaw points out, good practitioners are asking the right questions while not necessarily providing any answers. How do they know what the right questions are? They look to history. Perceptive technicians who have lived through or at least studied previous bull and bear markets are able to discern connections between the current phenomenon and the precedent. Since history tends to repeat itself, this enables them to focus their thinking in the right direction. Academics attempting to dissect and systematize technical analysis have their work cut out for them.

The technicians we interviewed were clearly frustrated that their craft is not more widely recognized by the institutional and academic establishments. John Murphy's and Paul Desmond's candid admission of their disappointment over the widely perceived inferiority of technical analysis to other forms of financial analysis, Ralph Acampora's efforts to gain wider acceptance of MTA-administered certifications, Robert Farrell's and Laszlo Birinyi's refusal to be labeled "technicians," and Birinyi's publication of the pamphlet titled *The Failure of Technical Analysis* are just a few telltale signs of their displeasure with the aura of skepticism attached to their field. Indeed, the very fact that these successful practitioners willingly spent three hours of their precious time being interviewed by us demonstrates their desire to be heard.

Contrary to the tendency to deny their displeasure at the widespread suspicion with which their craft is viewed, the practitioners we spoke to openly voiced their concern with what they see as the academic world's "reinvention," via behavioral finance, of technical analysis. In many instances, academic definitions and technical practices closely mimic each other. For example, the *representativeness heuristic* of Tversky and Kahneman (1974) echoes the technicians' emphasis on drawing on the historical phenomena to understand the current ones.[4] However, while critical of work that tries to "reinvent the wheel," technical analysts support the research efforts that take active interest in what they do and which they hope will earn the field the respect they consider long overdue.

◈ A New Beginning

Since we are only now beginning to explore the many aspects of technical analysis that may be relevant for our academic research agenda, we cannot yet say what kind of common language will emerge between academics and technicians. However, we hope these interviews and our ongoing work contribute to the development of such a language. We have no doubt that by pooling their respective bodies of knowledge and by reconciling their seemingly antipodal modes of inference and discovery, both the academic and the technician can profit enormously.

For too long, academics have ignored technical analysis, and technicians have ignored the discipline and structure of rigorous scientific inquiry. But, as Shakespeare wrote, "The fault . . . lies not in our stars, but in ourselves . . ." Although it may be too much to ask of our academic colleagues to start studying astrological signs, just as it may be too much to ask of technicians to start proving theorems, we do think that the stars are aligned for more meaningful dialogue between the two communities, and we hope these interviews will serve as a starting point.

◈ Notes

1. The interviews in this volume were conducted throughout 2004 and in the first half of 2005, so the references to current events made by the interviewees should be interpreted in that context.
2. Examples include Treynor and Ferguson (1985), Pruitt and White (1988), Neftci (1991), Pau (1991), Brock, Lakonishok, and LeBaron

(1992), Neely, Weller, and Dittmar (1997), Neely and Weller (1998), Chang and Osler (1994), Taylor (1994), Osler and Chang (1995), Allen and Karjalainen (1999), and Lo, Mamaysky, and Wang (2000).

3. See, for example, Cowles and Jones (1937), Kendall (1953), Osborne (1959, 1962), Roberts (1959, 1967), Larson (1960), Cowles (1960), Working (1960), Alexander (1961, 1964), Granger and Morgenstern (1963), Mandelbrot (1963), Fama (1965), and Fama and Blume (1966).

4. Indeed, each and every participant emphasized the importance of studying the history of the markets. Laszlo Birinyi even goes to the extent of collecting and analyzing major newspaper articles that appeared over the last seventy years.

1

Ralph J. Acampora

When you're practicing technical analysis, you have to be totally eclectic, because there will be a time when the approach you're using doesn't work. If you're not flexible, you'll self-destruct.

———◦∽⊙∾◦———

With forty years of experience, Ralph J. Acampora has been instrumental in the development of modern-day technical analysis. He is the New York Institute of Finance's (NYIF) director of technical analysis studies and has taught at the institute for thirty-seven years. Before joining NYIF, he was director of technical research at Knight Equity Markets and worked for fifteen years at Prudential Equity Groups as its director of technical analysis. His career has included positions at several of the financial industry's top firms, including Kidder Peabody and Smith Barney.

One of Wall Street's most respected technical analysts, Acampora is regularly consulted for his market opinion by major business news networks as well as national financial publications, and he has been consistently ranked by *Institutional Investor* for more than ten years. He is a chartered market technician (CMT), a designation he helped create and which is now recognized by the National Association of Securities Dealers (now FINRA) as the equivalent of a chartered financial analyst (CFA).

Acampora cofounded the Market Technicians Association (MTA) in 1970, is a past president of that group, and continues to be an active member of the society. He also founded and was the first chairman of the International Federation of Technical Analysts (IFTA), comprising more than four thousand colleagues around the world. As an educator, Acampora also participates in the Securities Industry and Financial Markets Association's annual Wharton seminars.

Acampora is a trustee on the Board of the Security Industry Institute (SII) and is involved in the establishment of the Securities Traders

Association University (STAU). He is the coauthor of the CMT examination and the author of the book *The Fourth Mega-Market, Now Through 2011: How Three Earlier Bull Markets Explain the Present and Predict the Future.*

❖ What led to your interest in technical analysis?

I came to Wall Street in 1966 after a couple of years in a Catholic seminary. My educational background is in history and political science, and I worked on a master's degree in theology, so I had absolutely no background in this business. I had a major spinal fusion operation, which ended my theology studies. My father's best friend was William Downe, who was a specialist on the floor of the New York Stock Exchange, with a firm called Spear, Leads & Kellogg. Bill Downe was able to get me a very fine back surgeon. Every day Mr. Downe would come to the hospital and visit with me, and he'd have publications like the *Wall Street Journal, Forbes* magazine, *Barron's.* I was in a body cast for three months, so I was like a little inverted turtle. Downe would throw everything he was reading on the bed. I was a captive, so for three months I read all this stuff about Wall Street.

When they took the cast off, I told him I was not going back into the seminary, and he asked me what I wanted to do with my life. I told him I enjoyed reading the stuff he had given me. "That's research," he said. That was in the mid-'60s, and research was in its very formative stages in those days.

Mr. Downe introduced me to Bill Grant at Smith Barney, which was probably one of the first brokerage firms to create what we know today as modern fundamental research. Grant told me to get an MBA, come back, and he'd give me a job. But I had had many, many years of schooling. I was twenty-seven years old. I didn't want to go back to school. That frustrated Mr. Downe because he couldn't help me. I didn't have the fundamental background for research.

I was still on crutches, and I literally hobbled around Wall Street. I went from job interview to job interview. After a while, I realized I wanted to be an analyst. Finally, I interviewed at a firm called Distributors Group, which was a small mutual fund, and they hired me. My working day was split in half. The first half was devoted to maintaining a point-and-figure chart library of more than two thousand charts that I did by hand. The second half was devoted to calculating price-to-earnings ratios for companies our firm had an interest in. I was spending half of my life doing technical analysis and the other half doing fundamental analysis. These people were so kind and wonderful that they kept pushing me, and I apparently excelled at technical analysis.

The man who started this mutual fund at Distributors Group was Harold X. Schreder, who had been an economic adviser to President Eisenhower. Mr. Schreder ran a very successful business and he insisted that every portfolio manager plot the stocks they owned in their respective portfolios. Every Thursday we would meet, and portfolio managers would stand with charts of the stocks that they owned in their portfolios. If anything looked suspicious on a chart, people would whistle, make noises, and say, "Hey, how can you own that ugly thing?" That was discipline. That was my first introduction to technical analysis. It was in the late '60s.

By 1968 they sent me to the New York Institute of Finance, so that one day I might become a portfolio manager. The New York Institute of Finance is a school of Wall Street, and I took a series of classes. One of the classes was taught by Alan Shaw. Alan became my mentor and dear friend. We started working together in October 1969. I can't begin to tell you how much Alan taught me.

Around 1970, Alan was to have lunch with a man named John Greeley. John was also running a technical department, and he had a young fellow with him by the name of John Brooks. Alan couldn't make the lunch, so he sent me. At that luncheon Brooks and I asked each other, "Who do you know in technical analysis?" I told him about Alan Shaw, and he knew a fellow by the name of Bob Farrell at Merrill Lynch. Those were important names, and that was the beginning of the Market Technicians Association. It was actually John Brooks and I, with a little help from Greeley, who started it. In those days the only place Wall Street analysts met corporate America was at the New York Society of Security Analysts. Getting a ticket to go to a luncheon to listen to the chairman of General Motors was virtually impossible for junior analysts like us. All of the fundamental analysts had their own little groups — the chemical analysts met, the drug analysts met, and the oil analysts met — to share their ideas. Technicians never met because we never had a formal group. So we wanted to unite the technicians of Wall Street. Of course, we went back to our old mentor friends—John Greeley and Alan Shaw—to get advice. We were able to get help from Bob Farrell, as well. While working at Harris Upham with Alan, I also met a man by the name of Ralph Rotnem, who was Alan's mentor. In the history of technical analysis, the great names are Edson Gould, Ralph Rotnem, Ken Ward, Edmund Tabell, Tony Tabell, and John Schultz.

The mission and the goal of the MTA was and is today to educate ourselves and the public about the true meaning of technical analysis. People think that the MTA started in 1973. It officially started in 1970, but it was incorporated in 1973. Our first president was Robert Farrell of Merrill Lynch. Alan Shaw was our second president. These people were very well known in their circles. I eventually started teaching technical analysis at the New York Institute of Finance, where I've been teaching it for over three decades.

◈ Which mistake taught you the most?

It was trying to make more of technical analysis than it is. The biggest mistake people make is to overburden themselves with indicators. The simpler you keep it, the better it is. In my early days, I was trying to do too many things with the subject, but we didn't have that many indicators anyway. Now, with the advent of the computer, they're back-testing everything and trying to reinvent the wheel, and I don't think you have to do all that. Keep it simple. I interviewed Richard Russell, who is the living guru of Charles Dow, and I asked him what advice he'd offer the younger generation of technicians. He said, "Always follow the major trend." If you understand the major trend in the market, then everything will fall into place. I agree with that.

◈ Describe your style of technical analysis.

I've been in the business for almost forty years. I think the biggest thing I bring to the table—and that's probably what distinguishes my style—is history. I was a history major in college, and I love it. A few reports that I have been successful in writing basically reconstructed historic events; I then applied the historic events to the current market. It worked. That's what technical analysis is; it's history.

◈ In what kind of market conditions do you make the most mistakes?

In a trending market, I believe, things are easier. In a nontrending market, which is by definition much more volatile, the odds of making mistakes increase. For example, moving averages are very helpful in trending markets. They keep you in a direct path. However, don't ever use moving averages in trendless markets, or at least be very careful when using them there, because you'll get whipsawed. But once you identify a nontrending market, there are certain things you do and certain things you don't do. For example, you don't use moving averages extensively. When do you use your indicator and when don't you use your indicator? That answer comes only with experience, after many years of trial and error.

◈ How much of what you do are you willing to share with others?

I have spent my whole life teaching. I share everything.

◈ If all patterns/indicators/strategies you use are in the public domain, what is it about the way you use these tools that accounts for your superior success?

I don't know about superior success, but I've been in the business for a long time, so I must be doing something right. In investing (or trading), you have to be honest with yourself and you have to be flexible. We all make mistakes, but we must not compound our mistakes. In technical analysis, you can correct the mistakes quickly, but you have to have the ability to admit a mistake. People will respect you for doing so. When you're practicing technical analysis, you have to be totally eclectic, because there will be a time when the approach you're using doesn't work. If you're not flexible, you'll self-destruct. I don't believe that any one approach works all the time. When in doubt, always default to price. People debate: "Oh, I'm a volume guy," or "I'm a put-call-ratio guy." You don't own volume, you don't own put-call ratio—you own price! That's my dictum. If a trend is going up—I don't care if it's going up on light volume—I am with it. If it's going down, I am with it. I own the price. Not everybody will do that.

◈ How do you deal with the problem of the tradeoff between early signal detection and sensitivity to random noise?

First of all, if you're a short-term trader—and I'm talking about day to day or couple of weeks to couple of weeks, which is not what I do—you're more susceptible to random noise. All the firms I worked for—and I worked for three major brokerage firms—invariably told us to have a twelve-to-eighteen-month time horizon, just like the fundamental analysts did. So I don't pay attention to little jiggles and wiggles. However, being human and having to call market turns, I get fouled up by an erratic move or two, which can distort things. But you can eliminate a lot of noise; it shouldn't impede or interrupt your long-term outlook. I just don't do short-term trading. I don't want to do it, though if I had to, I could, and then I would have to deal with the noise. There will always be noise there. That's why you use stop-losses to protect yourself.

◈ Is technical analysis more effective when used on its own or when combined with fundamental analysis?

If I were in charge of a portfolio or a mutual fund, I would always start with fundamentals. There would have to be a reason why I want to own a company, but technical analysis would always dictate when and how I would deal with a stock. So under those circumstances, I would want to have both. Now, when you step into my chart room, you're asking me my opinion, which is 100 percent technical. When we put out a market letter, it's a technical market letter. It's not dictated by any other outside forces except the technical ones. When I go on the road and I'm talking to a large audience, and especially when I'm talking to the public, I try to set up a fundamental case to back my picture, because it's easier to present a position that way. I can't just say, "Well, you've got to buy this stock; it has a nice bottom." That doesn't sell it. I could say that to a professional technical audience, because they would understand that. But for an audience that's not technically sophisticated, you have to gauge your terms. That's where the problem with technical analysis lies: It's not with what we do; it's with how we say it. We confuse people with our jargon, so I don't use that language. I use words like *overvalued* and *undervalued* instead of *tops* and *bottoms*. A base is a stock that is undervalued, and a top is a stock that is overvalued. Believe me, fundamentalists understand exactly what that is.

◈ So your approach is purely technical. You bring in fundamental analysis only when you're explaining your purely technical approach to a nontechnical audience. Correct?

At Prudential, I created a unique product. It starts with the universe of fundamental stocks that the firm follows. Out of those stocks, I'll take only the ones that are graded as buys. Then I'll ask, "Of these fundamental buys, how many are quantitatively graded positive or negative?" I take that list of fundamental buys, and I run it through the quant screen. Let's say starting out with five hundred stocks, two hundred are fundamentally attractive. One hundred of them are positive quantitatively. I'll take that one hundred, and I'll look at them technically. Maybe seventy-five of the one hundred will look good technically. These stocks now have gone through a triple screen, so I call them "trice blessed"—from fundamental, quantitative, and technical points of view. We do that report once a month. We also have fundamental analysts who have sell ideas. Stocks graded as sells are "cursed." They may be "twice cursed" or "trice cursed"; that is, they can be cursed from a fundamental, quantitative, and/or technical point of view. Clients love this system because they understand that I'm using all three of the disciplines. Although I'm a technician, I use the other two disciplines before I get to the technical recommendations. So I use other research disciplines, and it's a very popular product.

◈ Does political or global analysis influence the decisions you make in your chart room?

I have the TV on all the time. I read many newspapers and magazines. I try to follow what's going on in the real world. We can't live in a complete vacuum. Does the news change my market opinion? No, my market opinion is technical. Can it have an impact? Oh, sure.

Things like presidential cycles certainly can have an impact. We did a whole study on the impact of wars on the markets. When wars start, the market usually goes up. People don't believe that. That's all history, and it's fun. I think technicians make better fundamentalists. You do it backwards, because when you see something on a chart, you've got to find out why. A good technician is always asking why.

◈ Why do you eventually share your inventions with others, rather than keeping the edge for yourself?

I don't explain everything in detail. I explain what I'm trying to do, but I don't give out the formula. The formula is proprietary, and I tell people it's a proprietary indicator. It makes it a little mysterious, too. It's not all that complicated. I do fairly basic technical analysis. Up is good; down is bad. Seriously. I know it's hard for some to believe that, but it's true. The trend is most important. People tend to make more out of the subject than it really is. Keep it simple.

◈ How often do you use the technical tools you developed yourself?

As frequently as possible. They're not trading tools. I might use a particular formula a couple of times a month for a report. My work doesn't depend on a computer program. If computers all disappeared tomorrow, I'd still be the same technician I am today.

◈ Describe your working day.

I get into the office around seven o'clock in the morning and leave about six. I live nearby. By the time I get there, I've already read the *Wall Street Journal* and watched the news on television, all in order to get a feel for what the day might hold in store. By the time I walk into this building, I think I know exactly what the market is going to do. Everything seems perfect. But the problem is, when I get in the elevator, I talk to a few people, and by the time I get off the elevator, I am totally confused because I have to deal with the real world. Right across the hall is the conference room, where I listen to the fundamental analysts at 7:30 a.m. They talk about different industries, and I take notes. I accept everything the analysts say, but when I step into our chart room and close that door, I don't listen to the fundamentals anymore. I'm religious with my graphs. I wouldn't buy anything that's going down, despite what the analysts say.

Moreover, I talk with clients and write all the time. Monday, when I do a considerable amount of writing and have two to three conference calls, is the worst day of the week. Traders call here as well, and that's a minute-by-minute application of charting. The two other technicians are always discussing indicators, market reactions, etc. The ideas are constantly being brought out. At times, the room is quiet as a library because we're in the research department, and we need time to think.

Laszlo Birinyi Jr.

My approach is to dissect the stock market. I ask, 'What is going on in the market? What are the trends and the dynamics?' Then I let the market tell me the story.

———◦✎◦———

Laszlo Birinyi Jr., president of Birinyi Associates, began his career as a sales trader and joined Salomon Brothers in 1976. While at Salomon Brothers, he conceived the money flow analysis, created the Salomon-Russell International Index, and authored *The Equity Desk,* a book originally intended for a Salomon Brothers' training course. Birinyi also wrote the firm's first weekly market commentary, *Stock Week,* and topical studies on volatility, flow of funds, market structure, and transaction costs. In 1974, at Mitchell Hutchins, he conceived and introduced the idea of the trading calendar. In 1989, while a director at Salomon Brothers, he left to form Birinyi Associates, a money-management and research firm. Birinyi is a regular contributor to *Forbes* and also a frequent guest on CNBC and other media outlets. He was a contributor to *Bloomberg Personal Finance* and a panelist on *Wall $treet Week with Louis Rukeyser* for fourteen years and was inducted into the W$W Hall of Fame in 1999. In 2004, Birinyi was named to *SmartMoney's* Power 30 list of the most influential market players.

❖ What led to your interest in technical analysis?

I started as a trader after working in the operations departments of several Wall Street firms. In my generation, traders tended to be people who came from Brooklyn and Staten Island, who were pretty bright and street savvy and started trading literally in their late teens or early twenties. At twenty-eight or twenty-nine, I was somewhat behind the crowd. To be successful, I had to close the gap between myself and the other twenty-eight-year-olds who already had at least five years of experience. You can close that gap in several different ways, one of which is to become a really good trader, which is difficult, with the markets being the way they are.

Perhaps because I had the good fortune of having taken some classes at business school—I was getting my MBA at the time at night—I realized that to move up the ladder, I had to do something, and I started to become very interested in how markets worked. I looked for all sorts of articles and books on trading and market movements because we were sitting at a trading desk; we weren't looking out twelve to eighteen months. I spent a lot of my time and energy getting all sorts of articles and publications. One of the issues I explored was transaction costs. Around 1975, there were only about five articles ever written about trading costs, one of which was in *Mississippi Review*, a really obscure journal. If you took all the publications about trading costs available at that point, the stack would be only about a half-inch high. So I kept looking for things of this kind.

At the same time, there were many public newsletters; that was a very big business in those days. I subscribed to all these newsletters, and having been a history major as an undergraduate, I had a sense of how to compile facts. That's when I first got interested in the whole idea of what moved the market and how the market worked.

◈ How did you come to focus on technical analysis as a field?

All the work on markets in the short term was technical at that time. I got interested in technical analysis because it gave me a unique input in my dialogue with portfolio managers and other traders.

◈ Did someone or something in particular in the field inspire you?

Not really. If anything, there was a lack of inspiration. As I gathered information, I kept it, collated it, and worked with it. My first experience out of college was in the computer business. I was a systems analyst, so I was used to structures and databases. The more I interrogated, investigated, and learned, the more disappointed I was that so much of this was clumsy and inconsistent.

One of my contentions and criticisms of technical analysis is that the range of indicators is almost limitless. Someone once wrote a paper tongue-in-cheek about snow in Boston on Christmas day, relating the amount of snow to what the market did the following week. People would look at all sorts of things. They would have a bullish stance on the market and say that a certain indicator was also bullish; then the indicator would change, but their stance wouldn't change. So all of a sudden they would talk about volume instead of the advance/decline line. Ultimately, I got interested in technical analysis because I was cynical; I mean, this wasn't working.

The other disappointment to me was the flexibility—to put it nicely—that technicians showed. The market would do something and I would read in the newsletters "As we've been suggesting, the market has done XYZ." And I would go back and review the past newsletters and say, "I don't see where you were suggesting this in the last four, five, or six newsletters." They would be very vague in their commentary, suggesting investors look for solid companies with great prospects. A month or two later, after this or that company had risen, they would suggest that those were the exact companies they were recommending.

◈ Did you learn the craft by studying the literature on your own, or by studying with a teacher?

I took a class at the New York Institute of Finance, but the only thing I got out of it was how to calculate the 10-day advance/decline oscillator. Over the years I've spent a lot of money buying old books. You may be familiar with Fraser Publishing, which has all these old market books. I also got the old issues of the *Financial Analysts Journal,* and I did a lot of bibliography work.

For so many things, I found that the case was not on solid ground. Let me give you one example that came much later. There has always been this contention that the bull/bear ratio is a contrary indicator; that is, when 50 percent of the newsletter writers are positive, that's an indicator that the market is going to go down, and vice versa. Well, we got all the data since day one, examined it, and found that it was not consistent. Sometimes when everyone is bullish, the market goes up; other times when everyone is bullish, the market goes down. The numbers are pretty random; it's not like 80 to 20 or 70 to 30, where the tendency is there. It's just not a very good indicator despite the myth that it's a great contrary indicator.

Later on we discovered that the odd-lot indicator, also supposed to be a contrary indicator, didn't work either. In the entire 1980s, of the two thousand plus trading days, there were only around eleven trading days when the public was a net buyer. So you might ask, "Is it really a great indicator? The public was so stupid that they missed this big rally in the stock market?" But you know what the public did in the 1980s? They bought bonds. They bought U.S. government bonds, which gave them double-digit returns and no risk. It was not a bad investment. It was interesting that in the 1990s all of a sudden the odd lotter showed up. There were a huge number of days in the early 1990s in which the odd lotters were net buyers, and the timing was very good on their part.

As I looked at these things over time, I found they were inconsistent, so I have gone off and done my own thing, which is one reason I hesitate to label myself a technical person. I call my work *market analysis,* because that's what I am trying to do.

❖ Are there things you learned only after you started applying technical analysis to real markets, things you never saw in the literature?

One thing that disappoints me about the practice of technical analysis is that people don't fully realize how dynamic the market is and how things change. There is a cliché, "It's not your grandfather's market anymore." When you have a market that's dominated by traders, when your commissions are one or two cents a share or less, the dynamics are totally different from when you're paying a commission of fifty to sixty cents a share, as people were paying in 1976. In all investing, you look for these wonderful underlying truths, and the more statistically valid they are and the longer they persist, the more confidence you have in them, whereas actually it should be the other way around. We should recognize that what worked in an environment in which we had a historical classical long-term investor is totally different from what works in an environment where people are day-trading. We still think that charts and indicators work in the same way, when in fact they work differently now.

For example, one of the indicators that we have looked at over the years is mutual fund cash. The contention was that when mutual fund cash got to be above 10 percent, it was bullish; below 5 or 6 percent, it was bearish. It may have been a pretty useful indicator in the '70s and early '80s, but now you have mutual funds that are worth 5, 10, or 20 billion dollars. A mutual fund manager cannot go to 10 percent cash, because at 10 percent cash he is not making a market bet, he is making a business bet. If he is wrong, he is dead. The guy in the '70s who had a $100 million fund and was 10 percent cash could get back into the market in a day or two. Now you cannot do that. The failure of many technical analysts to recognize what's really going on, how things have changed, and how these changes have affected their approaches is really disappointing for me.

❖ Which mistake taught you the most?

One mistake stands out. In 1979 I introduced into our work the idea of ticker tape analysis. When we first started doing that, it was a very useful indicator. In the first version of it, we would look only at block trading. We would look at every single block trade to see if it was in an uptick or in a downtick, and that proved very helpful. Then we thought that since we were interrogating every single trade to see if it was a block, why not analyze every single trade further, and therefore we developed the idea called "money flows."

Money flows proved to be very useful until 1982. In 1982 they did not have quite the predictability that they had previously. We had to recognize that starting in the early 1980s the dynamics of the trading desk had changed. Before then, when volume was much lower, the specialist on the floor of the New York Stock Exchange controlled the marketplace. You did not really want to antagonize the specialist. He was a partner in what you did. I remember trading Motorola in the early 1970s and putting on a small trade without really checking with the specialist to see if he wanted to participate. The order came from the floor, from John Coleman, who was one of the great powers on Wall Street: "That young man will not trade Motorola again without my permission!"

In the 1980s, institutions grew, commissions were still very significant, and liquidity increased, so upstairs block trading became a bigger and more important force in the marketplace, and the control of the marketplace went from the specialist to the trading desk. Firms like Salomon Brothers, where I worked, would put on large prints—which in those days were twenty thousand to thirty thousand shares—tell the specialists that this was what they were going to do and to move out of the way. Our money flow concept was not as useful as it had been, because, with block trading, gradually the information did not seep into the marketplace. More and more prices were being set too often; prices were being set by retail investors. It was a unique circumstance because the NYSE was at that time, and to some degree still is, the only market in the world where retail sets wholesale prices. A hundred shares of Ford up a dime was a new price. Even though there were many millions of shares outstanding, that was the price that showed up on your screen. So we recognized that we had to differentiate between the retail and the wholesale markets, and we started doing money flows on block and nonblock trades, and we looked at them in different marketplaces.

◈ Describe your style of technical analysis.

First, we don't do any marketing. My criticism of technical analysis is not so much of technical analysis as a craft as it is of technical analysts who don't recognize what they're doing. They're basically in the marketing business: show up at CNBC, get your name in the paper, speak at some function. That's where many analysts go wrong.

Technical analysts also go wrong in making dramatic predictions. The best you can do in the market is to give some very strong tendencies and some direction. Because they're in the marketing mode, analysts try to go overboard and be dramatic. What I try to do is tell you we're going to have a cold day tomorrow and a lot of snow. Technicians say we're going to have 6.4 inches of snow and that the temperature will go down to 15 degrees. That is impossible to predict, but it's what people like to hear. They like to have this degree of certainty; they like to have somebody who really knows. Technicians cater to that. My style is characterized by recognizing the limits of what we're doing. That's the best you can do in the market. Very few people even get close to being right. We try to find tendencies.

Our style is unique in the industry. The common characteristic among technical, quantitative, and fundamental approaches is that they begin outside the market: somebody runs a computer program, somebody goes through a book of charts, somebody goes out and kicks the company's tires. And after they're all done, they go to the stock market to try to prove their ideas. My approach is to dissect the stock market. I ask, "What is going on in the market? What are the trends and the dynamics?" Then I let the market tell me the story. That's the major difference. I let the market direct me in trying to distinguish the trends and the developments that are durable, lasting, and profitable from the noise, which is 70 to 80 percent of what goes on.

◈ How do you go about this dissecting of the market?

We do a lot of historical studies and spend a lot of time on them. Peter Drucker once said that the failure of American business is that it knows no history. This is very true in the stock market. One thing I do that is unique in the industry comes from an idea I got from Joe Granville [a prominent technical analyst who popularized on-balance volume]. He suggested keeping track of market participants and what they're saying. We have in the past done charts of the market versus comments by well-known strategists and commentators. We started in the mid-1970s to cut and save major news stories. It's always a great puzzle to our summer interns, many of whom come from places like MIT and Yale, when they're given scissors, glue stick, and a Xerox machine and asked to cut and save major stories from the *Wall Street Journal* or the *New York Times*. They look at me as if to say, "You're kidding?" but I'm not. We have clippings going back to 1962. It gives a great insight into the sentiments and into what people were talking about and what was in the headlines. So we look at a lot of history to know what to look for and what not to look for.

What distinguishes us the most is our analysis of money flows. Money flows is ticker tape reading. It's the contention that the market is a discounting mechanism. We find that 90 percent or so of all stocks go up because people buy them and they go down because people sell them. But the 10 percent of stocks that have really significant moves—in which people make or lose unusual amounts of money—are stocks that told you so long before the news developed (the market being the discounting mechanism). That's really what distinguishes us.

Increasingly, we recognize that in markets such as we have now, which are dominated by traders, it's not possible to be a long-term investor. You have to recognize that the circumstances are different. We know that stocks tend to trade in bands or channels, and we focus a lot on buying stocks that are oversold and selling stocks that are overbought. And again, the only big difference is that we are not suggesting that the stock is 10 percent above its trading range or that it will go down 7.3 percent. We're just saying that this is a stock for which the light is red.

So our view is not one of absolutes. General Motors does not tend to get above its 50-day moving average, and if you buy General Motors at 15 percent above its moving average, you have to realize that you're making a long-term investment, because the probability of that stock moving significantly higher from that point in the next two to three months is not very strong. In today's environment, we are focusing more and more on intraday-trading and on the importance of information that one gleans from after-hours trading.

◈ How much of what you learn from others do you directly apply in your trading?

Very little, because most people who practice technical analysis don't invest. We had experience at Salomon Brothers with a group of quantitative analysts who allegedly were doing a good job and getting some commission business for the firm, and their calls had been more right than wrong. They realized that to really make the big bucks and get in on the significant bonus pools, they had to contribute directly to the bottom line, so they asked to be given some money with which to put their efforts to work. They were given several million dollars, and they did poorly. All these labora-tory experiences do not translate into real-world results.

One of my earliest disillusionments came in 1975. I was on a trading desk, and I was friendly with a young lady who worked for one of the major firms at a large technical department. We had a stock at 39.75 and she called and said, "We're trying to figure out what to do with this stock. At 41 it's a breakout, but what do I do with 39.75?" In the real world, you can't pass this because it's not at 41; you would be interested in buying it. Nothing in trading and investments is black or white, and we have no room in the trading room for "interesting," "developing," or "potential."

◈ How do you learn what works for you and what does not, without taking big losses?

Be willing to take little losses. Be willing to realize that if you have a huge body of information that leads to a conclusion, it's probably not that useful, because to get that information you have to go back in time. We're now developing patterns of pre- and posttrading. So in the morning someone announces that earnings are up 3 points premarket, from 8:00 a.m. to 9:15 a.m., and once we have just one or two data points, we try it; we buy five hundred shares. That's because premarket is a relatively new phenomenon.

I consider whether something is logical, whether it makes sense; then I do it. I don't need to have four decimal points to do it. We trust that we have enough experience, and we try to get a very logical approach. A lot of my ideas, such as the money flows, make a lot of sense and are very logical, but one of my great disappointments is that people don't like them because I don't have forty-seven thou-sand examples over twenty-seven years with statistical significance. As I keep suggesting, the market changes, it's dynamic.

◈ In what kind of market conditions do you make the most mistakes?

Probably in a bear market because you pull the string too much. I found too that in a bear market, if you do the right thing, the cus-tomers aren't happy. Like everyone else, customers want to make money. We've had problems in bear markets when we had high cash and customers said, "We're not paying you to do that." We did the most complete study ever done on market rotations. It was three volumes and twenty-five hundred pages. We found that in the last quartile of the bear market absolutely nothing works. There are just no hiding places. People are pushing you, and as a result you push yourself to look askew at the indicators in trying to make money, instead of recognizing that sometimes it's useful to be in cash.

◈ How much of what you do are you willing to share with others?

We publish our research. We have a very significant institutional product. We have a newsletter and a website. We share all of our work. One disappointing trend in the business today, especially on the institutional side, is that people aren't interested in the market anymore. People aren't practicing investments. Too many asset managers are in the business of just collecting assets, getting more and more money under management, just getting you 50–60 basis points a year, grinding out the numbers, and the whole idea of per-formance and market achievement has really gone by the wayside. Twenty years ago, when I had dinner with a bunch of money man-agers, we talked about the market; now they talk about how much money they raised.

◈ If all the patterns/indicators/strategies you use are in the public domain, what is it about the way you use these tools that accounts for your superior returns?

I understand the market, and being a trader helped me gain that understanding. For example, one of the issues with money flows is that it looks like a chart. People familiar with charts try to interpret money flows in the same way, so they look for certain points at which the money flow trades through the price. But our approach is totally different, because we're analyzing the tape. We may have a pattern in which stock is going down and money flow is positive. People have a lot of problems with that. They say, "How can a stock go down when people are buying? What does it mean?"

If you've been on a trading desk, you've seen that situation a hundred times. Say you have a stock that's down 0.50 or 0.75; it's been down five days in the last week and a half, and it just doesn't look good at all. Say it's broken its 50-day moving average and hit a new low, and yet you see positive accumulation. Someone will come in and talk about the disappointing action in Johnson & Johnson, General Mills, or whatever. As an old trader, I know he is a buyer. And since you know—or you should know—that he is a buyer, you tell him that you've been in touch with some sellers. You tell him, "I have a portfolio manager down the hall who might be able to use General Mills. Why don't you see if he can make an offering for you?" So you contact your position trader. The stock may be trading at 50.25, so you say, "I can offer you fifteen thousand shares at 50.75." And again he tells you that the stock is going down and so on. To which you respond, "Let me call my sellers again," and you say, "I can sell you fifteen thousand shares at 50.50." He says, "Done." Somebody is buying stock. When somebody is buying stock aggressively even though it's in a downtrend, that's the kind of thing we look for. But many people don't understand how this works in the marketplace.

◈ How do you deal with the problem of the tradeoff between early signal detection and sensitivity to random noise?

In money flows we want to see at least two weeks of continual, persistent buying as the stock goes down or sideways. Consider a stock like Apple. At the end of 1997, Apple went from 10 to 7. In that first quarter as it went down, there was something like $150 million worth of buying on the upticks and of being on the offering side on the downticks. That's not random noise. That's now a raw trader; that's the market. In the money-flow approach, we look for a lot of money verifying us, not just one or two trades or one or two institutions over a very short period of time.

◈ Is technical analysis more effective when used on its own or when combined with fundamental analysis?

We've had a lot of success over time combining disciplines. To me a discipline is like one hand clapping; it doesn't really do much. It's when you add another hand that you end up making noise. We pursue a lot of journals and newspapers, and I like to see a stock recommended by someone who is a visit-the-company, tear-the-balance-sheet-apart type of person, as well as by a chartist. Then we put our own overlay on it. Those are the most desirable situations and those in which we tend to be more aggressive.

◈ What percentage of your analysis is intuitive?

Having been in business for thirty years, it's probably more than I recognize. I would say it's 20 percent and it's declining. One thing that makes trading the markets difficult is that every day you have fifty different experiences, and by Thursday you forget how you felt on Monday. What do you do if a stock reports good earnings and is up 3 points and then goes up another 2? We're trying to catalog more and more of these experiences so that we know what the tendencies and trends are. We're trying to identify situations that we can quantify: at least 60 percent of the time it does this, 20 percent of the time it does that, 10 percent of the time it does that, and the other 10 percent of the time it's totally random. I'm trying to get the percentage of my analysis that's intuitive as close to zero as I can.

◈ What drives your innovative process?

Just seeing what's going on in the market and realizing that we're not picking it up, realizing that 75 percent of activity is programmed trading, and realizing that when you have decimals there is a different circumstance.

◈ Were there times when you felt that relying on classical patterns and indicators was simply insufficient, and that developing new technical tools was necessary?

The classical technical tools were probably pretty useful in the '60s and the '70s, because what you saw was what was happening, but they're no longer useful since the markets have changed. Now you have the surface market, which is just price, but then you have the dimension of what happens intraday. So the classical ideas, like Joe Granville's on-balance volume, were probably very useful in their day. But now, 5 million shares on a stock that's up a half doesn't mean that 5 million shares traded up a half.

◈ Describe your working day.

I come in at seven thirty–ish. I check what has happened overseas. I look at our tools, including a sheet that gives me a technical stance to the market by looking at the S&P advance/decline line and the spread from the 50-day moving average. I look at stocks that are overbought or oversold, and I look at the news events that are likely to affect the markets that day. When the market opens at nine thirty, I reassess everything. I work off the market—what's happening, what the trends are. We do a lot of daily pattern recognition. If the futures are down 1 percent and the market opens down 1 percent, there is an 85 percent chance that the market will rally. That's a very useful indicator. Then we look for opportunities to day-trade or get into a position that we may want to hold for a short or long period. In the afternoon, I may do a little bit of research or have meetings with people to direct them on what to do, but quite frankly, I am not nearly as industrious as I was twenty years ago. When the market closes, I go home. I let the young people stay. I find that today's managers are not as interesting as the managers of twenty years ago; they are not as interested in the market. In the old days, we still had a lot of old people around who listened to the market and focused on the rhythm of the market. Now everyone has an MBA, and everyone follows the same sort of model.

◈ To what extent does your trading control your life?

This is definitely a business of type-A personalities, and the people who are successful in this business are consumed by it. The best book I've read about the stock market is *The Money Game*. In that book, Adam Smith says that if you're not consumed by this business, then you're not going to be successful, because most of the players are consumed by it. It's not really for the money, he says. We could be doing this for whale's teeth or beads. We're playing to play. And, as someone once said, the next best thing to playing and

winning is playing and losing. For the really successful traders—
not the technicians, but the real traders, the real portfolio pros—
the business is what they eat, sleep, and breathe.

When my daughter was in a posh nursery school in Manhattan,
on Father's Day, all the fathers would come in with their three- to
five-year-olds and get down on their knees to play with their kids.
After about twenty minutes, everybody would be talking about the
market. So for about twenty minutes, you paid attention to your
kids; then it turned to the market. These are people who have found
their role in life. People like me wouldn't even dream of doing anything else. We would be total, dismal failures in anything else we
did. Mike Epstein, former NYSE trader and now a visiting scholar
at MIT, is one of the few people who've escaped. For most of us,
there is no afterlife. That's what makes us good at it. It consumes
us. We're not satisfied with the mundane.

3

Walter Deemer

Whenever you think you've got a key to Wall Street, somebody comes along and changes the lock. Whatever indicators work, however well, however long, something will come along to change them, and you always have to be alert for new things to do.

Walter Deemer began his Wall Street career in 1963 as a Merrill Lynch research trainee. The following year, he moved to the firm's market analysis department, where he worked directly under Bob Farrell, and he has been a full-time market analyst ever since. In 1966, Deemer joined Tsai Management and Research just before the initial offering of the Manhattan Fund. Then, in 1970, he went to the Putnam Management Company in Boston, one of the most prestigious money-management firms in the world, and headed Putnam's market analysis department throughout the ten years he worked there. Deemer became a full member of Putnam's investment policy committee and was promoted to senior vice president in 1976. In 1980, he formed his own company, DTR, and has successfully offered his market strategies and insights to institutional clients on a consulting basis since that time.

Deemer is a founding member and past president of the Market Technicians Association. He has twice addressed the Conference on Technical Analysis, held in Cambridge, England, and has also addressed the Boston Security Analysts Society, the San Francisco Society of Security Analysts, and the Contrary Opinion Forum. He has appeared on the *Nightly Business Report* and has been the special guest on *Wall $treet Week*. And, last but hardly least, Deemer is the featured technical analyst in Dean LeBaron's book *Dean LeBaron's Treasury of Investment Wisdom*, joining such luminaries as John Bogle, Peter Lynch, and George Soros as the chosen gurus in their fields.

❖ What led to your interest in technical analysis?

I first got interested in technical analysis when I was at Penn State. I was on the main campus in 1961, 1962, and 1963. There was only one brokerage office in town and two of the three people there were very much into technical analysis. One of them was also a part-time teacher at the university. In 1962 the stock market crashed. It was something that was easily predictable using technical analysis, and I was impressed that they were able to predict it. They essentially bent the twig for me, and from then on the tree was inclined toward technical analysis.

❖ How is your style of technical analysis distinct?

If you had to choose a phrase, it would be *anticipatory analysis*. When I went to work for Putnam Investments in 1970, in my very early days, I told one of the big fund managers that IBM had just broken out. "Fine, but I can't buy it," he said. "It's already broken out and moving, the price is rallying. I can't really buy it in size. So what I need you to do is tell me before it breaks out." So I went back to my office and spent quite a bit of time working on that, but I soon found out that when you're dealing with major institutions, managing large sums of money, you need to tell them that the only time they can really buy in quantity is during the decline, and the only time they can really sell in quantity is in a rally. So, I needed to tell them just before the market or stock makes a top. Or, tell them just before the market makes a bottom, so they can buy that last supply and sit there with a basket and have everybody throw stocks in it. Once it starts back up, it's much more difficult for people to buy in major sizes. A lot of technicians can say, "As soon as the rally is over and it starts back down, I'll get out," but I don't have that luxury. Or they say keep tightening up your stop in a long position. Well, you can't sell 2 million shares on a stop on the floor of the New York Stock Exchange; you just can't handle it that way. I need to look at things that give me an idea that the trend is starting to reverse rather than waiting for it to reverse. Unlike a lot of my colleagues, I've been dealing only with institutional investors for thirty-four years.

◈ How much of what you learn from others do you directly apply in your analysis?

Practically everything I use is from others. I build on it. Information comes from various places, and I've been lucky enough to be with some very smart people, like, for example, Dean LeBaron, the fellow who started index funds, an investment genius. He is so contrary that when index funds became popular, he got out of the index fund business. I talked with Dean when Fidelity Investments came out with some of its sector funds. These funds are very small, narrowly focused mutual funds that invest only in a single sector of the market, such as energy services, precious metals, or semi-conductors. They price these things hourly. They're designed for very aggressive traders, and they're run by Fidelity analysts who follow a particular industry. We talked about what this might mean, and Dean said, "I think there is some information in there, somewhere." What Dean was telling me was that Fidelity funds give you a chance to follow actively managed portfolios rather than following industry groupings that an organization like Standard and Poor's puts out. These are the best-perceived biotechnology stocks versus the best-perceived precious metals stocks versus the best-perceived electronics stocks. You're measuring the best of each group at any particular time. So, in 1986, we started doing relative-strength work on the Fidelity sector funds. We've done a lot with that, and it's been very helpful. But the original idea was not mine; it was LeBaron's. I picked up the ball and ran with it.

◈ Is technical analysis more effective when done working individually or in teams?

In my opinion, it's done better individually, because technical analysis is part contrary—you're leaning against the prevailing wind all the time. In coming up with the ideas, you're standing on your own. Basically, I'm selling clients experience. I've been following this for forty years. I've seen it all. I've done it all. I've made a lot of mistakes and learned from them, so when the market does something, I know how to react.

❖ Since all the patterns/indicators/strategies you use are in the public domain, what is it about the way you use these tools that accounts for your superior returns?

Interpretation.

❖ How do you deal with the problem of the tradeoff between early signal detection and sensitivity to random noise?

If I'm dealing with the longer term, I don't get as much random noise. Random noise is generated more on a very short-term basis, on a day-to-day, or an intraday, basis. What I'm doing, essentially, is stepping back. I let the trading desk at the institution worry about the noise, and I worry more about the longer-term trends.

❖ How much of your technical analysis is intuitive?

Quite a bit, but then you try to back it up with facts. Again, it's the experience of having been there so many times. You first try to grasp the precedents and then to relate the current experience to the precedent. So the intuition, perhaps, is in trying to figure out what part of the precedent is most applicable in the current situation, and then the analysis is in trying to back it up with some numbers.

❖ What drives your innovative process?

Fear of being wrong and losing all my clients; greed, in trying to be more accurate in the market; and a desire to hone my skills. Somebody once asked me why I didn't manage any money, but that's a whole different set of skills than market forecasting. When I perfect my skills in market forecasting, I'll try another field, but those skills aren't perfect yet.

❖ Were there times when you felt that relying on classical patterns and indicators was insufficient, and that developing new technical tools was necessary?

All the time, because as somebody once said, "Whenever you think you've got a key to Wall Street, somebody comes along and changes the lock." Whatever indicators work, however well, however long, something will come along to change them, and you always have to be alert for new things to do.

◈ Describe your working day.

The first thing I do for my clients in the morning is send them a daily update. It's like a daily weather forecast. You don't necessarily run your life on a daily weather forecast, but it's nice to know whether it's going to be warm or cool, wet or dry. If there's a question on their minds, my job is to answer it in that update before they ask it, so that they don't have to call me at nine o'clock. The daily update goes out at twenty minutes to seven in the morning. So I get up at twenty minutes to six and go into the office, get the numbers that come out at midnight (such as the assets of the Rydex Investments funds), look at the overnight trading to see what's happened, and issue my daily update. I wake up without an alarm clock because the stock market is such a fun thing to analyze. I come into the office, thinking that I know what I am going to see, but it never turns out exactly that way. There is always some wrinkle or something new that's happened.

After I send out my update, I collect statistics, I do the things needed to run the business, and then I start collecting the closing statistics, which come out starting with the closing of the bond market at three o'clock. I keep a number of broad sector averages, which we started at Putnam in the early '70s. We actually had some sector averages at the Manhattan Fund in the '60s, so I've been following the market sectors for a long while. We followed currencies and the bond market at Putnam in the 1970s, so we were doing intermarket analysis before some of the people who popularized it were even born, I think. After collecting the closing statistics, we issue a rough draft of the daily update, sometime around six or six thirty at night, because there are some people in Tokyo who want an idea of what's going on as their market opens. Once every two weeks, I publish an in-depth report, which takes the better part of three days to prepare.

Paul F. Desmond

People tend to get too specific about theories and say that it doesn't matter what the market is doing, this is what the market is going to do. That's really dangerous. They're saying that their theory is right, and the market is wrong. The market is always right.

⸻◦⟨◉⟩◦⸻

P aul F. Desmond is president of Lowry Research Corporation, the oldest technical investment advisory firm in the nation. Lowry is particularly unique in the advisory field in that its analysis, which is based solely on the law of supply and demand, has been conducted in exactly the same manner since the 1930s. About 85 percent of the Lowry subscribers are professional investors, and almost 20 percent of them have subscribed for twenty-five years or more. Desmond joined Lowry in 1964 as director of research and advanced to the presidency in 1972. He is past president of the Market Technicians Association and was the recipient of the Charles H. Dow Award in 2002, sponsored by Dow Jones and *Barron's*.

◈ What led to your interest in technical analysis?

I got interested in technical analysis before I knew what technical analysis was. My father taught me how to read point and figure charts and how to plot them. We kept five hundred point and figure charts every day, but I wasn't really aware of the distinction between technical analysis and fundamental analysis. Then, in 1964, I was doing some research in the Miami library, and I bumped into the Lowry market analysis material and was fascinated by it. I got very caught up in the analysis they were doing and wanted to be a part of it. I actually offered to work for them for nothing, just so I could learn from L. M. Lowry.

◈ Did you learn the craft by studying the literature on your own, or by studying with a teacher?

A little bit of both. I had taken a lot of economics courses in college, and Chapter 1 of almost any college-level economics textbook is always about the law of supply and demand, and the fact that the law of supply and demand is the starting point, the foundation of all macroeconomic analysis. And for some reason, it stops there. Chapter 2 ought to discuss what indicators one can use to measure supply and demand. It's frustrating to know the foundation, but not how to use it, measure it, or take the next step.

Lowry was very helpful from that standpoint, because he started out working for a bank in Miami in the early '30s, during the time of the 1929 to 1932 crash. He was young, and he thought he was going to learn a great deal from the bank officers, the older men. But instead of learning from them, he found that they spent most of their time wandering up and down the hallways and saying, "Nobody can blame us. We don't understand what's happening here. We bought good-quality stocks, but they just keep going down." He realized that these educated, trained, experienced analysts really had no idea how to deal with the forces of the stock market. There was more to it than just buying good-quality stocks and hanging on for the long term; some other element was missing.

Lowry got frustrated and quit the bank. To figure out what the missing element was, he went back to the college textbooks. Everywhere he looked, there was the law of supply and demand, and yet no explanation as to how to measure supply and demand. So he decided to figure out how to measure them. He concluded that all of the forces of supply and demand are related in six numbers. First, there is price. There are two parts to the price equation: the number of stocks rising, which is captured by the advance/decline line, and the dollars gained by all of the advancing stocks, which is captured by points gained, an indicator that Lowry created. Then he looked at the amount of volume traded on stocks that were advancing, which is called upside volume. He was the man who first broke down the total volume into the upside volume and the downside volume. So, for stocks advancing, he had the number of stocks advancing, the amount by which they were advancing, and the amount of volume that accompanied those advances. Similarly, for stocks declining, he had the number of stocks declining, the amount by which they were declining, and the amount of volume that accompanied those losses.

And no matter what you're trying to measure—it could be real estate, gold, silver, soy beans, stocks, or bonds—supply and demand is all you have. You could measure sentiment, you could take surveys of people, but what people say and what they do are very often entirely different things. Lowry actually wanted to see them put their money on the line before taking them seriously. The advance/ decline line was already in existence, but he created points-gained and points-lost indicators, and upside and downside volume numbers. Starting from there, we've developed over the years a series of indicators that use those six numbers to measure the pressures of supply and demand in force. I learned all of that from him, and carried on with it.

◈ Are there things you learned only after you started applying technical analysis to real markets, things you never saw in the literature?

There is a big difference between theory and reality. That shows up in a number of ways. For example, over time, as you meet people involved in various areas of investment, you start to notice distinct differences in their personalities. There are analysts, there are traders, and there are portfolio managers. To be successful at any one of those disciplines requires personality traits that are substantially different from those required to be successful at the other two. Traders make decisions very quickly. They don't stop to think very much about what they're doing; they just act. If a trader sees a situation that looks good to him, he'll act on it and buy; if he realizes he was wrong, he reverses himself very quickly. He controls his ego to the point where it does not bother him to take losses; he knows it's a normal part of his method of operation. A very successful trader may find that as much as 60 percent of his trades are losses, but as long as he adheres to the rule of cutting the losses quickly and letting the profits run, he knows that he is going to be successful.

An analyst is a completely different creature. I am an analyst. I tend to think about things to a fault. I'll study things, look at the probabilities, and by the time I finish thinking about it, a lot of opportunities are gone. But I could not be a trader. I am a long-term investor, not only because I think that's the best way to operate, but also because that's the only way I could survive. It takes me a long time to make a decision. But when I make a decision, I've cut down the odds of being wrong substantially.

If I were going to write a book on the stock market, the first four or five chapters would be on psychology. You need to know yourself, what risk you're willing to take, how quickly you can make decisions, how difficult it is for you to accept making mistakes, how quickly you can change your mind. These things are critically important to being a successful investor. If you don't know yourself, nothing else matters. The charts and the measurements don't mean a thing unless you know how to put that information to work.

◈ How is your style of technical analysis distinct?

Too many technical analysts do not really recognize how pervasive supply and demand are. Almost everything that's considered technical analysis is nothing more than the form of measuring supply and demand. All you're trying to do with the chart patterns is determine whether there is more buying or selling going on, or whether there's more money going into stocks than flowing out of stocks, and all of that is basic supply-demand analysis. A lot of people think that what we do here at Lowry's is unique in that we concentrate on supply and demand. In many cases, they do not realize that what they're doing is also supply and demand, just in a different way. We simply measure the flow of money into and out of the markets, and the changes in investor psychology that are reflected in those flows of money. That's the only thing we do.

◈ Is technical analysis done better working individually or in teams?

There is probably an advantage to teams, but you have to pick your teammates carefully. You're trying to get an objective, disciplined, controlled, and factual analysis. The reality is we're all human beings, and we're all heavily influenced by our emotions. If you can have a few people around you who are like-minded, and who are trying to get at the same thing you're trying to get at, and you can bounce ideas off of each other, and correct each other, you can probably end up a little bit closer to remaining on that narrow, objective trail.

◈ Are there certain market conditions that increase the likelihood of your making mistakes?

Absolutely. If you take a long-term chart of the Dow Jones Industrial Average or of the S&P 500, you can see changes in patterns. You will see periods in which the market averages are in clear, strong trends, either up or down, usually up. Once these long trends end, the market goes into a choppy pattern. The reason for this is that an uptrend typically starts at a low price and then rises to a high price, at which point a lot of investors start to feel that prices and valuations are too high, and they can't get excited about buying stocks at these levels. So you go through a choppy period in which investors can't really make up their minds whether or not to commit. A lot of investors try to take profits at these levels, and that holds the market down. Then you go through another long, clear, well-defined trend, usually on the downside. After that you sometimes go through a basing pattern for a period of time, in which the prices are low and move sideways. Unless you're a very-short-term trader, you're going to make a lot of mistakes during these sideways periods. You're going to think that the market is going into an uptrend again when it is not. You'll have to turn around and get back out again. The market keeps doing this to you; it whips on you. A number of analysts spend a considerable amount of time trying to develop indicators that will tell you when the market is in the trading mode and when it's in the trending mode. The distinction between the trading and the trending mode is clearly visible when you look at the long-term chart of stock prices. During a strong uptrend, it's hard to do anything wrong, and during these choppy periods, it's hard to do anything right. You either have to endure it, keep making little mistakes and correcting yourself very quickly, or find a way to identify the trading mode and stay out of it.

❖ If all patterns/indicators/strategies that you use are in the public domain, what is it about the way you use these tools that accounts for your success?

Part of it is objectivity. It's relatively unusual to find real objectivity in the stock market. The stock market seems to attract egos. People will have some theory that guides their analysis, and many times they put that theory in front of reality. There are some popular theories around. One of them is the Elliott wave theory, which says that there are certain waves that take place in the stock market, and that's generally true. It's as true as saying there are generally seasons to the year, but if you try to get too specific about the temperatures during the seasons in a year, you can make some bad mistakes. And people tend to get too specific about these theories, and say that it doesn't matter what the market is doing, this is what the market is going to do. That's really dangerous. They're saying that their theory is right, and the market is wrong. The market is always right. So we don't have any built-in biases, and that partly accounts for our success. We simply believe that if there is more money going into the market than there is coming out, prices will rise, and vice versa.

The market is much more complex than it has been—or has been thought to be—and I think this recognition is a big part of the future of technical analysis. Bull and bear markets are all mixed up inside each other. For example, during the bear market from 2000 to 2002, there was also a bull market going on at the same time. The bear market was primarily in technology stocks, and the bull market was in mid-cap and small-cap stocks. If you didn't know that, you would have missed an incredible opportunity. While the vast majority of investors were losing money, you could have been invested in midcaps and small caps and making a substantial amount of money. I think that phenomenon has existed all through history to one extent or another, and we're working on identifying those phases in the past when bull and bear markets existed simultaneously. We're moving toward segmenting the market into pieces, so that we can see those trends within trends. I think it makes an enormous difference. So simply knowing where to position your money, rather than just treating it as *the* stock market, even in an uptrend you can double the standard benchmark, which is the S&P 500.

◈ Is technical analysis more effective when used on its own or when combined with fundamental analysis?

I prefer to operate entirely on technical factors. Some parts to fundamental analysis cannot be applied to certain investment vehicles. For example, it's pretty hard to apply fundamentals to exchange-traded funds, mutual funds, or derivatives. You just can't look at an option and effectively apply fundamentals to it. I prefer to operate purely on technical indicators, because fundamental analysis has an influence on stocks, but it does not control them. The law of supply and demand controls stocks: if there is more money flowing in than coming out of stocks, prices will rise. And that's not saying that *maybe* they will rise; it's saying that they will rise. If the company has good earnings, you cannot say with certainty that the price of its stock will rise, all you can say is that there is a strong likelihood that the price will rise. I prefer to use supply and demand, because they control the price movement, rather than just influencing it.

◈ Were there times when you felt that relying on classical patterns and indicators was insufficient and that developing new technical tools was necessary?

No. We're using the same classical indicators, but we're applying them to a much more complex animal. For example, people have always had the tendency to think of a stock market as a single entity. It's not. Big caps move differently than small caps, technology functions differently than finance, utilities tend to be different animals than transports. These are markets within markets within markets, and you have to uncover the crosscurrents. International securities is almost a brand new field. As recently as the '70s the idea of international investing was almost unheard of. People just didn't do that. Today, it's a very important area of consideration.

◈ Describe your working day.

The first thing I usually do is go over the numbers from the previous day's market and look for inconsistencies. At the end of the day, we go through the closing numbers; we go through the analysis and reach the conclusion as to what today's action meant. The next morning we'll check the data even more closely, make sure it conforms to what we thought the previous day. If it doesn't conform, we make the necessary adjustments. We may even send a report to our clients to tell them that something has happened that we didn't anticipate the night before. Later in the day, I'll go through a deeper analysis of the market, looking for smaller trends in individual stocks or groups or sectors that I hadn't seen before. I also take calls from clients with questions. Usually, a part of the day is spent developing a new idea. We're going to start on some new research projects that are going to be substantial, which are going to take a long time. It's important to plan those out. At the end of the day, we reanalyze the market as it approaches closing and when it closes. We write a commentary right after the market closes each day to tell our clients what we think happened, why it happened, and what actions they should take or not take accordingly. Usually two nights a week I work until ten or eleven o'clock at night purely on research projects. When you're trying new ideas, you can't be interrupted, and working late at night has the advantage that everybody is gone, allowing you to be immersed in your research.

◈ To what extent does your work control your life?

Too heavily. My wife has often told me my first love is the stock market. There is at least some truth to that. It's a lifelong search for knowledge. Someone long ago said that the stock market is the world's biggest guessing game, and to have the sense that you have found some order to what appears to be total disorder is fun, challenging, and just never grows old.

Gail M. Dudack

Few things in life are perfectly black or white. That is the art of analysis—describing the gray. A large part of technical analysis is science. It's measuring supply and demand. But I'm good at guessing the picture behind the puzzle when I don't have all the pieces.

Gail M. Dudack, CMT, is managing director of Midwood Securities in New York. Before joining Midwood, she was a managing partner and director of research products at Dudack Research Group in New York, managing director of research and the chief investment strategist for SunGard Institutional Brokerage, and the chief investment strategist for UBS AG and its predecessor S.G. Warburg PLC. Dudack began her Wall Street career at the Pershing division of Donaldson, Lufkin & Jenrette (now Credit Suisse First Boston Corporation).

Dudack is a frequent guest on CNBC, PBS's *Nightly Business Report,* and Bloomberg Television and a popular speaker at many business forums and societies. She is a past president of the Market Technicians Association (MTA), a founding member of the International Federation of Technical Analysts (IFTA), chair emeritus of the SIFMA's Securities Industry Institute, a past arbitrator for the NASD, and an ex-member of the Department of Labor's Business Research Advisory Council for consumer and producer price indexes. She received an MTA award for best price analysis and market forecasting in 1997 and a special achievement award from Skidmore College in June 2001 and is featured in the book *Bull! A History of the Boom, 1982–1999* by Maggie Mahar (Harper Business, 2003). She earned the chartered market technician (CMT) designation in 1990.

❖ What led to your interest in technical analysis?

My interest began when I was in college, but I did not under-stand at the time that the independent studies I had set up were technical analysis. I had a summer job on Wall Street my junior year in a research department and I substituted for everybody and anybody who was on vacation. One man there was called the quantitative analyst. These were the days when technical analysis was truly viewed as voodoo, so he was not called a technical ana-lyst; he was called a quantitative analyst. But he was studying the internals of the market. He showed me how to update his charts so that when he went on vacation I could update them for him. I was fascinated. When I returned to Skidmore College, I chose two topics for my senior thesis: short interest and odd lots. Both were data sets of information used to analyze the psychology of the stock market.

❖ Are there things you learned only after you started applying technical analysis to real markets, things you never saw in the literature?

Whether you're a technical analyst or a fundamental analyst, what-ever you look at—a chart/balance sheet/income statement—you must put this information into the context of the world at large. For example, 90 percent days are one of my favorite tools. It tells you oodles about investor emotion. But you need to know the backdrop of the market to understand the meaning of a 90 percent day. You have to ask, "Was this 90 percent day triggered by a one-time event?" If it *was,* I do *not* believe it's as significant as it would be if it were *not* triggered by a one-time event. How to put informa-tion into the context of the current environment (and the environ-ment is always changing) is something a book cannot teach you. For example, today's trading environment is very different from the trading environment of ten or twenty years ago. There is more program trading, more derivatives, and more recently we've had the addition of exchange-traded funds. As the trading environ-ment changes, tools or indicators change as well. I have never found a book that explains this concept to anybody. You simply learn it through experience.

◈ Which mistake taught you the most?

I've made so many mistakes I don't know which one to choose.
I've learned over time as an analyst (and I write for professional
investors) that if you're wrong on your view of the market, it's
important to be honest about having been wrong. Explain why
you were wrong and what you learned from that mistake.
Through this process, your clients will trust you. It took experience and confidence to be able to do this. I've also learned that
my stomach churns before I'm even conscious of being wrong.
Somehow my stomach knows first. So if I'm sick to my stomach
for three days, my market call is probably wrong. I should go
with my gut at that point. This comes from having made many
mistakes.

◈ How is your style of technical analysis distinct?

I would call my style eclectic. I will look at absolutely anything
that moves if I think it will be helpful to me. Some of my fellow
technicians believe one should be a technical purist. I am the
opposite. I'm a strategist. I work with technicals, fundamentals,
and economics. My degree is in economics, with a minor in math,
so I like numbers. I follow economic data; I look at sector fundamentals; I use valuation models; I believe in theme investing; I
take both technical and quantitative approaches, and I believe we
are in a *global* environment. I'll look at skirt lengths if it's going
to help me. I look at many things, and I'm always looking for
something new. So I don't believe I have a definitive style. My
approach to technical analysis is very basic. I do a lot of plain and
simple chart analysis. I also look at relative strength and sentiment. What I add to my collection of indicators that may be unusual is flow of funds. This simply means looking at where money
is invested. I look for extremes (over or under investment) in any
asset class as the sign of the end of one cycle and the beginning
of another. These statistics define the larger supply and demand
cycle. Charts tell us about current supply and demand. So I start
with the bigger supply and demand picture and then look at the
current supply and demand picture. It is a basic approach with
my own twist to it.

◈ Are there certain market conditions that increase the likelihood of your making mistakes?

The hardest part of the cycle for me is the middle- to late-stage bull market. This is also the middle of the economic cycle, which means that the economy has done well for a long while and investor complacency has set in. It can be difficult to outperform in such an environment. Stocks are generally moving up, yet there are no obvious signs of a top. It's as if everything is on hold. Economists provide good guidance in the middle of a cycle, but they do not have the tools to see the train about to hit them when the end of the cycle is near. On the other hand, technical analysis excels at tops and bottoms. It's excellent at defining turning points. That's where technicians can step up to the plate and hit a home run; we can "see" the extremes. Since I find that fundamental analysis works best in the middle of an economic cycle or the middle of a bull market, I might switch my focus in midcycle to relative sector value, stock strength, and earnings strength.

◈ If all the patterns/indicators/strategies that you use are in the public domain, what is it about the way you use these tools that accounts for your superior success?

That is the greatest mystery of all. I think it comes down to two words: *your gut*. How can two technicians look at the same chart and not necessarily have the same view? I don't know. Few things in life are perfectly black or white. That is the art of analysis—describing the gray. A large part of technical analysis is science. It's measuring supply and demand. But I'm good at guessing the picture behind the puzzle when I don't have all the pieces. The pieces are flow of funds, charts, sentiment, etc. Some people can figure out the picture; others can't. I am not always right, but it intrigues me. If you can be right more than half the time, you're successful. I would also say that I'm successful because I *am* so eclectic. I'm not a purist. I use different tools at different times, because some work at tops, others work at bottoms, still others work in the middle. I'm constantly changing and adding other nontechnical things to the mix.

In today's environment it is important to understand how the stock market has changed. These changes impact the technical tools you use. We have a completely different trading structure now. I mentioned flow of funds, looking where money is invested and where it might go next. It's important to understand which investor is driving the stock market. There have been times—it started in the mid-1960s and went through the 1980s—when we had a huge growth in mutual fund assets and a tremendous increase in pension fund assets. This growth in managed fund assets drove the markets for most of that period. It was *before* the 1973–74 bear market that the average investor began to leave equities and stepped to the sidelines. Simultaneously, the drivers of the stock market became the professional money managers. The managers—of pension funds, mutual funds, or independent advisers—acquired assets and made decisions that defined the market. In the 1990s, it was the household sector again. I have always monitored mutual fund flows as a sample of demand much like everybody else. But my approach to those flows differed. Mutual fund managers were not the drivers of investment decisions in the 1990s; people who felt those managers were controlling the market were wrong. The managers were the conduits, not the decision makers. The public gave individual money managers the money. I looked at mutual fund flows to see which funds acquired assets: it was technology funds. It was obvious that the market would trade differently in the 1990s because it was driven by the public. In fact, it was the public's irrational exuberance that created the bubble. Professional money managers would not have been aggressively buying stocks when they were trading at forty times earnings. But they *had* to. Today, the asset class acquiring the most assets is hedge funds. Hedge fund managers are different from mutual fund managers or the public. Since hedge funds are very short-term oriented, they drive the market in different ways. There is a greater amount of noise in daily market action; this is primarily generated by hedge fund money managers as they scramble to find absolute returns any way they can. They tend to "rent" stocks, not "invest" in them. With that in mind, we may need to measure the market and the major trend differently.

◈ How do you deal with the problem of the tradeoff between early signal detection and sensitivity to random noise?

I have a natural filter for "noise." First, I don't try to forecast every 10 percent move in the market or in a stock. In today's market, to try to do that is suicidal. I create filters to take out random noise, and I attempt to get early signals. I want only *good* signals. For example, we had a 90 percent up day that I believe was a result of Ronald Reagan's passing. When I saw it, I said, "Technically, this is a signal, but it's not really market related; it's a special *tribute*, in my view." *You can't chart this stuff!* Ronald Reagan was the first president to ever visit the New York Stock Exchange floor. The NYSE membership is a big fan of Ronald Reagan. In short, what happens on that floor—the supply and demand for stocks—has a strong emotional component. I'm trying to find investments, rather than day trades, and that makes it easier for me to filter out random noise.

◈ What percentage of your analysis is intuitive?

I would say 10 percent. I'm very statistically driven. I look at numbers. My clients need to have a clear explanation for my decisions, and this is only possible through the data. They're making big decisions on huge amounts of money. They may be managing someone's pension. They may believe in you, but they still need a statistical explanation on how you got there.

◈ Why do you share your inventions with others rather than keeping the edge for yourself?

Because it's my bread and butter. I write for my clients, and my clients are my business partners. If I were at home trading my own account and that was my source of income, it might be a different story. I'm paid for my ability to discuss the market and be different, creative, innovative, and correct. Hiding it does not have any interest for me.

◈ Is it possible for you to completely stop thinking about the market?

Let's put it this way: People should go on a cruise at least once. My first day on a cruise, I did go nuts. I did not believe them when they said there was no newspaper. I checked the news posted daily on a bulletin board, and it was only short AP news headlines. It was nothing! For twenty-four hours I was in shock because I had been cut off from the world. It was total isolation. I enjoy staying on top of world news, and I am analyzing all the time, thinking about what it means for the market. If the news is important, I will work on the weekends. But I do not come home and talk about it, and I avoid people at cocktail parties who want to talk about the market. I think a break from the market is good. Try a cruise. You realize that the world goes on without you, the news goes on, and the markets function just fine.

6

Robert J. Farrell

I look at the message of the market. I believe in long-term cycles;
there are no new eras, only old eras that go to new excesses, and
there is the return to the mean.

———◦◦◦◦———

R obert J. Farrell was at Merrill Lynch for half a century before he retired
in 2004. He was chief market analyst until 1992, when he assumed
a new role as senior investment adviser. He published Wall Street's first
report on longer-term theme and sector changes in the market. He ranked
first sixteen times in the market-timing category of *Institutional Investor*
magazine's All-America Research Team, and in 1993 was inducted into the
Wall $treet Week Hall of Fame. He is a founder and first president of the
Market Technicians Association.

Farrell holds a bachelor's degree in economics and finance from Manhattan College and a master's degree in investment finance from the
Columbia University Graduate School of Business.

◈ What led to your interest in technical analysis?

Everything with me was simultaneously accidental and planned. I
went to Columbia University Graduate School of Business in the
mid-'50s and had both Benjamin Graham and David Dodd, the
authors of *Security Analysis*—the bible of stock market analysts—
as teachers. My expectation was that I would get a job on Wall
Street as a security analyst. When I got to Wall Street, I had no
background in technical analysis and no particular interest in it. I
was in a training program at Merrill Lynch in research, and I
wanted to find some way to distinguish myself, because a lot of

people at the firm were security analysts and were very smart. The job of a technician at Merrill Lynch opened up when I was in the training program, and they offered the job to me, even with no background in technical analysis. It was just me and a girl who kept up the charts. Since I was the only one doing this, I figured that maybe I should learn something about it.

After the second year at Merrill Lynch, the head of the research department, Bill Dunkak, was replaced and put on the president's staff, and he asked me to go with him. In addition to his background in fundamental analysis (he headed the research staff of fundamental analysts), he was very interested in markets, in the behavior of people, and in how markets were affected by people. He became my mentor and my teacher. I learned a lot about analyzing the market from him. As time went on, I thought it would be important to shed the idea that a technician is a short-term trader. I realized that if I were to have a future in this field, I had to cultivate the institutional market, and to do that, I had to have more of a long-term perspective than a short-term perspective. I believe the most useful technical and market analysis has a longer-term focus, because there are more nonrandom long-term movements.

As time went on, it became apparent to me that being a technician was not something that was going to put me on any kind of pedestal. It was not a profession you could be proud of at that time. Most of the institutional customers I dealt with were skeptical about what it could offer. Through my mentor I was able to study the psychology of the markets to a much greater extent than just looking at whether a chart broke out or had a reversal formation. We spent a lot of time analyzing various types of data generated internally at Merrill Lynch, such as the buying and selling by margin accounts. The margin trader was the aggressive buyer of stocks. When he was skeptical and selling, that was a good sign; when he was piling in and buying, that was a bad sign.

At that time, I was also introduced to a friend of Dunkak's named Sandy Landfield. Landfield was the partner in charge of floor positions in the Carlisle DeCoppet odd-lot house. At lunch, he would discuss how the odd-lot mentality was evolving, how he was positioning his brokers' stocks, and how much inventory they would carry based on how the book looked and how orders were flowing. It became increasingly apparent to me that this whole sub-jective area of market psychology, or market sentiment, as we iden-tified it in the '60s, was not developed to any great degree. We had the stop-loss orders, short-sale and short-covering trades data avail-able, and we were examining that data on a total basis to see which way people were going with their transactions. I also read the au-thors who had some original insight about the history of the mar-kets. For example, Garfield Drew was the original odd-lot theorist. Humphrey Neil wrote a book about contrary opinion. Everybody talks about contrary opinion today, but back then it was not as com-mon. Gradually, I was learning a style, and the style was not to be identified as a chartist or a technician, but as someone who had historical insight, like Dunkak. Every day after the close, Dunkak and I would go over what was happening in the market. He would chart the Dow Jones industrials, the transports, and the utilities and say, "I remember that formation. It looks just like 1938." Then he would go back to look at 1938. I did that so often with him that I committed to memory what all the markets looked like at each given point in time since the 1920s, and I gradually became aware of the cyclicality of the markets.

In any event, I went into technical analysis almost by accident. I became the first president of the Market Technicians Association. I had achieved a little more professional respect for the kind of analysis I did, and I was representing a major firm. Again, I was almost dragged into [the association], rather than being the big pioneer. So I was part of the group that put the MTA together. I put some effort into it and organized a lot of programs in the beginning.

Starting out, I also figured out that Wall Street has all these smart people, most of whom are quantitative types, and I knew I could not compete with that. I was more right-brained intuitive and more street smart, and I thought I should develop that to add something extra to the equation that would help investors. Every-thing I've done was not typical of technical analysts. I did not want to be called a technician even though I was the first president of the MTA. We named our group at Merrill Lynch the Market Analysis Department, and I emphasized the psychological and the historical relationships I thought were important, and cycles would come into that as well.

◈ Did you learn technical analysis mostly on your own or with a teacher?

I really never had a teacher in technical analysis. Most of the academic world did not regard technical analysis as worth much. I learned by doing and from my mentor, though at the time I did not realize he was my mentor. I also learned how important communication was, so I became a reasonably good writer. To communicate ideas and to get people to act on what you think takes some doing; you have to get their attention. When I started out, I was dealing with Merrill Lynch retail offices, and that was the short-term trading. Then I realized I should cultivate the institutional clients. They have portfolios and have to keep turnover down and try to find important long-term trends.

In 1968 my mentor retired, and I was made head of a technical department of sixteen people, which was the largest on the Street. We had a meeting every day before 8:30 a.m., and everybody at the department was encouraged to contribute their ideas. I encouraged all of the technical analysts who worked with me to specialize in something. For example, one would specialize in Elliott wave and another one would specialize in odd-lot theory or cycles. That way each one of them would know more than I knew about any given area. Their contributions could help formulate the opinion, but somebody had to make a decision. You're going to have lots of different ideas as to what you should do, but the best decisions in the stock market or in running money are not committee decisions. Committees don't take chances; they stay bunched in the middle.

I gradually found that I was better off being a contrarian and looking at what the markets were saying versus what people and the economists' surveys were expecting. When they all agreed in one direction, I at least had one alternative to rule out. So I had a starting point. Often it was more intuitive than quantitative. I do chart by hand a bunch of things even today, but I look at the numbers as a representation of how people are reacting. I ask myself whether the numbers represent an extreme in one direction or the other, and whether the extreme is a good extreme or a just another opportunity to sell or to buy because it's a modest extreme.

◈ Are there things you learned only after you started applying technical analysis to real markets, things you never saw in the literature?

Once you put your money to work, the work is much more emotional. It's very easy to tell people, "This is the way it should be," but when you have to pull the trigger, that requires a special skill. That's why the best analysts don't necessarily make the best portfolio managers. I learned that you never take a position on a technical basis and then say, if it doesn't work, "Well, this is fundamentally pretty good, so I'll keep it." You want to integrate the two, but you can't use one as an excuse for the other or as an excuse for the failure of what you're trying to achieve, which is a trading gain or a trading short-sale gain.

◈ Which mistake has taught you the most?

For a while I didn't learn to cut losses. I made the mistake of using fundamental analysis as an excuse for the failure of the technicals. I'd say, "That's a good stock anyway," despite the fact that the technicals looked bad. That's always wrong. After quite a few years I realized that the most effective analysis was sector analysis rather than general market analysis. I've spent a lot of time analyzing where we were in a market cycle and what the general market was likely to do. I found I was not as accurate in identifying the top and the bottom as I was in identifying the time to own oil and the time to own consumer growth stocks, and so on. I resigned as the chief market analyst at Merrill Lynch in 1992 because I wanted to be a senior investment adviser doing theme and profile investing. So I wrote reports on long-term themes, like the aging population and the benefits that the aging population could have for the drug companies, for example. I felt this was something needed on Wall Street, and I wrote about it for eight years or so. It was popular with some of the institutions, but it never caught on more broadly. In any event, the mistake I made early on was to concentrate too much on what the overall market was going to do, and not spend enough time on major sector trends.

◈ How is your style of technical analysis distinct?

It's basically looking at the message of the market. I believe in long-term cycles; there are no new eras, only old eras that go to new excesses, and there is the return to the mean. I have some very simple premises. When you have a boom or a bubble, the same pattern follows each time. There is a big break, as in 1929–32, and I call that an "A" wave. Automatically that wave goes so far that you get a return move—not a new bull market, but a partial or maybe even full retracement in some cases. Most of the time it's a halfway or a third-of-the-way retracement. That's what I called the "B" wave. Then you go into a long period of markets either going down and making new lows or going sideways for a long time in a "C" wave as the excesses are purged and as what got overvalued winds up being undervalued. I still write about these A, B, C patterns today. A lot of my style sounds more fundamental than technical. That's because I try to integrate the intermarket relationships, for example, the idea that there is a relationship between the gold and the dollar. I comment on or try to integrate a lot of different markets into my analysis, so I'm a broad generalist with a historical bias.

◈ In what kind of market conditions do you make the most mistakes?

The late cycle market—particularly the late bull market where you have more trading range behavior and where the market is not showing a clear trend (for example, more stocks are failing than earlier)—becomes a more difficult environment to operate in, especially if you're short-term oriented. But I'd rather not do mainly short-term trading.

◈ Are all the indicators/strategies you use in the public domain? And if so, what is it about the way you use these tools that accounts for your superior returns?

Yes, they are. It's an art. We can all have the same information, but we have to figure out which information to emphasize at any particular time. It isn't something that you plug into a formula. You can't say that everybody has the same information, and, therefore, everybody is going to do the same thing. People act differently on the same information. That's why we never had any problems sharing our internal data or the results of our internal data with our clients. We found that they were very interested in it, but not all of them knew what to do with it. So, it's the experience and the art that makes it work for some and not for others. In some markets it's hard to distinguish random noise from something that is signaling a real breakout or a new trend, but you give a trend the benefit of the doubt until you go beyond your parameters, where you're too far in the other direction. If you're trading too actively and using intraday charts, and everybody has the same information—only nuances may be different—somebody is going to say, "If they're all going to buy on that, I'm going to sell, just to be a contrarian." But why is it that you get a better answer from the same data than somebody else does? It's because of your understanding of where you are in the cycle and because of your experience in dealing with the data.

◈ Is technical analysis more effective used on its own or combined with fundamental analysis?

I prefer to know what the economic background is and what the fundamentals are in a company. It's like knowing the yield on a stock. Suppose you don't like the chart. You think it should be a top and it's going down, but the yield is much higher than the normal yield level and you see that there is steady increase in the dividend. You're likely to be more leery of shorting than you would be if you didn't have that information. There are lots of other examples. When I was doing theme and sector investing, I would look for long-term trends that were fundamental trends, such as increases in the older population, which could help the drug and medical device companies. I started looking at the charts of the companies that made hips and knees after I got a new hip five years ago. That was a fundamental factor, that the population is aging. Then I looked at where the leadership was. Where were the stocks that were going to do the best in this situation? That was an integration of fundamentals with the technicals in a crude way. I don't get down to the analysis of the balance sheet or looking at the basis for the earnings.

❖ How much of your technical analysis is intuitive?

A lot. I would say it's probably 60–70 percent. *Intuitive* covers a lot of ground; it's not just having a hunch. I believe that if you have a good or bad feeling about something, you should go with the feeling, looking for evidence to support it.

❖ What drives your innovative process?

My innovative process has been evolutionary. I look at different things. I measure psychological extremes and look at where we are in a cycle. I don't use the same tools all the time. That's the intuitive part of it. It's not something that you plug into a computer. I've learned that when a signal does not seem to work, I need to explore it further, see if there is something else, see if something is changing with that indicator.

❖ Were there times when you felt that relying on classical patterns and indicators was insufficient, and that developing new technical tools was necessary?

Yes.

❖ Why have you shared your inventions with others rather than keeping the edge just for yourself?

Because technical analysis is an art. I can tell someone how I think an indicator should work, but it takes a lot of time for someone to get to the point where he or she can rely on it. I have never had a problem with sharing, because all analysts have different experiences with which they go into the stock game.

❖ Is your confidence in the ability of technical analysis to forecast future price moves strong enough to relieve you of stress?

There are always stressful moments, usually coming about because of the short-term noise, such as when you feel you were too soon on something or got one wrong. I had much more stress when I worked at Merrill Lynch than I do now, even though I'm writing about what the market is doing just as I did before. Maybe that's because I travel less and I don't have a bunch of people calling me. There is always some stress in anything you do well. It's usually self-imposed stress, and that was true with me. I wanted to be right and to do something well.

7

Ian McAvity

The market is right. The market will make me wrong and find out where my pain threshold is. It will find out when I will change my opinion. It takes a number of years to learn to be less stubborn.

───◦⟨⟨◦⟩⟩◦───

Ian McAvity started his professional career in 1961 as a banker at the Bank of Montreal. In 1965, he went to Wall Street to work in the research department of Dominick & Dominick, a major brokerage firm, and remained in the brokerage business for ten years. Since 1972, McAvity has been publisher and editor of *Deliberations on World Markets,* a technical analysis-based newsletter that provides charts with commentary. *Deliberations* offers insights on the major world equity, bond, forex, and precious metals markets and is renowned for its timely and unusual graphic presentations.

McAvity was a founding director in 1983 of Central Fund of Canada, a bullion fund, and of Central GoldTrust (listed on TSX and Amex since 2003). He was written up in leading financial newspapers and magazines, including *Barron's* and the *Wall Street Journal,* and was a guest on *Wall $treet Week* several times in the 1970s and 1980s. Since the 1990s, he has opted for a lower public profile, although he has been a featured speaker at investment conferences and technical analyst societies in Canada, the United States, Britain, France, Germany, Switzerland, Holland, Denmark, and South Africa.

During the 1960s, McAvity was a world-class squash champion. In 1969, he played on the doubles team that was Canadian National Doubles Champion and was ranked No. 1 for several years.

◈ What led to your interest in technical analysis?

I started as a banker. I then became a broker working in the research department for Dominick & Dominick, which was then a major Wall Street brokerage firm. That was in 1965. Very quickly I discovered that when we published a research report, the price on the report was just one moment in time. One month later, I would be talking to a client and telling them, "Buy Schlumberger at 60," and the client would say, "But Schlumberger is 70." So I started charting stocks just to be aware of the price, and quickly I realized that when they started going up, they kept going up. If a stock came up to 70, the odds were it was going to 80. So I started keeping charts on every stock that the research department was recommending. I increasingly got to recognize that the patterns on the charts were far more reliable than the analysts' opinions, because in those days the analyst never went negative even when you saw a chart go up, stall, and start coming down. I became progressively more of a chartist in the late 1960s.

◈ Are there things you learned only after you started applying technical analysis to real markets, things you never saw in literature?

The nature of trend is something that you're always learning. I have been working with this material now for nearly thirty-eight years, and I'm still learning. There is always something a little bit different in the way a trend behaves. Simply, there are four stages to a trend: It's bottoming, it's rising, it's topping, it's falling. And, really, it's a question of continually keeping it simple. I see so many young traders who are looking to buy the open, sell the close, and they get so mechanical. They have computers screening where this morning's open is relative to the yesterday's close and to the midrange of three days ago. I don't even understand these formulas. To me, open, high, low, close, and volume is all I need to know. When somebody shows me a formula that includes one letter of the Greek alphabet, I close my ears. I am anti-academic in that sense.

❖ Which mistake taught you the most?

Invariably, I develop a hypothesis, a longer-term view of what I expect, and then I watch the evidence in support of my case weaken, but I stay stubborn. The market is right. The market will make me wrong and find out where my pain threshold is. It will find out when I will change my opinion. It takes a number of years to learn to be less stubborn. There was an old timer by the name of Abe Cohen, who was the founder of *Investors Intelligence,* the newsletter that measures investors' sentiment. Cohen was at a conference, and a very young fellow, in his twenties, was giving a presentation. It was in a bull market, and the youngster started walking people through two years of charts, saying, "It crosses the moving average, you buy, you sell, you buy, you sell." It seemed like a perfect system; in other words, there was a very select two-year period where it worked perfectly. And I've never forgotten Cohen going up to the podium and saying, "I remember when I was so young and so sure." Now that I'm older, I understand what Cohen meant.

❖ If all patterns/indicators/strategies that you use are in the public domain, what is it about the way you use these tools that accounts for your superior returns?

When you say superior returns, I don't know. I have not measured. I don't know how to measure it, because I don't try to tell people what to do. My newsletter is called *Deliberations*. Basically, I let people look over my shoulder, and see what I'm concerned about. Most of my focus is on anticipation or identification of changing conditions in trend. I don't make calls and say sell or buy. I don't make that kind of analysis. I'm more focused on relative change. For example, I will note that small caps have been strong, but that they're weakening relative to large caps; that the dollar is weakening against the euro, but that it's holding against the yen; or that gold is rising against the dollar. I am typically looking at (1) chart patterns, (2) moving averages, and (3) the VSMA (versus MA) ratio, which is basically price as a percentage of moving averages. The VSMA ratio is a chart method I believe I originated. It helps me identify how far price is from a moving average. For example, if a 200-day moving average is my basic definition of trend, am I too far away from it? Am I making a peak in momentum, then cooling off, coming back, making a higher high in price, but a lower high in momentum? In other words, is my trend maturing? Is the most recent strength as strong as the prior strength? So I watch for price-momentum divergences.

❖ How do you deal with the problem of the tradeoff between early signal detection and sensitivity to random noise?

Mr. Market will make a lot of noise because he does not want it to be easy. But it's impossible to determine what is random or to know precisely what is not random. I am an artist, and I just say the music is changing a little bit. To try to define it too much is a mistake, and this is one of the challenges for the academics, because virtually all patterns of behavior change over the course of a trend. The simplest way to define a trend would be "anything measured by free price," because free price is a function of buyers and sellers, greed and fear. Fear is a more urgent emotion than greed. Bottoms are very easy. Tops depend on how greedy people get. So you can think of these two emotions at either end, but as you progress, it's always going to be a little bit different, and that's very difficult to quantify.

❖ How much of your technical analysis is intuitive?

Probably half. I am still very influenced by what I see. My newsletter shows I'm a very visual person. My twenty-four-page forecast issue is probably 70 percent charts.

❖ What drives your innovative process?

Almost invariably it comes back to how to express something graphically. I think of myself as a storyteller. I gather vast quantities of data, and I'm driven by the pictures that I can create. I'll do ratios of this to that, and then I'll fiddle with the scale so that there is enough of a range to show me if the trend is going up or down.

Then I'll throw a moving average on so that I can see if this is a reasonably projectable trend.

◈ Were there times when you felt that relying on classical patterns and indicators was insufficient, and that developing new technical tools was necessary?

Over the years, all indicators will change. Parameters will change over a course of a trend. In the 1970s, for example, there was this thing called the "specialist short sales ratio," which is the percentage of the short selling that was done by the specialists. Before the advent of options trading, that was probably the single most reliable ratio for about seven or eight years. But then they changed the floor trading rules so that the specialists could lay off part of these trades upstairs on the desk, not on the floor. Then options came along, and within a period of about three years, the specialist short sales ratio was useless, when viewed in the context of prior rules and extremities for signals.

Odd-lot short sales had varying values at times. I quickly learned that with a lot of market sentiment measures, like the market vane or the bullish consensus surveys, the range of interest is constantly changing. For example, in the later stages of a recognized downtrend, you'll recognize a swing up from 10 to 50 percent in a lot of bulls, but as soon as you realize a new trend is in place, your range of interest may become 50 to 85 percent in a bull market trend. It's a question of studying prior cycles in different markets, because every market will generate different degrees of enthusiasm.

I stay away from trying to define a signal level, because signal levels are always moving. I don't understand the math of constructing a Bollinger band, but it's one good measure, because it's a continually moving measure. I want parameters that are constantly adjusting to the current market. There is a mathematical term for it, essentially "dynamic trendlines," or something that is continually adjusting to the latest information, but with respect to what it did in similar trend conditions in the past. It's not continually generating new parameters on its own. I spend a lot of time relating what's happening now to what happened in the last bull market, for example.

❖ Why do you share your inventions with others, rather than keeping the edge just for yourself?

It's largely egotistical at this stage, but my primary income for many years was publishing my opinions in my newsletter. My subscribers own my thoughts; I work for them. I have never worked for anybody else since the mid-1970s. I've seen a few people trying to create or market black boxes, but I'm against such an approach because (1) it lends itself to fraud if it's abused, and (2) I'm very dubious of something that cannot be explained fairly simply. If someone starts explaining an algorithm that's far too complicated, my reaction is this: open, high, low, close, volume. What else have you got to work with? It's either going up or down, and if it takes you three pages to say that, I think you have a problem.

❖ Is your confidence in the ability of technical analysis to forecast future price moves strong enough to relieve you of stress?

Forecast future price movements? I think trends are predictable without being too precise. In terms of forecasting, the old joke is never put the price and the time in the same paragraph, which means, never try to suggest that next Thursday at three o'clock this will be the price. I have very little confidence in that. But I can identify a trend that would appear likely to continue, based on cumulative characteristics.

❖ To what extent does your trading control your life?

I am the antithesis of that. For example, if the market is at a critical juncture and doing something I've anticipated, and I have a tee time at the golf course at eleven o'clock, I'll find out when I get back from the golf course what happened that day. I'm able to do that because I'm not going to put myself in a position where I can blow up, because, again, I am not paid to play. When I retired from the mining business in the mid-'90s, I put out a letter that said I would only continue doing my newsletter and that I would remain as a director of Central Fund, the gold and silver bullion fund, because that's more of a trustee's role than a trading-decision-making role. My primary ambition right now is to work on my golf game in the summer and on my skiing in the winter, and when I have time, I'll decide what I want to be when I grow up. If you take life too seriously, you'll shorten your life. Those who are most compulsive typically burn out very quickly. This comes back to the assurance and the arrogance of youth. If you go down to the floor of the Chicago bond pits, you won't see many sixty-year-old traders on the floor. You'll see an awful lot of people who are twenty or twenty-five, with a lot of bruises and very sharp elbows. And many of them are working for the sixty-year-olds, who graduated from that floor a long time ago. It's the nature of the business.

◈ Describe your working day.

I spend a tremendous amount of time just gathering data. I've tried not to get dependent on computers, but I am now basically an attachment to my notebook. I am continually behind in updating things I've done at one time or another. If I have an idea, I'll work on it for twenty-five or thirty hours. When I write my newsletter, I live on cookies and coffee. I'm a heavy smoker as well, so I started a radical medical thing a couple of years ago called chelation therapy to get the plaque out of my system or, as I say, to make the sludge move. For example, I started my last forecast issue Sunday, and I got it to the printers Thursday night. I had five or six hours of sleep that week, and I smoked two cartons of cigarettes. I ran out of coffee twice, and I remembered the medical person saying it was important to have some protein, so I think three times in those four days I had a hot dog. When I'm interested in doing something, I won't bother to eat and I'll forget to go to sleep.

John J. Murphy

You have to be comfortable being in the minority. If you're right about the market most of the time, you're going to be in the minority, because the majority is usually wrong.

John J. Murphy is a chief technical analyst of StockCharts.com, providing investors analysis online. Previously, he was a director of technical research at Merrill Lynch and president of MurphyMorris Money Management Company. Murphy is a popular author on the subject of technical analysis. His book *Technical Analysis of the Financial Markets* is regarded as the standard reference in the field, and in *Intermarket Technical Analysis,* he pioneered a branch of technical analysis emphasizing interrelationships between various financial markets. *The Visual Investor,* which applies charting principles to sector analysis, is his third book. A former technical analyst for CNBC, Murphy has appeared on major financial television programs such as *CNN Moneyline, Nightly Business Report,* and *Wall $treet Week with Louis Rukeyser,* and on Bloomberg Television. He has been quoted in leading financial newspapers and magazines, including *Barron's* and *Stocks & Commodities* magazine, which described his intermarket work as "unparalleled." In 1992, Murphy received the first award for outstanding contribution to global technical analysis given by the International Federation of Technical Analysts. In 2002, he received the Market Technicians Association's annual award. He holds a BA in economics and an MBA from Fordham University.

❖ What led to your interest in technical analysis?

I did not set out to be a technical analyst. I got a bachelor's degree in economics, and I wanted to work on Wall Street, primarily as a security analyst, because that's what I knew about. One fellow who interviewed me had just become a portfolio manager with a very large company. He was sort of a technical analyst. He kept charts, but he was a little bit of both (fundamental and technical). "I need someone to come in and help do charts for me," he said, explaining that was a good way to get your foot in the door. "When you're ready, in six months or a year," he said, "you can move into a fundamental area." So I started keeping his charts. There were bar charts and a lot of point and figure charts, as well as a stock portfolio. I became fascinated by it. I read every book, though there were not a lot of them then. There were only two or three really good books, like *Technical Analysis of Stock Trends* by Robert Edwards and John Magee. I took a course that Alan Shaw and Ralph Acampora taught at the New York Institute of Finance, and I never did move on to the fundamental area.

About two years after I started, in the late '60s, the stock market went into a decline that lasted a long time. I was probably the most junior person at my firm, so I got laid off and started looking for a job. No one was hiring in the stock market area. Then, by accident, I saw an ad for a commodity analyst with Merrill Lynch. Again, they were looking for a fundamental guy, but I was pretty desperate at that point because there weren't a lot of jobs being offered. So I went in, and one guy said, "I see you have some charting experience." I said, "Yes, that's what I would really like to do." He said they had an opening for a chartist, and I thought that was wonderful.

Alan Shaw had told me in one of his courses that you can use technical analysis for commodities. As luck would have it, although the 1970s were not very good for the stock market, they were great years for commodities. We had hyperinflation of oil and grains, and gold went to $800. I just happened to be in the right place at the right time. The commodities I was dealing with were originally just oil, gold, pork bellies, and things like that. But then they started to introduce financial futures, like currency markets, bond futures, stock index futures, and commodity index futures; so we were trading everything at that point. Later on, I gravitated back to stocks. Interestingly, not a lot of people have both stock market and commodity experience.

◈ Did you learn the craft by studying the literature on your own, or by studying with a teacher?

In those days—over thirty years ago—most of the learning was self-education. There were only two or three books: Edwards and Magee, Bill Jiler's *How Charts Can Help You in the Stock Market*, a couple of point and figure chart books, such as the one by Alexander Wheelan and another one by Abe Cohen, who started the Chartcraft method. I took one or two courses here and there, but after that it was largely self-education. There was no Market Technicians Association. Everyone was scattered, and there was not a lot of sharing of ideas. So it was very much a matter of self-education. Now it's very different. We have the MTA, we have meetings, we have newsletters and journals, people write articles, we have books (some of which I wrote) all over the place. It's much easier to learn about technical analysis now.

◈ What were some of the first things you learned when you started working as a technical analyst?

I learned that the technical work is the leading indicator of the fundamental work. I learned that very early on and in a very dramatic fashion. It was in the early 1970s, and the commodity markets started going up in a way that had not been seen in forty to fifty years. I was writing very, very bullish reports, and there must have been forty or fifty fundamental analysts who said, "This is crazy. Commodities can't go that high." I remember being severely criticized for being irresponsible. As it turned out, commodities went through the roof. So I learned you had to be comfortable being in the minority. If you're right about the market most of the time, you're going to be in the minority, because the majority is usually wrong. Another thing I learned early on is that there is a difference between analyzing something and making research recommendations as opposed to managing money. Towards the end of the '70s and in the early '80s, I started managing money. Trading tactics became a lot more important. It's not enough to be right on the direction of the market. The timing has to be especially good, and that timing is almost completely technical.

❖ Which mistake taught you the most?

I've made two big mistakes over the years. One was seeing something on a chart and not pursuing it because everybody disagreed with it. You have to believe what you see even when people disagree with it. There were occasions when I missed a very good trade because I decided that I would be criticized if I followed it. I learned over the years not to do that. My other big mistake relates to the old trading axiom "Let your profits run and cut your losses short" and to the discipline this axiom implies. You have to be very disciplined. The biggest mistake you can make in the stock market, commodity market, or any other market is to get out too soon. That had been one of my flaws over the years. You have got to have the discipline to stay in, and you shouldn't sell something unless there is a really good reason to.

❖ How is your style of technical analysis distinct?

Over the years it's become a bit more classical. I rely on classical chart patterns, trendlines, moving averages, and oscillators. What I've become best known for is intermarket analysis. I wrote a book on it back in 1991 called *Intermarket Technical Analysis,* and I did another one in 2004. This was an outgrowth of my having worked in the futures markets, where we were trading bonds, stocks, commodities, and the dollar, and where I started to notice all kinds of correlations. The whole idea of the book is that all these markets are related. For example, if you're trading the stock market, you also have to follow bonds, since what happens in the bond market has an impact on stocks. And bonds are very much affected by commodity prices. For example, when commodities turn up, that's an early sign of inflation. Commodities' turning up pushes interest rates higher, and, in time, that becomes bearish for stocks. Now what pushes commodity prices higher is the falling dollar. You can't look at any one of these markets all by itself—you have to understand the impact they have on one another. Also, global markets are very important. Then there are sector rotations; depending on where you are in the business cycle, you need to understand which sectors of the stock market you should be emphasizing. That comes out of the whole body of intermarket analysis.

❖ Describe your approach to the practice of technical analysis.

It's not complicated. I look at all the markets. The stock market is the most important. I do a top-down approach. I try to determine if the stock market is a good place to be at any given time. I do a lot of sector work and industry group work. When the stock market is going up or down, and even when it's going sideways and doing nothing, there is always something going up and there is always something going down. The sector work is actually one of the best places to use technical analysis, because there is so much going on beneath the surface in the stock market. We have about ten major market sectors and about ninety industry groups, and some of them are always going up and some down. And since the turns come fairly quickly, they can be spotted very easily on charts. So mine is a more active trading approach. I use relative-strength analysis, for example. We divide all the various sectors by, say, their performance relative to the S&P 500. We trade only those sectors that are outperforming the market, and we try to capture them as early as possible.

❖ Is your analysis more effective when you're working by yourself or when you're working with others?

Definitely by myself. I work in New Jersey now, and I have an office all by myself. I don't keep the television on anymore. Once in a while I may turn on CNBC or Bloomberg to hear a bit of what's going on, just in case I'm missing something. Ultimately, I think you're better off being away in a quiet spot by yourself.

❖ In what kind of market conditions do you make the most mistakes?

Probably in a trading-range market. When the market is trending, it's hard to make too many mistakes, because the market bails you out. When the market is going down, our technical work keeps us out of trouble. The really difficult situation is when the market just trades sideways. You get frustrated, and your clients get impatient. I manage money now, and when the market is not going anywhere, my clients say, "Why aren't we making any money?" So sometimes you start to force things, and you get a little too aggressive when you really shouldn't. If you do get a quick profit, you might take it a little too soon.

◈ If all patterns/indicators/strategies you use are in the public domain, what is it about the way you use these tools that accounts for your superior returns?

I think there is a skill level, just like in the medical field. People go to medical school and learn the same things about the human body and how it works, and yet you have good doctors and bad doctors. That's true in any field. There is a certain artistic, creative element to it as well. Over time, you develop an intuitive element.

◈ How do you deal with the problem of the tradeoff between early signal detection and sensitivity to random noise?

This is an ongoing problem with our technical work. If you get too long-term oriented, you give up too much in the beginning and in the end: you get in too late and you get out too early. If you become too short-term oriented, you run the risk of getting caught up in noise. You can't avoid it totally, but you can try to minimize it by looking at things from both the short-term and the long-term perspectives. For example, even if you're looking at a short-term chart, you should always look at the long-term chart as well. This is where the intermarket work comes in. I'm looking at the stock market, but I'm also looking at what's happening in the dollar or in the bond market, and sometimes that helps clarify things. You can't avoid being affected by the noise; it's going to happen on occasion, but if you look at the weight of the evidence, you can minimize it.

◈ Is technical analysis more effective when used on its own or when combined with fundamental analysis?

Some of the intermarket work I do is sometimes considered as having a bit of fundamental analysis in it. For example, I pay a lot of attention to the direction of interest rates because it has an impact on the stock market. I also analyze currency trends, trends of commodities, and inflation. These are sometimes considered fundamental factors. I don't necessarily agree with that, but I've been accused of sounding almost like an economist when I'm on television, which I'm not.

The trend in the industry now is to blend the two approaches. I've often said to fundamental analysts that the price action is the leading indicator of the fundamentals. If you're not following price action, you're really not doing fundamental analysis. I often hear people say that a particular analyst may be very bullish on a certain stock, despite the fact that the charts look very bad. They say the technicals may be bad, but the fundamentals are good. I say that can't be. Technicals and fundamentals are not divorced from each other. If the technicals are bad, then the fundamentals have to be bad. Most of the audiences I talk to are not technical people; they're fundamental analysts. I tell them, "I'm not suggesting that you give up what you do; I'm just suggesting that you should be looking at the technicals to improve your timing."

There is a big problem with fundamental analysts. If they issue a bullish forecast on a particular industry, like technology, what do they do if it starts to collapse? The fundamentals haven't changed, so they still issue buy recommendations all the way down. They have no stop-loss. Whereas in the technical work, if I issue a bullish forecast and it starts to break down, I say something is wrong here, and I get out.

There are two ways to combine the two approaches. First of all, if you're a fundamental person, you should first form your fundamental judgment as to whether you like something or not, and then look at the chart to see if it's in an uptrend or in a downtrend. If it's in a downtrend, you may want to wait a little while—just use it to help you with the timing a bit. The second way of combining the two is something I experienced many times when I worked at Merrill Lynch back in the '70s: When you see something happening to the market on a chart—it suddenly breaks out on the upside or it suddenly breaks down—you go running to the fundamental analysts' offices and say, "Something is happening in your market," and they say, "No, nothing is happening. There's no fundamental news." Then, three months later, they find that something has happened. Technical analysis becomes an alert. If you're a fundamental analyst and you see something unusual—maybe a lot of volume coming into a particular security—it should alert you that something is obviously changing.

◈ How much of your technical analysis is intuitive?

I think that, as you get older, more and more of it is intuitive. You try not to do that. You try to be disciplined and follow the rules. It's not good to trade just from hunches. But there are times when I look at all the evidence and I decide to make a move—to get in or get out of something before it happens—and if someone were to ask me why I made that decision, I would have to say, "I am not quite sure; it just felt right." I don't want to overemphasize that, but I do think that over time your memory bank remembers certain things, and that's where the skill level comes in. You learn to spot and anticipate certain situations. Whether we want it to or not, the subconscious is always going to creep into it.

◈ At this point in your career, would you say that classical technical tools are sufficient?

I wouldn't say that. Some of the useful technical indicators are still fairly new. I wrote *Technical Analysis of the Futures Markets* in 1986. I wrote about a lot of timing indicators that have been developed in the futures industry—like the relative strength index and stochastics—which have become quite popular in the stock market. So there are always new things coming along. Generally speaking, my intermarket work is a new approach.

◈ How soon after you develop a particular technical tool do you make it accessible to the public? Why do you share your inventions with others, rather than keeping the edge just for yourself?

I talk less and less to the public these days. If I give a speech or if I'm on television, I may share some ideas, but I don't share everything. Wouldn't you be suspicious if someone found something that worked for him and then he suddenly broadcasted it? We all have little tricks that we use, our favorite things that we don't necessarily talk about. My responsibility, since I manage a mutual fund now, is to my clients. It's no longer my responsibility to go on CNBC and tell people how we do it. So I've become a little more selfish. Not that the techniques we use are that complicated, but I don't feel any responsibility to share those ideas.

❖ So there are tools that you've developed but never shared with the rest of the world?

Well, not so much the tools, but how you put it together. How can you share? I'm not sure I can explain to you exactly how I do what I do. I look at a lot of things in a very short period of time, and I form an impression. I'm not sure I could completely explain to someone how I do it.

❖ Describe your working day.

I usually wake up around six thirty. I put Bloomberg radio on, and I don't get out of bed until I've listened to it for about half an hour. What I like about Bloomberg is that they give all the overnight data about what the markets have done in Europe, in Asia, and about the dollar, gold, oil, etc. That gives me an idea which stocks to watch that day. Before I even get out of bed, I have a snapshot of what kind of day this is going to be or how it's going to start. Then I read the *New York Times*—the sports section first, but then I get to the financial stuff—and *Investor's Business Daily*. I go through that rigorously. I also read the *Wall Street Journal*. When I get to the office, I scan everything that's happened overnight. I look at what's been up and at what's been down. Then, after the market opens, I go though a checklist of stuff. So I put in a good three or four hours in the morning just trying to get a feel and find out what's important, because there is a lot of noise out there.

By nine or nine thirty, I've gotten all the data for our decision model. I review our positions, see if I need to upgrade or downgrade something, or make any changes. These decisions are usually made before ten o'clock. I also write for our website, StockCharts.com. Then I do some analysis, and answer my e-mail. Usually, by noon I take a break. I go away for a couple of hours. Sometimes I take a nap, sometimes I go to the health club, but I just get away from it in the middle of the day, because there is really nothing going on. I come back in the afternoon. There may be a trade we were looking to make near the close, and I usually write a market wrap-up. I may work till five or six o'clock. Very often I'll watch business shows like the *Nightly Business Report*. Saturdays I read *Barron's;* Sundays I read the *New York Times*.

◈ Is your confidence in the ability of technical analysis to forecast future price moves strong enough to relieve you of stress?

Live without stress? I haven't gotten there yet, but I'm getting there. I started meditating recently and working out a bit more. I don't think you can ever eliminate stress. As you get older, you have a bigger perspective on life. When you're younger and raising a family and trying to climb the corporate ladder, it's almost a life-and-death situation. It isn't that anymore for me. It becomes more of an intellectual exercise. If you connect the dots right and follow the rules pretty closely, you're not going to go too far afield. And if you make a mistake or something doesn't work once in a while, you say, "Well, it didn't work this time."

◈ Did the market have a strong hold on your life in the beginning of your career?

Yes. After about fifteen years of trading, I had to quit. I was so burned out and so emotionally drained that I started developing physical problems. You know the old joke where you go to a doctor and say, "Doctor, my arm hurts when I do this," and he says, "Don't do this!" I remember going to see the company doctor quite often, and he said to me, "God, you've been through an awful lot. Your medical file is gigantic." He asked me what I did for a living, and I told him I was a commodities trader. He said, "Don't do it anymore. You've got to make a life-style change." Yes, for me it was emotionally draining. I'd walk out of the office at the end of the day, and my mood would be determined by the market. If I had a bad Friday, I would be grumpy all weekend. I think this is true if you're trading a large amount of money in very volatile markets. And I was trading by myself, which is true of a lot of traders. By my midthirties I was a basket case. I decided to do something else for a while. But now that I'm back to it again a bit, I have a more detached attitude about it, and I think I'm better than I was then.

9

Robert R. Prechter Jr.

Being wrong in forecasting a market does not mean you have made a mistake. This is a probability business. If your principles are sound, you will be right a certain percentage of the time, which means that you must be wrong a certain percentage of the time. So being wrong is a consequence of doing the right thing, not "making a mistake."

⟶ ❧ ⟵

Robert R. Prechter Jr., CMT, is founder and president of Elliott Wave International, the world's largest independent financial forecasting firm, which provides round-the-clock analysis on global financial markets. He has been writing market commentary since 1976.

Prechter served for nine years on the national Board of the Market Technicians Association and in 1990–1991 served as its president. In 1989, Financial News Network (now CNBC) named him "Guru of the Decade," and in 1999, he received the Canadian Society of Technical Analysts' (CSTA) first annual A. J. Frost Memorial Award for Outstanding Contribution to the Development of Technical Analysis. In 2003, Traders Library granted him its Hall of Fame Award.

Prechter has written thirteen books on finance, beginning with *Elliott Wave Principle: Key to Market Behavior* in 1978. His 2002 title, *Conquer the Crash: You Can Survive and Prosper in a Deflationary Crash and Depression*, was a *New York Times* best seller. In *Socionomics: The Science of History and Social Prediction* (1999–2003), Prechter presents a theory of endogenously regulated social mood and its manifestation in social action. His articles have appeared in the *Journal of Behavioral Finance* and other publications. Prechter speaks to groups worldwide on socionomic theory, including the London School of Economics, Georgia Tech, MIT, SUNY, and at academic conferences. In 2005, he created the

Socionomics Institute, which is dedicated to explaining socionomics, and he funds the Socionomics Foundation, which supports academic research in the field.

◈ When did you first get interested in technical analysis?

I was exposed to it in the late 1960s and got really interested in the early 1970s.

◈ Did a mentor play a role in your development as a technical analyst?

My mentor, from a distance, was [Richard] Russell. I wanted to do what he did for a living. His letter [*Dow Theory Letters*] was the first place I saw a discussion of the wave principle. But many people have taught me things over the years, including the staff at the Merrill Lynch Market Analysis Department, where I started in 1975. That's where I learned about indicators.

◈ Did you learn the craft by studying the literature on your own, or by studying with a teacher?

I got most of my education from books, and I read a lot of them, mostly on Dow theory and cycles, and of course R. N. Elliott's books and articles, which I went to great lengths to locate. I focused on approaches that gave you a prayer of *predicting*. Everything else was irrelevant, as far as I was concerned. I never had a teacher. In fact, in 1975, market analysis departments at brokerage firms were typically one guy. There was nobody to do the teaching, and no one was holding seminars. In college, twice I tried to get into a course on mass psychology, but it got canceled both times. But it turned out to be my field.

◈ Are there things you learned only after you started applying technical analysis to real markets, things you never saw in the literature?

Two things: First, I discovered things about waves that others hadn't noticed—subtle, remarkable things, such as quantitative relationships between certain waves. Second, and more fundamentally, I came to the realization in 1979 that the *implications* of the validity of technical analysis for society and history are utterly unappreciated. I am trying to found a whole new field, which I call "socionomics," to explain this idea and use it to forecast financial, macroeconomic, and social trends.

❖ Which mistake taught you the most?

The biggest mistake I ever made with respect to market forecasting was to use up valuable effort thinking about fundamentals from time to time in causal terms. They never help in forecasting stock market trends, or even currencies or commodities. I have always known to ignore 99 percent of fundamental data, but I did not fully root them from my mind until the summer of 2002, when I wrote the essay "A Socionomic View of Central-Bank Causality." Truth comes in principles. You can't have exceptions to a valid principle. If you do, either your principle is wrong or you haven't thought through the matter hard enough.

I want to clarify something here, though. Being wrong in forecasting a market does not mean you have "made a mistake." This is a probability business. If your principles are sound, you will be right a certain percentage of the time, which means that you must be *wrong* a certain percentage of the time. So being wrong is a consequence of doing the *right* thing, not "making a mistake." I hate it when journalists ask what error we made last month when the market didn't go our way. Most people wouldn't ask a .400 hitter what *mistake* he made in grounding out to first base in the fifth inning. Most people can understand that baseball is a matter of percentages, but they don't see this when it comes to forecasting. The best analysts are still wrong a lot. Now you can see why the public always loses. It thinks that being right means *always* being right and being wrong is a "mistake."

Of course, we're learning more all the time about market analysis, so some miscalls come from a lack of knowledge. That's the excuse I use, anyway. But let me give you an example of what I'm talking about. If I'm a market historian, I take history as a guide to what's possible. When markets make new history by breaking all previous measures of extremity, my knowledge of history kicks in and I get increasingly adamant that the trend should end soon. Sometimes it

goes on way longer than I could imagine. Now, should I "learn" something from this rare outcome? Should I learn, for example, that you
can't trust history? But I know that you *can* trust history, but only as
a basis for *probabilistic* expectations. If I were to "learn" that you can't,
I would be in a state of uncertainty all the time, and I would abandon
a tool that has given me some successes. There's being wrong, and
there are mistakes; they are not the same thing.

❖ How is your style of technical analysis distinct?

I use a model of the market called the wave principle, which is a
robust hierarchical fractal comprising quasi-geometric forms. It is
not a designed model but a distillation of empirical observation of
what markets actually do. The wave principle is the template against
which to judge every market action and indicator. It gives me a context in which to think.

❖ Is technical analysis better done working individually or in teams?

Individually! Read Irving Janis's *Groupthink*. He was a professor
of mine at Yale. When you are a member of a group, the natural
tendency is to abdicate responsibility. The best analyst is one who
abdicates nothing. He blames or credits only himself.

❖ How much of your approach to analysis are you willing to share with others?

Absolutely everything. I used to run into technicians who didn't
want to let their secrets out. Some got annoyed in 1978 that we wrote
a book on the wave principle. What a joke. As if the public as a whole
will ever wise up. It's fine to teach interested, talented people. They
love it, and it's fun.

❖ How do you deal with the problem of the tradeoff between early signal detection and sensitivity to random noise?

I don't think there is much random noise in markets, and what is
there usually lasts only minutes and never more than a couple of
hours. My definition of noise is what markets do when leveraged

traders react to news. It creates a brief repatterning of *activity*, but it never alters the pattern of the underlying cause of market trends, which is aggregate *mood*. So mood always reestablishes its motivational hold over activity very quickly.

◈ Is technical analysis more effective when applied on its own or when combined with fundamental analysis?

To me, that's like asking, "Is food more effective when used on its own or when combined with arsenic?" Keep in mind that I'm not talking about Benjamin Graham and David Dodd and individual stocks here, and I'm not talking about valuation. I'm talking about discussing the possible impact of exogenous forces on the prices for a market. I am not aware of a reliable predictive correlation between any type of external data and prices for an aggregate financial market. Talking about exogenous causes lulls you into thinking that you have an important insight when you don't, so it encourages rationalizing, which is deadly. When you take this approach, it allows the limbic system to run wild and do what it wants, while your neocortex is otherwise occupied logically card cataloguing unhelpful data.

◈ How much of your technical analysis is intuitive?

None. The whole point of analysis is to *overcome* the unconscious, which is trying to force you to follow the herd.

◈ Some technicians believe that structures such as the Elliott wave, Gann's natural order postulates, Fibonacci numbers, etc., underlie market action. What is your opinion?

I studied Gann, and all I could see was numerology. Years ago I wrote a report refuting three of his claims, but I haven't published it yet. I wouldn't say that Fibonacci numbers "underlie" market action, but they are manifest in waves. In my view, the wave principle—Elliott waves—are *the* market fundamental. It's a form that markets follow, just as trees, lungs, and blood vessels follow a robust branching system, and just as hurricanes, whirlpools, and galaxies follow spirals. As with trees and spirals, Elliott waves constitute a fundamental organizing principle of nature. More specifically, they are an organizing principle of life forms.

◈ Is your confidence in the ability of technical analysis to forecast future price moves strong enough to relieve you of stress?

This is a false dichotomy. I'm stressed because I push myself. Yet I have no uncertainty regarding the validity of technical analysis. Again, technical analysis is a matter of probabilities, so once you take a stand, you can't avoid stress, not because it's inherent but because your readers or your clients impose it on you. They want every call to be right and every trade to be profitable. So they transfer their expectations to you, causing stress for no reason but their misunderstanding. Is a baseball player stressed? Sure, but does that mean he doesn't believe in his approach to hitting if he's batting .380? Now, trading is another matter. If you over-leverage, you invite stress. But that has nothing to do with technical analysis. Fundamentalists trade, too.

10

Linda Bradford Raschke

Sometimes the best moves happen when nobody can figure out why, so I'm purely interested in basic supply and demand, and in the balance that's there. I don't care why the market is doing what it's doing. I'm a purist. I don't do any fundamentals at all.

⎯⎯⎯◦❦◦⎯⎯⎯

Linda Bradford Raschke is president of LBRGroup, a registered commodity trading adviser (CTA) and money-management firm, and president of LBR Asset Management, a commodity pool operator. She began her professional trading career in 1981 as a market maker in equity options. In addition to running LBRGroup's CTA program, she is the principal trader for the Granat Fund.

Raschke was recognized in Jack Schwager's critically acclaimed book *The New Market Wizards* and is known for her own top-selling book, *Street Smarts: High Probability Short-Term Trading Strategies*. She has been featured in dozens of financial publications and on financial television and radio programs, and has served on the board of directors for the Market Technicians Association. She is a past president of the American Association of Professional Technical Analysts and currently on its board of directors.

Raschke has presented her research and lectured on trading for many organizations, including the Managed Futures Association, the American Association of Professional Technical Analysts, Bloomberg, the Market Technicians Association, and the International Federation of Technical Analysis, and has lectured in more than sixteen different countries for Dow Jones Telerate. She received a degree in economics and music composition from Occidental College in 1980.

◈ What led to your interest in technical analysis?

I traded for a good six to eight years before I truly got a handle on technical analysis. My dad was interested in markets, and he always had chart books, and he'd tell me to scroll through a couple of thousand stocks and look for stocks just breaking out of a base. I didn't know anything at the time and he didn't either. Then I went to Occidental College, where I got a degree in economic theory. There was a fund called the Charles R. Blyth Fund, which ten of the students got to trade. Again, I knew nothing about technical analysis, but we were making transactions in the market off of fundamentals.

I later became a floor trader on the Pacific Coast Stock Exchange, trading the equity options, which, at the time, was more oriented toward pure arbitrage. However, the person who backed me and took me under his wing was a technician. This was back in 1981 or '82 and we didn't have computers, so we would update the charts by hand. We would also call a hotline at night where we would get an oscillator, which was essentially a normalized difference between a 3-period simple moving average and a 10- or a 16-period simple moving average. So you had a momentum oscillator with your bar charts. Then, at the end of the day, I was always taught to keep things like 10-day moving averages, advance/decline lines, put-call ratios, and volume characteristics. So that's how I started getting into the routine, and much of the processing of data is a bit of a ritual or a routine.

In 1982, we were about three blocks away from the San Francisco business library, which had one of the largest selections of books on technical analysis anywhere in the country. So I would go there and read. For example, I read about chaos theory and about the equivolume charts, where you're plotting the volume relative to the price. I even plotted the equivolume charts for a while. So, I had an exposure to technical analysis since very early on in my trading career. However, being a floor trader, I worked in the bid and the offer a lot, and technical analysis was not a critical element of my trading right away, in terms of analyzing the directional play. In fact, much more of our analysis went into applied volatility and really basic stuff, I think, because we didn't have the computing power.

It was not until at least six or seven years of being a very successful floor trader that I felt I really did not understand how to use the tools to forecast the market properly. In the summer of 1987, the market just kept going up and up. It was the middle of July. By then, I had left the trading floor, and I was trading from upstairs. I used to do a lot of index futures and things like that, and I remember thinking, "I have no clue what this market is doing, where it's going, or why." Despite all my experience and the reading that I'd done in the business library, I realized that I didn't have the tools or the knowledge to figure out what this market was doing.

I truly did everything the figure-it-out-yourself way. Most of the work I did at first comprised really simple bar chart patterns and a 2-period rate of change, and that 3–10 momentum oscillator that I used to use. I was also watching the movement from the perspective of a 2- to 3-day time frame, the swings of having 2 to 3 days' markup, 1 to 2 days' markdown. I wasn't really getting into intraday charts or anything like that. When I started the research partnership with Steve Moore in 1993, my research got a lot more formalized. I went on a binge, just trying to quantify everything.

That gives you an idea of just how long it took before I felt I got a real handle on technical analysis. A big part of my journey was investigating everything, before finally arriving at the conclusion that it's just price, price, and price that matters, and then figuring out the best way to quantify the price, whether it's going to be via a momentum function or a range function, etc.

◈ Did you have a mentor?

No, my mentor was experience, which is the ultimate master, the best teacher. I remember that when I got my charting software, I was the first one who had it. I had all these little stochastics and moving averages, and this was a big thing back in 1986. Before getting the software, I made money for forty-eight consecutive weeks. Then I got my first software program, and I lost money for three months. I was like a kid in a candy shop, seeing what wasn't working and playing with all these different things. So everything I've learned about technical analysis, about quantifying patterns, was always the hard way: by investigating what didn't work and why. I do a lot of probability modeling. Let's say I have something that says I have a 66 percent success over a sample size of two thousand, which is a very nice, reasonable edge. Or let's say I have a pattern that works 80 percent of the time. Then I'm going to try to learn more about why these things didn't work 34 and 20 percent of the time, respectively, and what the factors are that I could decently model that would set that up. So it's always the investigative and inductive reasoning, considering all the different routes I could go.

◈ Was experience your teacher because you could not rely on the information you found in the literature?

I was an ignoramus. I didn't even know there were books out there. I was a floor trader; we would laugh at books. The people who write the books are the ones who can't trade and don't know anything about the markets anyway. Come on. If you have something that works and it's good, are you going to write a book about it when you can make money off of it? No! Of course, there is basic stuff, like the bar charts that you should know, and that's why in the mid-'90s I became a big promoter of classic technical analysis and its forefathers, including Charles Dow; [Richard] Schabacker, who is the father of chart patterns; and [W. D.] Gann, for his observations about the way the market trades around swing highs or swing lows. I don't do any Fibonacci or weirdo calculations; I don't believe in that stuff. But I respect [Richard] Wyckoff for his attempt to organize the way we think about the market by distinguishing among the distribution, the accumulation, and the markup phases. Then there is [R. N.] Elliott. I don't practice Elliott wave analysis, but you have to understand that this was the way these people tried to organize data at the time. They didn't have computers; they didn't have ways of crunching numbers that we do now. So they had to try to put this overwhelming amount of data into some type of framework or structure. It was just their attempt to process it. You had your basic theory that the price behavior was a reflection of crowd dynamics, so bar chart patterns are a reflection of crowd dynamics. But then, some of these guys tried to take it one step beyond that and say, "Well, how do I fit this into some macro cycle, maybe a parallel business cycle, a broader span?" That's all they were really trying to do.

◈ How is your style of technical analysis distinct?

I am pretty much 100 percent price based. I don't use volume, because most of the work I do is on the futures side, and it's difficult for me to get timely volume data. I've also found that the volume is pretty highly correlated with the range, so if I have a contraction in the range, I'm going to have contraction in the volume, unless it's at a certain point in the structure. So I look at volume characteristics intraday for a buying climax or a selling climax type of thing. I do use volume as a confirming factor if there is a good trend move. The analysis I do every night is pretty much all price based. I rely on momentum functions and spend a lot of time on volatility indicators.

◈ How much of what you learn from others do you directly apply in your trading?

Zero.

◈ Is your analysis more effective when you're working by yourself or when you're working with others?

Every night I do my homework on twenty-five different futures markets. I do the currencies, the bonds, the index futures, metals, and grains and other stuff. I go through one market at a time, and I pretty much use the same tools on all of them. Each has its own subtle nuances, and some markets have more noise than others, but I am basically looking for two or three main patterns on each of them. Then, usually on the weekends, I do broader analysis on the stocks. But I have a methodology, a routine that I follow. I always do my analysis when the markets are closed, in terms of preparation for what I'm looking for. It's like taking a test with a No. 2 lead pencil: your first guess is always going to be your best one.

◈ In what kind of market conditions do you make the most mistakes?

I tend to make more mistakes when I haven't had enough sleep. I spend a lot of time making sure that I eliminate stress from my life, that I eat right, that I exercise right, because what I do isn't

100 percent automated or mechanical. There is a big connection between the body and the brain. In terms of market conditions, I never look at it that way—that I make a mistake because of a market condition or a market environment. I always make my best educated guess as to what the probability models are telling me to do. And there is always going to be a percentage of time that the trade does not work out. It's not because I've made a mistake; it's because those are the numbers. I know I'm going to lose a certain percentage of time. I know not to overtrade when there are high levels of noise, and I know the types of conditions that lead to very noisy markets. If I'm trading in a noisy market, I need to trade in a different style; for example, I'm going to trade lower leverage, and I can do more aggressive countertrades.

One of the more frustrating environments to trade in is a very low volatility environment, because you don't have the swings there, and there are just not as many setups that occur. When you have low volatility, it often means you have a strong trend, because a characteristic of some of the strongest trends is declining volatility. That's telling me to jump out of my time frame, because at that point I can't be as accurate in trading the intraday swings. I need to be an investor at that point, just to position myself and stay with the trend. That's probably the hardest thing for me to do, because I enjoy trading. It's fun. So a strongly trending market, where you need to put a position on and walk away, is frustrating, but it isn't a matter of making a mistake, unless, too early, you get out of a position that is hard to reestablish.

◈ Which mistake has taught you the most?

My biggest mistake is trying to guess a directional outcome from a low volatility point, trying to guess a breakout. It's a very seductive little game, but if I have a fifty-fifty bet, I'm going to be wrong 90 percent of the time. It's like Murphy's law. That's why I did so much work on volatility filters.

◈ How much of what you do are you willing to share with others?

I'm willing to share anything, as long as it's something that can't be 100 percent automated. I'm not going to share anything that somebody could take and use the specifics of to run a half a billion dollars. That would be a pretty stupid thing to do. I've come up with these things myself to get my own fund back up and going.

◈ If all patterns/indicators/strategies that you use are in the public domain, what is it about the way you use these tools that accounts for your superior returns?

You always have two functions that are going to be attributable to your long-term success. The first one is trying to manage the risk; that's more important than anything. What's going to be your strategy for managing the risk? The second one is leverage. At what points in the market—in the market environment or in the overall structure—are you going to use bigger leverage? That's a key part of money management, because you get to certain points, and you have to make those big wins count. Or at what points are you going to have to cut back on your leverage, again due to either liquidity conditions or a different type of market environment? So, the two functions are (1) the money management and (2) the use of leverage. Then you have to consider how you're playing your exit strategy. Whether you're playing for a small target or for a larger target has a lot to do with it. Maybe 80 percent of the time you're playing for a small target. It's really a low percentage of the time you're playing for a big target.

◈ How do you deal with the problem of the tradeoff between early signal detection and sensitivity to random noise?

I always use two time frames. If you step out to a longer time frame, you're going to overcome that noise. The markets just have a noise factor; that's inevitable. In a strong trend, you're not going to have the noise. Perry Kaufman did a lot of nice work with the efficiency ratio there. In more of a trading range, you'll get an increase in noise, and if you go down to a shorter time frame, you'll get an increase in noise. The noise is a function of the liquidity of the market you're trading, of the swings it has. I've made my living on noise, trading off of the bid and the ask. Noise is not a bad thing. It's a good thing. If we didn't have the noise, we wouldn't have the opportunity.

◈ Is technical analysis more effective when used on its own or when combined with fundamental analysis?

I'm a purist. I don't do any fundamentals at all. I'll look at liquidity or monetary measurements, such as money flows or money supply, but I don't know if I would call that fundamental analysis. Before long, you start opening a whole can of worms. You start asking about the weightings of the market, about what the traders' reports are saying. Are the commercials or the funds too long or too short on one side? What are the sentiment readings? You enter a nebulous area. I don't do any research along those lines. I want to be aware of them, but in the long run they do me more harm than good. Sometimes the best moves happen when nobody can figure out why, so I'm purely interested in basic supply and demand, and in the balance that's there. I don't care why the market is doing what it's doing. If I were to try to figure out what would happen if the currency did this or that, it would affect my ability to process information. I don't watch TV, I don't read newspapers, I don't want anybody else's advisory letters, I don't want to know what anybody else thinks. I work best in a total vacuum.

◈ What drives your innovative process?

Losing money. Any time I get caught on something, I'm frustrated. When I can't figure something out, I think about how I can be on the right side of that the next time.

◈ Were there moments when you felt that relying on classical patterns and indicators was simply insufficient, and that developing new technical tools was necessary?

It's not that the indicators are insufficient, and I think it's a mistake to say that there are new tools. It's more a matter of what type of framework you put the data into, how you organize the data, as opposed to what particular tool or indicator you use. For example, if I'm looking at a particular set of data, I need to look at it in the context of a daily chart, a weekly chart, or a broader structure, and see how that's going to change the picture. It's not going to require a new tool, and the indicator is always going to be the price and the momentum type of stuff. The indicators with which I feel most comfortable are all range-based functions.

◈ Are there things that you developed but never shared?

I've shared everything that I've ever come up with, but that doesn't mean anything. You still have to figure out the risk, how you're going to manage that risk, where you're going to get in, and where you're going to get out. An indicator is meaningless. It's an indicator; it indicates something. And that's a whole lot different from knowing how to trade and manage the emotions. So I don't mind sharing any indicator I've come up with.

◈ Describe your working day.

I am usually in my office at my desk at 7:30 in the morning. At 8:00 a.m. I'm watching how the foreign markets are trading. Pretty much between 8:00 and 4:15, I'm sitting in front of my monitor. I go into the house to get lunch for ten minutes, and have my lunch in front of my monitor. I've got two trading assistants. Over the Internet during the day, I input stuff regarding what I'm watching and what I'm doing. That way I can communicate with the fellow who works for me in New York and the fellow who works for me in Chicago. They're comedians; we joke around if it's boring, or else I can bounce an idea off of somebody. So it's pretty much like being on radio live. At 4:10 or 4:15 the markets close, and I usually write all my numbers in a book. That takes half an hour. I do my trade analysis briefly and post it on the website. I'm usually out of the office at about five, and I'll immediately go hop on a horse. I have to do some physical activity, working out at the gym or riding a horse, where I get my mind 100 percent off the markets and get totally absorbed in something else. I come back into the office anywhere between 8:00 and 9:00 in the evening. I watch the way the night markets are trading, post some charts and commentary, and then maybe do some research and play around with indicators or data-based functions. I may spend an hour or so on the market-related stuff. And sometimes I'm in the office for six or seven hours on the weekends. We do research, testing different functions. Sometimes we do that till midnight. It's fun. Will I ever use it in trading? Most likely not, but you always have to be asking questions.

◈ To what extent does your trading control your life?

I can walk out of the office and turn it all off. I can instantly switch to something else. I can go out gardening. I can have the worst trading day and make the stupidest mistakes, but I'm like your ultimate poker player; you're never going to see it on my face. I have someone else in my life, and I can immediately go and be with them 100 percent and just enjoy them. I have the perspective that it's just a game, and I can quit the game any time. I love life, I love nature. Even if I'm having a bad day, I can go outside and totally enjoy myself. I'm happy to be alive. I wasn't always that way. I had some health challenges maybe fourteen years ago; they make you reevaluate what the priority is in your life. And the priority for me is people and relationships, being grateful for the things that I have and for the universe, being a spiritual person, not that I'm a religious person. The markets have made me very, very humble, because I've come to realize just what a little peon I am. I'm nothing more than a stupid little ant on this earth who is going to die someday. When you put it into that perspective, it becomes a game that you can turn off at any time.

Alan R. Shaw

Smith Barney had an elite, well-known, and well-respected fundamental research department in 1976, but it had no one doing technical analysis, so the merger with Harris Upham & Company was perfect. I was privileged to sit on the prestigious investment policy committee. The technical analysis discipline had just as strong a voice on this committee as any of the other disciplines, and I think this was a first for Wall Street.

───── ✥ ─────

A lan R. Shaw spent forty-six years on Wall Street in various research roles, specializing in technical research analysis. At the time of his retirement in April 2004, he was a managing director in the technical research department at the brokerage firm Smith Barney. He currently serves as consultant emeritus for Louise Yamada Technical Research Advisors, an independent research source in New York.

Shaw joined the brokerage firm Harris Upham & Company in 1958, after attending Susquehanna and Adelphi universities. He began his career as a fundamental securities analyst, and in the early 1960s he became actively involved in practicing technical market analysis. He served as research director at Harris Upham before its merger with Smith Barney in 1976 and was appointed to the firm's prestigious investment policy committee, where he offered often quite vocal input, right up to his retirement.

A member of the New York Society of Security Analysts, Shaw was a founder and the first president of the New York Society of Junior Security Analysts. He was also a founder of the Market Technicians Association and served as the association's second president. From 1966 to his retirement, he was an instructor of technical analysis at the New York Institute of Finance. He also was a lecturer at the annual Securities Industry and Financial Markets Association's Wharton seminars. Shaw authored the chapter on technical analysis in the *Financial Analyst's Handbook* (Dow Jones-Irwin, 1988).

For more than two decades Shaw was on *Institutional Investor* magazine's All-America Research Team in the technical analysis category, taking the No. 1 spot in 1993 and holding that ranking for many years. He has appeared in *Who's Who in America* since 1988. In 1997, he received the annual Market Technicians Association lifetime achievement award. Over the years, he has been the subject of numerous featured interviews in *Barron's* and other media, and appeared a number of times as special guest on Louis Rukeyser's *Wall $treet Week*. In May 1999, in recognition of his Wall Street accomplishments, he received an honorary doctor of laws (LLD) degree from Susquehanna University. Shaw is a chartered market technician (CMT) and was an allied member of the New York Stock Exchange and a supervisory analyst.

◈ What led to your interest in technical analysis?

I went to work for a firm called Harris Upham & Company in 1958 as a clerk in the research department. I slowly began to take on additional responsibilities assisting the firm's analysts, until I finally saw an opportunity to become a junior securities analyst. In our research department, the analysts followed particular industries like steel, paper, oil, etc., and there was an opening in the consumer goods area for someone to follow food and beverage stocks, and other consumer staples. The director of research was Ralph Rotnem, one of the greatest market historians of Wall Street in his day, an astute market analyst. I was his statistical assistant, and I asked him if he would consider me for the analyst job.

I did get that opportunity. It was the summer of 1960. I spent a great deal of time writing a research paper called "Investment Opportunities in the Food Industry," which was published in September. I went through all the basic qualitative and quantitative "fundamental" thought processes, including the investment thesis that food stocks should be looked upon as growth stocks, rather than income stocks, because of something called "convenience" foods, or frozen foods. These convenience foods carried extraordinary profit margins, and that was a major reason I thought the stocks should be looked at as growth stocks. Well, I had no idea that my report was going to be published during what was, at the time, an extraordinary bull market for consumer staple stocks. Over the next year, just about every stock we recommended in the report doubled in price, and, in fact, some even tripled in value. So I immediately thought that I was the smartest person in the world.

Mr. Rotnem used to commute from Princeton, New Jersey, with a fellow by the name of Jim Morgan, president of a Wall Street firm called Morgan, Rogers and Roberts. In those days, Morgan, Rogers and Roberts was the sole, principal purveyor of point and figure charts and the statistics for maintaining the charts. One day Mr. Rotnem gave me a copy of a new book that Morgan had given him called *Study Helps in Point and Figure Technique,* by Alexander Wheelan. "Mr. Rotnem," I said, "you really want me to read about this tic-tac-toe stuff?" He said I might find it interesting. So I read the book, and I found it absolutely fascinating. Of course, I didn't believe everything I read. It just didn't make sense to me that you could look at these "squiggles" and determinate whether or not a stock was going to go up or down. But I was intrigued. One day I went to Mr. Morgan's office and told him that I wasn't a wealthy person but I was interested in experimenting with this point and figure charting technique. I asked him if he would be willing to give me a head start, and I said I'd pay him back over time. For a very reasonable price, he gave me the back studies (charts) for about twenty of the stocks that I had recommended in my report. I kept these charts up-to-date by hand and hid them in my desk drawer.

In late 1961, I started to see some "formations" appear on the charts that looked very suspicious to me. I went back to the textbook that Mr. Rotnem had given me, and I found the patterns illustrated there. They were under a column called "tops." "This can't be," I thought. "How could these stocks be making tops when my fundamental news is right on line and when earnings are coming through for all my companies? It doesn't make any sense." So I confessed to Mr. Rotnem that I was keeping these charts and that I was starting to see these "distribution" patterns, these top formations. "How can these stocks be topping out when the fundamental news is so good?" I asked him. He leaned back in his chair, and I knew I was about to hear something prophetic. "I think you're about to learn how to separate a company from its stock." I was confused because I had always thought they were the same thing: "You mean the stock price might go in a different direction from the trend of the fundamentals?" Then he impressed upon me that the stock market is a *discounting* mechanism. That is one of the most important assumptions that one must appreciate and accept to practice technical analysis. The stock market is always looking ahead. It seldom looks to its side, and it definitely never looks behind. Stock prices oftentimes can, and do, move ahead of the fundamental progressions. Indeed, the food stock prices had already discounted the improved fundamentals I was reading about in the paper, and I was starting to see the technical patterns of distribution emerge in the fall of 1961.

There are three animals that prowl on Wall Street: the bull, the bear, and the pig. The bull and the bear both make money, but the pig usually loses money. In the fall of 1961, we sent out a bulletin to our brokers saying that the stocks that we had recommended in our basic report had possibly reached their upside expectations and that we would have no objections if clients wanted to "lighten up" in their holdings. Well, the rest is history. In 1962, the stock market experienced a significant bear market. Stock prices fell 50 percent or more in 1962.

The decline was called by the pundits of the day a "valuation adjustment." Well, in fact, it was. I didn't know that 47 times earnings was expensive for General Foods, and that was the price-earnings multiple that General Foods achieved at its top before the stock collapsed in 1962. And, indeed, the earnings didn't collapse; the multiple did. And yet the charts were displaying to me that there was this distribution going on. Of course, those top patterns got even bigger, leading me to another assumption I've worked with through the years: movements in the stock market tend to have relationships to each other. Some people say that the bigger the top, the bigger the drop, or that the bigger the base, the higher in space. But the point is that there is a relationship between the extensiveness of patterns and the moves that follow.

I was hooked on this point and figure methodology, and in 1963–1964 I expanded the number of charts I was keeping, and that became the backbone for the development of the technical analysis research department at Harris Upham, which I headed. In 1976, Harris Upham & Company merged with Smith Barney to form Smith Barney, Harris Upham. Smith Barney had an elite, very well-known, and well-respected fundamental research department, but they had no one doing technical analysis, so the merger from my perspective was perfect. I was privileged to sit on the prestigious investment policy committee. The technical analysis discipline had just as strong a voice on this policy committee as any of the other disciplines, and I think this was a first for Wall Street.

◈ How is your style of technical analysis distinct?

I wrote a piece in 1995 called "Japan vs. U.S." With the use of semi-log graph paper, I discovered that there was a pattern in the U.S. stock market developing that could be overlaid on the Japanese stock market with a thirteen-year time shift. This was the Japanese Nikkei, which at one time was the second-largest stock market in the world in terms of market value. Our conclusion was that if this pattern were to continue, by the end of 1995 the Dow Jones Industrial Average might begin to accelerate to the upside, perhaps going to 10,000 by the year 2000. It was 4,700 the day we published that piece, and it reached 10,000 by 2000. The likeness of supply-and-demand characteristics we were comparing was phenomenal. Did we really know that was going to happen? Of course not. But our research allowed us to suggest the question, is it possible that the Dow is on the same trend as the Nikkei before it topped out at 40,000? We created a lot of followers by the publication of that piece, because it turned out to be so accurate.

My swan song, so to speak, my last good piece of research, was published in March 2004, a month before I retired. It was called "Will Dow 10,000 Become Dow 1,000 and/or Dow 100?" I lived through seventeen years of the Dow Jones average bumping against 1,000. I had to go back and do research about the Dow 100, because that was in the second decade of the twentieth century to the 1920s. And I found incredibly interesting similarities in patterns. For example, there were five cyclical bear markets and four cyclical bull markets at or around 100, and there were five cyclical bear markets and four cyclical bull markets at or around 1,000. We concluded that maybe we had the first cyclical bear market in 2000–2002 and that we were in the process right now of concluding the first cyclical bull market and therefore looking forward to the possibility that there would be another cyclical bear market that we would see. It doesn't mean that this is set in concrete, but it's a research piece that we constantly go back to and reference, because it's possible that our experience will mirror those two experiences—the bear and bull markets at 100 and the bear and bull markets at 1,000.

◈ Is your approach to technical analysis both art and science?

Yes, it's both. For example, do we embrace the principles of relative strength? Yes. The principles of momentum? Yes. The principles of trendline analysis (which you can implement with a pencil and a ruler)? Yes. I used to kid everybody that you don't have to be wealthy to be a technician; you need forty cents for the ruler and ten cents for the pencil. You only need fifty cents worth of equipment to make multimillion-dollar decisions. So if I had to define my personal style, I'd say it's in the common land: relative strength, momentum, moving average convergence divergence, and stochastics. The reason our approach was embraced so readily by clients was that we always tried to educate them. We let them know how we arrived at the conclusions and what was behind the research. For instance, I've always found it interesting that a lot of people blindly conclude that an oversold condition is bullish and that an overbought condition is bearish. If you think about it, it's just the opposite. You see, by definition, if the stock market becomes overbought, that's bullish. If you understand the statistical makeup of an overbought/oversold oscillator, you'll see that the fact that it reaches the oversold condition is bearish, not bullish. Listen to many of the people on the cartoon network—CNBC—and what you'll hear is stupidity. They say they're bullish because the market is oversold. You know what? On October 12, 1987, the stock market went into an oversold condition, and a few days later it crashed 500 points in one day. It wasn't until the 3rd of November that it came out of the oversold condition. So what was the better day to have bought? The day it went oversold or the day it came out of the oversold? These are the misconceptions that we try to educate our clients about.

People used to think that technical analysis was a self-fulfilling prophecy because if you show the chart to three technicians, you're probably not going to get the same answer. That's not true. There is an interpretation. Just as if you show a balance sheet to three fundamental analysts, you're probably going to get three different opinions. When you ask people about the definition of technical analysis, sometimes someone will say, "You look at the past to predict the future." Well, I stop them in their tracks and say, "Tell me what a balance sheet is. Is that a look at the future or a look at the past?" It's obviously the past. What's an income statement? A look at the past. What's today's PPI [producer price index] report? It's the past. What's the unemployment number? It's the past. All forms of analysis look at the past to get a feel for the future.

◈ How much of what you do are you willing to share with others?

It comes down to recognizing why you're here. I'm not doing this for my own portfolio. I am doing this because I'm an employee of a prestigious firm, and I have a responsibility to share my knowledge with my clients. We share our weekly policy meetings, our weekly writings. That's why we're here.

◈ If all patterns/indicators/strategies that you use are in the public domain, what is it about the way you use these tools that accounts for your superior success?

Forecasting the direction of the Dow is a no-brainer. All you have to do is a very thorough analysis of the technical condition of the thirty stocks that comprise the average. There are only thirty of them, not five hundred of them, and you can take particular interest in the higher-priced ones because you know that the Dow is a price-weighted average. It's not capitalization weighted like the S&P is. Now, suppose that the highest-priced stock is down 10 percent, or 10 points, and that the lowest-priced stock goes down 10 percent, which could be 1 point, say from 10 to 9. Because the Dow is a price-weighted average, that little stock has no real effect on the direction of the average itself. Every 1-point move in a Dow stock currently translates into 7 points in the average itself. So, you have to know this if you're going to forecast this average. People are going to come to you and ask where you think the Dow is going, and you have to have an understanding of how the average is computed and what stocks influence the average the most. Otherwise you have no right telling someone your opinion of the average. Let's say I think the Dow is going to drop 500 points. The client is correct if he says, "Okay, big shot, which Dow stock would you sell short?" If I don't have a short-sell candidate, how can I say that the average is going to drop 500 points?

◈ When you encounter a classical indicator that's no longer working, do you try to change your interpretation of it, or do you discard it and invent something new?

Both. Decimalization, for example, has not only affected the advance/ decline line; it has affected the high/low statistics as well. Nowadays it's possible for a stock to go up one cent and make a twelve-month high. Decimalization has distorted these statistics somewhat, but we still keep them on the wall. However, whereas in the past we used to give them the strength of 10, we now give them the strength of 6. We may not pay as much attention to these high/low statistics as we used to, but they're still worth doing.

◈ Describe what your typical working day was like before you retired.

A working day would typically start with an assessment of the environment, which is everything around us. We would have writing assignments every week and our conference call every Thursday at four o'clock with fourteen thousand brokers. A great deal of our time would be spent in communication. I traveled a lot. I would be out of the office maybe three or four months a year. I was always communicating our thoughts to our clients, domestically and internationally. I used to love to travel, not so much to see the geography—most of that was out of the window of a taxi anyway—but because I'd pick up ideas from the clients. Clients asked questions that would give me ideas about new things to work on.

12

Anthony W. Tabell

If I felt that relying on classical patterns and indicators was sufficient, I would have done nothing but read Alexander Wheelan's book and look at point and figure charts. I've tried to go beyond that, though the charts never became useless. You can't have too many tools.

———— ✺ ————

A nthony W. Tabell's career started in 1954, when he joined his late father Edmund W. Tabell at Walston and Co., doing technical research and consulting with institutions. He became senior vice president, a member of the board of directors, and the director of technical research—all at the same time—in 1965. In 1970, Tabell left Walston to form Delafield, Harvey, Tabell in Princeton, New Jersey, where he continued to consult with institutions and provided research input to investment advisory operations. When Delafield, Harvey, Tabell merged with United States Trust Company in 1992, he became senior vice president of U.S. Trust Company of New Jersey. Tabell began applying computers to technical research in the late 1950s and headed one of the first computer installations devoted solely to technical analysis. He was a founding member of the Market Technicians Association, serving as its president in 1975–1976 and a member of its board of directors until his retirement in 1993.

◈ What led to your interest in technical analysis?

I got involved with technical analysis when I went to work for my father, Edmund Tabell, who had been involved in technical work since the early 1930s. He would come home with a portfolio of charts almost every night as I was growing up. My mother's uncle was Richard D. Wyckoff and he offered my father a job in the 1930s at the *Magazine of Wall Street*. That's how my father got started in technical analysis. When I went to work with my father, he had just broken the ice as far as getting technical analysis accepted by some institutional investors. He was running a brokerage business and was serving a number of institutions. I joined him in 1954. I built on what he had done before.

Wyckoff, of course, had done a lot of work with point and figure charts, which, right through my retirement, were the basic tools I used. My father didn't last long with Wyckoff—nobody lasted long with Wyckoff—but he lasted long enough to develop an interest in technical work. He then worked for a brokerage firm for many years as a conventional registered representative. During this time, he was building up a library of point and figure charts, which, by the mid-1940s, was probably one of the few complete libraries of point and figure charts available on the Street. This was his basic research input in conducting his brokerage business. He then conceived the idea that he could convince institutional investors to use technical analysis. Gradually, he developed a set of contacts. By the mid-1950s, when I joined him, his business was basically institutional.

My father was one of a small group of people on the Street who were devoting as much time as they could to technical analysis. They were keeping the torch of technical analysis alive. It's hard to visualize, unless you've talked to people who were involved, how difficult this was in the atmosphere of 1930s and 1940s. The entire brokerage business was a basket case. Volume on the NYSE was under a million shares. This was the Depression. Nobody had any money, and if they did, they were leery about investing. Furthermore, technical analysis had been associated with the excesses of the 1920s. All of the various securities acts were designed to get rid of the manipulative market operations that had characterized the '20s. Since technical work, to a great degree—certainly point and figure charts—had been conceived as a means of detecting pool operations, confessing that you were involved in technical work at that point was equivalent to confessing you were some kind of a low-level criminal. I experienced some of this, because that attitude was still kicking around when I started in the business in the 1950s.

When I was eight or nine years old, my father taught me how to post charts. This was a precomputer age: We were dealing here with five thousand pieces of paper, and somebody with a pen had to make marks on these charts every day. When I graduated from Colgate University in 1952, it was the time of the Korean War, so I spent two years in the army, getting out in March of 1954. Over the years my father had brought up the subject of my carrying on the work he was doing. Through high school and college, I had been reluctant to say that I would do this. Finally, he leaned on me fairly hard, and I made a decision when I left the service to work for my father, who at that point was a senior registered representative at Walston & Co. on Wall Street. So when I started working, I was in the brokerage business.

My father's business was tremendously successful because he was a large producer. He was successful helping individual investors and later institutional investors. His stature was due to the bottom line. Nobody he worked for or that I subsequently worked for ever really cared about technical analysis per se. They were interested in whether technical analysis was enabling us to produce a lot of commissions. So I was in a brokerage business that was based on technical analysis, and 95 percent of that was point and figure charts. In 1946, my father started publishing a market letter based essentially on technical work. Luckily, he worked for firms at that point—DuPont and then Walston—willing to put their name on a letter that was based on technical analysis. This was a major breakthrough. I started writing the letter occasionally shortly after I came to work for him in the mid-'50s, took it over upon his death, and continued until my retirement.

❖ Are there things you learned only after you started applying technical analysis to real markets, things you never saw in the literature or heard from your father?

I learned from the application as I went along, and I am continually improving and learning. I have become better and better at analyzing point and figure patterns, as my father had become. When my father died in 1965, that was a major watershed for me. I worked for him for eleven years, until he dropped dead of a heart attack in a client's office. So there I was, thirty-four years old, obviously a junior partner in an ongoing operation, and the question was, could I continue the operation, could I continue to carry on a technical-research-based brokerage business? I was able to convince myself after a while that I could.

◈ Has your practice of technical analysis changed significantly since the death of your father?

In the late '50s, early '60s, one of the things that moved me personally was the use of the computer. I liked computers. I liked sitting down and writing computer programs in assembly language. But it was a natural marriage with what I was doing with technical analysis, because technical analysis is analysis of data. I can tell many stories about fighting my way through Wall Street in my efforts to merge computers with the practice of technical analysis. The whole idea of doing research on them was foreign to everyone involved with technical analysis. I'm probably one of the first people who tried to evaluate stock price returns on a computer, necessarily a mainframe. The PC was still twenty-five years in the future. This was an interest I pursued when my father was still alive, but I got involved in it more deeply when we started our own firm in 1970. I went out and bought a Digital Equipment PDP-11. This was to my knowledge the first computer to be 100 percent devoted to doing technical research. I regard the computer as a watershed in technical analysis.

◈ How is your style of technical analysis distinct?

Throughout my career, the major way in which I looked at individual securities was via point and figure charts. I continued to do it in the 1970s, when I started my own firm with money managers, and I was doing it in 1993, when I retired. So never at any time during this entire period of sixty years—between my father and myself—did we stop keeping point and figure charts. The last thing I did before I retired in 1993 was to finally get those charts onto a computer, where they still exist. Were we relying exclusively on point and figure charts? No, we were not. As time went on, the available techniques of technical analysis expanded. All manner of research work was being done. People like Sedge Coppock and George Chestnut were doing work on relative strength, and you were beginning to get various smoothing techniques starting with elementary things like 200-day moving averages. I was a technician, so you name it, I was doing it.

◈ Is your analysis more effective when you're working by yourself or when you're working with others?

It's more effective when it bounces off other people. I was always a part of the team. Until 1965 I was a junior member of that team; after that I was a senior member. We had eight or ten in charge of technical work at the peak.

◈ In what kind of market conditions do you make the most mistakes?

By definition, the easiest time to make an important mistake is at a major turning point. If I'm somewhere in the middle of a major bull market, I may make mistakes in that my clients could have made even more money if they had listened to someone else. The serious mistake is going to occur in an environment like August through October of 1982. So you make mistakes all the time, but there are times when these mistakes will cost you a lot more, and that's at a major turning point.

◈ If all patterns/indicators/strategies that you use are in the public domain, what is it about the way you use these tools that accounts for your superior returns?

I wouldn't even claim that I've had superior success. I've had success. The cardiac surgeon that performed a triple bypass on me nineteen years ago was using techniques that were in the public domain, but he was successful. He didn't have any secrets that he was hiding from the rest of the medical profession. Same thing here. I don't believe in secrets.

◈ Is technical analysis more effective when used on its own, or when combined with fundamental or other kinds of analysis?

When it's combined. I've always been trying to get other people to use it in conjunction with whatever else is in their arsenal, and in most cases that's fundamental analysis.

◈ How much of your technical analysis is intuitive?

A great deal. I would say 50 percent. That would seem to be at variance with what I did in most of the latter part of my career, which was to try to test indicators using standard statistical testing. If I could come up with an indicator and a way of interpreting that indicator that had a chi-square somewhere up through the roof, I would say, that's great, but I would still be intuitive about it.

◈ Were there times when you felt that relying on classical patterns and indicators was insufficient and that developing new technical tools was necessary?

Yes. If I felt that relying on classical patterns and indicators was sufficient, I would have done nothing but read Alexander Wheelan's book *Study Helps in Point and Figure Technique* and look at a whole bunch of point and figure charts. Instead, I've tried to go beyond that, though the charts never became useless. But clients were expecting more from me than simply opinions based on charts. I would love ideally to have one thousand more tools at my disposal than I am using now. You can't have too many tools.

◈ Is your confidence in the ability of technical analysis to forecast future price moves strong enough to relieve you of stress?

Oh, sure. There was stress involved, but I never felt stressed out because of technical analysis. That's something I developed early on. I could make a bad call and live with it, and I could make a good call and not think that I was the latest incarnation of Einstein. On the other hand, I found many aspects of being in business very stressful, such as clients, colleagues. All that stuff that goes into a day spent in human relationships is by nature stressful.

13

Stan Weinstein

If you follow the market properly, it's a slow, evolving process. And life should be the same way, an evolving thing. We need to learn from our mistakes. The market will test every strength and weakness you have. If you're open to learning what your strengths and weaknesses are, you'll grow, and that's what the journey should be about.

—————— ❧ ——————

S tan Weinstein is president and founder, in 1990, of Global Trend Alert, an advisory service that provides both intermediate and longer-term outlooks for global markets and equities to institutional investors. He was also publisher and editor of *The Professional Tape Reader* market letter, which he retired in 2000, as well as the author of *Secrets for Profiting in Bull and Bear Markets* (1988). Weinstein has appeared frequently as a guest on major financial television programs, was one of Louis Rukeyser's *Wall $treet Week* elves, and has been quoted in leading financial newspapers and magazines, including *Barron's, The Wall Street Journal, Investor's Business Daily, USA Today, The New York Times, Business Week,* and *U.S. News & World Report.*

◈ What led to your interest in technical analysis?

I've had an interest in the stock market since I was a kid. Like most people, I started in a more traditional way. I followed some of the big fundamentalists, and the techniques that were supposed to do very well did not do very well. I ended up losing my bar mitzvah money and figured there must be a better way. When I went to college, I studied economics, although they taught traditional methods, not technical analysis. One day, at the school library, I found a book called *Technical Analysis of Stock Trends,* by Robert D. Edwards and John Magee. I read it, and it seemed interesting to me—I'm willing to give anything a shot. So I started doing some charting, and at the time I didn't make a lot of money, of course. Initially, as I was learning the ground strokes, I found that I was losing less money, maybe made a few dollars. The more I dwelt on it, the more I started to feel that my future was with technical analysis. The Edwards and Magee book really talked to me, and I loved it when I read it. I thought, this is great, and some day I'd like to add a little something to technical analysis. Years later, I ended up writing my own book, *Secrets for Profiting in Bull and Bear Markets,* in which I took off from the good principles of Edwards and Magee. I added a few things of my own. Edwards and Magee didn't have moving averages, for instance. I also simplified some things. In fact, it was my purpose to really make it easy to read, because Edwards and Magee are terrific but very difficult to read.

◈ Are there things you learned only after you started applying technical analysis to real markets, things you never saw in the literature?

I've read so many books. I don't honestly know. I've been doing technical analysis now for well over forty years, and for many things you forget whether you developed them yourself or borrowed from someone. The more relevant question is this: What are the things that I think are important to bring to the market—not that I never saw them written anywhere. Certain truisms go way back into the '30s and are still relevant today. For example, a part of good technique is to always cut your losses quickly. A lot of the books—not just on technical analysis but on the stock market—talk only about the things that look so easy, but they don't talk about things that go awry. In my book I have a chapter about the mistakes I've made and the things they taught me about making money in the market, and that's one of the things I'm proud of.

The truth is, only liars are right 100 percent of the time. My book separates a real winner in the stock market from people who are going to be so-so. It's very important to learn how to take losses. Even if you're right only 50 percent of the time, though I think you can do much better than that, you can make a lot of money in the stock market by letting your good stocks run, by letting the trend work for you. You can certainly be right at least 70 percent of the time. If you make good money on a winning stock, and if you take small losses when you lose, it can become a very profitable endeavor. If you have a false breakout, it's very important to get out immediately, especially if you're trading. That's one of the tips I never saw written anywhere, but I've written about it. Let's say a stock XYZ breaks out above 20. If it closes at 20.5 or 21, that's usually going to work, that's a good thing. But if XYZ broke out and went to, say, 20.5 today, but closed at 19.5 tonight, I get a bad feeling. From a trading point of view, I think it's going to be a loser. The really, really good trades are going to be clean. They're going to break out and close above the resistance level and stay above it. That's one of the key factors to consider in deciding whether or not you're dealing with a false breakout. If it's a false breakout, take a quick small loss. It's better to take the first little loss than a big loss. Volume is the second key factor—this has been written about by others as well as by me. If you have two stocks and both look good, and one breaks out but the volume is only so-so, I would say that that stock doesn't have as high a probability of working as the stock that breaks out on significantly higher volume. The really good breakouts are usually accompanied by a volume level that is triple the normal average volume.

◈ Which mistake taught you the most?

All the mistakes I've made over the years—and I've made many—become like a total gestalt. It all comes together and it's slowly added to my discipline. It's a slow-building process. When I first started trading as a stockbroker, if a position didn't work, I would stay with it longer and wish and hope. I soon learned that it's better to quickly take a loss on a position that isn't working, and to stay with the ones that are working. Also, in the early years, I would look at charts more in a vacuum and not pay as much attention to the market sectors.

All of these things helped me develop my system, which I call my "forest-to-the-trees" approach. I look at the big things first. If the market is very bearish, the way it was in say 2002, even a good stock has less likelihood of working (even though some of them will). Obviously, you're going to bet less of your capital when the major trend is against you than when the trend is with you. That's an important thing to learn. You start with the forest, which is the big thing, the market, and work your way down. I also look to see which are the best sectors. You want to focus on the most positive sectors because they have a greater likelihood of working. At the same time, other groups are often negative and should be avoided even if the overall market is bullish. In my forest-to-the-trees approach, if I'm going to buy, I want to buy in the best sector, and when I want to short, I want to short in the worst sectors.

◈ How is your style of technical analysis distinct?

It's a very simple system to understand, very straightforward: basic charting and chart configuration. I look for patterns, such as a head-and-shoulders top or a double bottom. I also pay a lot of attention to moving averages. Moving averages are a key part of my system, which is one of the things that is not in Edwards and Magee's book. I use three major moving averages: first, a 200-day moving average, which is what most people use; second, a 150-day moving average, because I've found it usually gives you a head start by thirty-plus days over the 200-day one. And if you move above or below the 150, the probabilities are very strong that eventually you'll break above or below the 200. Third is the 50-day moving average, which is more for trading.

If I have a position I like very much, but it starts to roll over and break its 50-day moving average, I definitely do some "trimming" of the position. I am robotic and never violate my discipline. I never say, "This is a special case that I can ignore because I like the company." If a stock is in a long-term uptrend, and it's rising above the 50-, 150-, and 200-day moving averages, it would make for an excellent position, but as soon as it breaks and closes below the 50-day moving average, I trim it. Then I'll see what happens thereafter. I always try to move incrementally, in the stock market and in life. A lot of people will stay bullish until it breaks the 200-day moving average, and they give away a terrific amount of the profits. I like to move step by step by step. I don't think the market changes overnight. If the stock is terrific and we are riding it up, and it starts to make a little head-and-shoulders top, and it also breaks its 50-day moving average, I'll sell a third of the position. And then if it has a normal correction and holds above the long-term moving averages, I'll buy it again when the correction is over. Conversely, if it starts to go down further—let's say it breaks the 150-day moving average—I would sell another third, and when it closes below the 200-day moving average, then I am gone.

◈ Is technical analysis more effective when practiced individually or in teams?

In my experience, it's better to practice as a single practitioner, rather than in a team. But that's just my philosophy. If I have a strong feeling, I don't care about what anyone else says; I'm going to go with my feeling. I don't want to start factoring in somebody else's opinion. It won't work for me. But that doesn't mean that somebody else, who has a different type of personality, wouldn't perhaps be better in a team environment.

◈ How do you deal with the problem of the tradeoff between early signal detection and sensitivity to random noise?

That's becoming tougher, especially in this environment. In the old days, I used to have many more mutual fund clients; now more and more of my clients are hedge fund managers, and they do create a lot of "random noise." You can see their activity all over the tape! You can separate out the noise by following the big pictures on the chart. You have to separate the short-term and the long-term action. For example, yesterday's market may have been terrific, yet today it's suddenly down. In such a situation it helps to have a bit of an overview, to follow the big picture and to say that as long as my big "goal lines" are not violated, as long as I am comfortably above the 50-, 150-, 200-day moving averages, and as long as no serious violations have taken place in terms of patterns, I am okay. The long-term picture still looks fine. I think that's the way to factor out the random noise. As long as the big patterns are okay, and haven't done anything bad, and haven't broken levels that shouldn't be violated, even trading-wise, and you are still above all your moving averages, then the sell-off isn't serious. That's the best we can do to deal with the increasing volatility. But there is no doubt that in the past few years the volatility has become ridiculous. It's a fact of life that we have to live with, as hedge funds become a bigger and bigger part of the market and they move a lot of money in a hurry.

◈ Is technical analysis more effective when used on its own or when combined with fundamental analysis?

I am not antifundamental, but I think there are cases where technical analysis can be more effective when used on its own, especially in selling. It's easier to know where to buy than to know where to sell. On the sell side, technical analysis should be used by itself and not in conjunction with fundamental analysis at all. The market is supposed to be a discounting mechanism, and by the time the bad shows up in the fundamentals, it's too late; you've already topped. I do see the relevance of adding in maybe 20 percent of fundamentals with 80 percent of technicals on the buy side. Even though I personally trade 100 percent off of the chart, if a chart of stock A and a chart of stock B look about equal, but company A has a terrific new concept or new product, I'd choose stock A. I think that you're better off with something you can put your hands on. I'll still do the chart, but on the buy side—unlike on the sell side—if I can see something that makes sense and can get a fundamental edge, that's great. But all things being equal, if you do have a great chart and terrible fundamentals, I would still go with the chart. I'll be advising mutual funds, hedge funds, and they'll follow up with these terrific fundamental stories. And I'll look at the charts and say that these are awful charts; there is no way on God's earth that I'll buy that.

◈ How much of your technical analysis is intuitive?

When I was on the seminar circuit, I used to hold all these classes where I would teach people and they would "get it." So it's certainly at least 85 percent mechanical. I think there is probably about a 15 percent intuitive factor. I get a little bit more of a tingle so to speak than somebody else.

◈ What drives your innovative process?

I think it's the desire to be great. I kid around and call myself the Michael Jordan of technicians. I like to think that I'm one of the best. I think that's what drives me. At this point in life—I'm sixty-two—it's certainly not the dollars, but the desire to excel and the gratification I get from it, knowing that I am going against the best minds and the best computers on the Street. When you win and come out ahead, it's a great feeling. When I hear somebody pontificate about the random walk, saying there is nothing to technical analysis, I just laugh to myself. In fact, that's part of my growth process. When I was young, in my twenties, I wanted everyone to believe in the technical method. I've come to realize that it's really good we have so many people out there who don't believe in technical analysis. If we all did the same game, and we all see the stock is terrible, to whom are we going to sell the stock tomorrow? Years ago, everyone used to use *Barron's* confidence index, and it became widely followed; it became terrible after a while. It takes a certain kind of person to accept technical analysis. Large groups of people keep bringing out fundamental recommendations, regardless of the fact that they have been wrong so many times. Just the opposite is the case with technical analysis: most people, if they don't make it right away, if they lose money trying one or two trades, say, "Ah, I knew there was nothing to this."

Let's face it. Technical analysis doesn't make sense to people, especially to some of the academic types. It doesn't validate what they're taught. Some of these MBAs are really annoyed when I'm right and they're wrong. It bothers them because they've done all these theses, and they think, "How can a person just look at a crummy chart and have a higher batting average than somebody who's done all this work?"

❖ To what extent do you share your inventions with others?

I shared totally with the rest of the world. I developed my eleven o'clock indicator years ago, where I just took the net change from eleven to twelve o'clock. Then I saw that other people were saying in their market letters that it was their indicator. I developed the last hour indicator, and I've seen other people using it. I also developed my most-active-stocks indicator, where I took the net change of the fifteen most active stocks today and started running moving totals on it. And I developed my stage analysis—everybody at least gives me credit for this one—which says that any stock can be categorized into one of the four stages: stage one is the base, two is the advancing phase, three is the distributional top, four is the decline phase.

I always share. When I used to do the *Professional Tape Reader*, when I was doing the writing, I always felt like I was trying to talk to the readers as if they were in my living room. That's how I wrote my book, too. I asked myself, "What would they want to know, and what do I want to tell them?" A lot of times, systems are so confusing. I can't understand them, so I figure they're trying to confuse people. I believe that if you keep it simple, it works just fine. I don't do the *Professional Tape Reader* anymore; I now advise institutions with my Global Trend Alert service. Among my clients, there are hedge funds and some mutual funds, and some of them are very sharp, and they know their technicals well. But there are also some fundamentalists who want to hear what Weinstein has to say, not because they believe in technical analysis, but because they've heard that I have a high batting average.

◈ Why do you share your inventions with others rather than keeping the edge just for yourself?

If you and I are on the same page, I can be of more value to you, rather than if you just take it and say, "Okay, Stan said sell, so I'm going to sell." I think I can make you a better client of mine by showing you the world as I see it. In fact, one of my largest institutional clients today was a strict, 100 percent fundamentalist when he started with me thirteen to fourteen years ago. He just wondered about technical analysis. He said he'd heard I had a pretty good record. Many years later, my wife was laughing because he was now sending us an e-mail, saying let me know where to put my stops, where will it break down, etc. Before then, he didn't even know what stops or breakouts were. The more I can get you to see why I'm saying what I'm saying, the more value added I can be and the more you'll feel comfortable with my advice. For me, it's also very gratifying. All of us at some point—hopefully not for a long time—have to move on to the next world, and we have a legacy. I still get thank you letters from people who used to be *Tape Reader* subscribers. One said reading my book changed his life. He has retired, and he's been so successful. That makes me feel good. We are only here awhile, and we try to make the world a little better place; we try to help a couple of people and leave something positive for the world.

◈ Is your confidence in the ability of technical analysis to forecast future price moves strong enough to relieve you of stress?

Absolutely, but anybody who is in the market and says he or she has no stress is either a liar or a freak. We all have stress in the market, but I think technical analysis lowers the level of stress, even if something is going wrong. This is very unlike fundamental analysis, where, unless you found out the product doesn't work, you have nothing to hang your hat on when the sales are going bad. I have all these guidelines: Up to this point, it's a normal pullback, and I am okay with it. Now it's starting to violate what I thought was a normal correction, and I'm going to take some of that position off. Now it's gotten terrible, and it's breaking my long-term moving averages. I'm out of here! So technical analysis makes me feel that I am somewhat in control.

◈ Did you always have the balance in your life, or did you have to work at it?

No, I did not. I had to really work at it. I have to thank my wife, Rita, big time. She has definitely helped keep balance. And I also think that you mellow as you go through life. Life is a journey, and if you get anything from the journey, you start to learn. When I was starting out, at twenty years old, we wanted to set the world on fire, and all we were thinking about was making trillions of dollars. I don't think I had a balance there, although I always did have the family values. But as you go through life, you see bad things happen to some friends, and you start to realize what's really important in life. For me, it's all about my wife and my kids: I have a terrific family. Just seeing the good and the bad that can happen, you start to realize what's really important in life. We've had some terrific things going on here, and we've had some hard times. When you put it all together, that's what the journey teaches you, if you're open.

That openness, I like to think, is one of my strengths. It's one of the things that made me very good at technical analysis. I am always ready to be wrong and grow. I'm the same way in life; I've made my mistakes and I've grown. I always try to come down in the middle. The same thing in the market: I try to move incrementally. Some people are bullish on Monday, and on Tuesday they're bearish. To me, that's ridiculous. If you follow the market properly, it's a slow, evolving process. And life should be the same, an evolving thing. We need to learn from our mistakes. The market will test every strength and weakness you have. If you're open to learning what your strengths and weaknesses are, you'll grow, and that's what the journey should be about.

Conviction: Countering the Skeptics and the Scoundrels

I don't doubt the validity of technical analysis in general, but rather the validity of my own applications of it. The whole market is sort of a living being. It's a psychological thing. That's where having a feel for a trend comes in; that's where the art takes over from the science.

— I. McAvity

◈ **Have you always been convinced of the validity of technical analysis? Have you become more or less convinced since you first started?**

ACAMPORA: Almost always, yes. Otherwise I wouldn't have stayed in the business. I love practicing it; I love teaching it. There was a time in the late '70s when I said, "Oh, God, this thing isn't working." Maybe it was my naïveté, maybe it was my lack of experience, maybe it was one of the worst markets in the world. It was probably every one of those things. Now I am a little older, a little wiser, and a lot luckier, and I think technical analysis is fine. So I've become more convinced that it works.

BIRINYI: I was disappointed in it almost from the beginning. I felt that there was a lot of information in the marketplace, but that too many technicians and strategists were not in the market. They were in the office. Technicians would ask me things like why does an uptick trade have to be a buy? That kind of question can come only from someone who has never been on a trading desk. Let's say you're trading U.S. Steel. U.S. Steel is at 27.5, and somebody comes in and asks, "Where can you sell me ten thousand shares?" You say, "I don't want to sell you ten thousand shares." The customer says, "But I am a good customer," and you respond with, "Okay, I'll sell you ten thousand shares at 28, up a half a point." At that point the customer says, "I buy." Right then you know you lost money. And sure enough, ten minutes later, news comes out and U.S. Steel is up another dollar or two. And you sit there and say, "Hmm, I got picked off. Not only have I lost money, now my boss is asking me where I'm going to work tomorrow." So scientifically you cannot prove it to me that an uptick is good news, but I can prove it to you unscientifically.

I've gotten less and less convinced of its validity since I started out, because technicians have gotten a lot more into marketing. There are a lot more opportunities for people to be on TV and in other media. Joe Granville said that if you're going to be a newsletter writer, the way to be successful is to take some really ridiculous stance. No one will ever remember if you're wrong, but if you're right, you'll get a lot of publicity. That's what it's about. George Soros made $2 billion betting against the British pound. They don't tell you all the other times he lost millions betting against the yen. I am not sure how well he's done overall on his big currency bets, but we're always reminded of the one big win. That's unfortunately what this business is more attentive to. So you have to make a splash.

DEEMER: Yes, I've always been convinced of its validity. I've become more convinced because it's the basic underlying truth of the stock market. The only approach that analyzes stock or the stock market is technical analysis. You can come up with the value, but the underlying truth is the law of supply and demand, which is technical analysis. If I were working for Warren Buffett and buying companies, I would have a different perspective on life, but I am working for people who buy these little pieces of paper, and so I use technical analysis. If you want to follow and forecast the stock market, you have to use technical analysis. Everything else is just peripheral.

DESMOND: Yes, absolutely convinced. It's like with everything else in life. You think a certain principle ought to be correct, but you don't have absolute confidence in it unless you have a lot of experience. I am a lot more confident about the value of technical analysis and supply-and-demand analysis now. I am very confident that I will never be caught in a major bear market, and I will never miss out on a major market advance. And that's all that I can hope for.

DUDACK: I always believed in technical analysis, and the more I use it, the more I believe. Things may change, and you might want to adapt your tools to a new environment, but the basic principles remain the same.

FARRELL: I've always been convinced about the validity of market analysis, ever since I started studying it. I thought it was a useful approach, but it had so much more to it than just looking at charts. That was one reason I called it "market analysis" and did not want to be labeled as a technician.

McAVITY: I've always been convinced of the validity of various parts of technical analysis. In the earlier stages, I would get too set in my ways and refuse to recognize that characteristics of some things were changing. Over time, I've become much more respectful. People use the term *technical analysis* as if it is definable. In my mind, it is undefinable because market ingredients are always changing. There is always a different ingredient, and this invariably comes back to the fact that an ingredient is a reflection of changing market sentiment or changing price, but not necessarily a reflection of the change in what people would call the "fundamental rationale." When it comes to forecasting financial markets, the single most consistently wrong group of people are the economists. The economists cannot even construct a leading indicator that works and a lagging indicator that works. If they can't measure what has already happened, that is a problem. Just remember their declaration of the last recession. They declared it over on the day they recognized it! That was really useful information. The law of the investment markets supplied the Prudent Man Rule, which, the way I view it, says that it's perfectly okay to lose money, as long as everyone else in your peer group loses it the same way. My reaction is that if you're afraid to take risk, you're afraid to succeed.

I've become much more convinced of the validity of technical analysis over time, in large part because I've broadened my horizons. Early on, I would go through phases where I felt I could define precisely what the market trend was. And whenever the market disagreed—in my mind as a young arrogant beginner— the market was wrong. Over time I've learned to recognize that the market is always right. The question is whether or not I can recognize what has changed and adapt.

There have been various turning points in my career that have been critical in determining my level of confidence and conviction in the validity of technical analysis. For example, I have been very much involved in major-trend contrary opinion. There were times when I made a great deal of noise, with very high conviction that what I was seeing was unsustainable and that therefore it was practically over. I am a disciplined analyst, and when the market is up, it should be sold. The more opposition I get, the more strongly I feel. If I am alone in a position I'm comfortable with, that's probably my highest conviction. When an awful lot of people are saying, "You're so smart, and we agree," I get nervous. As the consensus grows, I tend to want to go opposite. You can't really quantify contrary opinion, beyond some statistical measures and surveys, but, for the most part, it comes back to identifying the herd. Too many people try to go contrary to everything they previously believed. Identifying what to go contrary to is often a major challenge.

Over time, I've become more confident of my ability to beat the market, but I have a luxury that many people in the business don't have: I am not paid to play. I trade only for my family and myself. I am not trading for the public. Somebody in charge of a mutual fund or a hedge fund is paid to play. I respect the fact that when somebody is uncertain they'll go to 100 percent cash and make no decisions. They'll explain to their investors that they're 100 percent in cash, and they'll be paid to guard that cash in anticipation of the next successful trade. I think that's the most admirable position they could take, but the odds are pretty good most of the money will leave the fund. People buy the fund because they want and expect the trading. Most managers will end up forcing opportunity where none exists. What probably damages most performance records is having a very good streak but then trying to beat a dead horse.

MURPHY: I liked technical analysis early on; it made sense to me. You only start becoming convinced over the course of several years, when you start applying it. In the early days, you close your eyes and cross your fingers. In those days, I was actually a little surprised when it worked. After you come up against the fundamental and the economic communities—these are very smart people and there are fifty of them for every one of us—and you see how often we've been right and they've been wrong, you begin to develop more confidence in it. Now I expect it to work. It doesn't always work, or I may not always read it right, but I expect it to be right, and I'm a little surprised when it isn't. When it doesn't work, it's usually because I've read something wrong.

PRECHTER: I've always been convinced of its validity. This might be a good time to point out that I have met many technicians who began as practicing fundamentalists and gave up on it, but I have never met someone who went the other way. I'm a purist now.

RASCHKE: There is nothing truer than price. Price is everything, and, to me, technicals are the price. Technical analysis works as it always has worked. In terms of your ability to forecast the price, there are times when it works, and there are times when it doesn't. You just need to recognize that everything is a matter of probabilities, and everything can be quantified. I can ask, "With three up days in a row, what is the probability that the next day is going to be down?" There might or might not be any edge to that. In terms of my conviction about the validity of technical analysis, I don't think anything has changed at all.

Certain moments in my career have been critical in determining my level of confidence and conviction in the validity of technical analysis. It's always easier to use technical analysis on a shorter time frame than on a longer time frame. My forecasting models have a very strong edge over the next twenty-four to forty-eight hours. If I try to look too far out—one month, two months, three months down the road—it drops way off. And it's not dumb luck; there are only a very few things that work out there. You can reduce everything down to the fact that you're trying to enter into a trending market, in the direction of the trend. My confidence in the technicals and the price never changes. But I'm always trying to be more on guard about the weaknesses of my game, in recognizing when there are going to be distractions, or where there could be execution problems, liquidity issues, or weaknesses in terms of mechanics. Those are areas where I have my doubts.

SHAW: Yes, I've always been convinced of its validity. I saw it work. I followed what the charts were saying in 1961, and I avoided the 50 percent declines of 1962. And remember, the earnings didn't change—it was the price-to-earnings ratio that changed, going from 47 to 20, and the stock went down 50 percent to allow that to happen. So that was what turned me on to the approach. There was validity in separating the company from its stock.

TABELL: Yes, I have, but it was in the family. I would have had to have some kind of psychological conflict with my father not to be convinced of the validity of technical analysis.

WEINSTEIN: Mine was a growing conviction. In the beginning, I was a little skeptical, and then as I started to use it, it certainly seemed more than random. As I got more proficient, I started to make some really good calls. I went from thinking, "There may be something to this," to "I know there is something to this." But there are limitations to technical analysis, just as there are limitations to fundamental analysis. And just as it's a problem when people don't believe in technical analysis at all, it's a problem when they believe in it without being aware of its limitations. Nothing is foolproof. That's why it's important to know to exit when something isn't functioning according to the game plan.

❖ Did the lack of credit many academics gave to technical analysis during the early days of your career ever discourage you or make you doubt the validity of technical analysis?

ACAMPORA: No. I was too naïve to know that that was going on. When I found out that academics were so antitechnical, it just made me work harder. I instinctively knew they were wrong. Did I back-test it? No, but I was working with it, and these academics were more involved with the fundamental side of the business. They didn't understand risk. They thought risk was a company going out of business. That's just one form of risk. That's not the risk we deal with every day.

BIRINYI: No. It encouraged me to come up with my own ideas that were valid and that withstood rigorous testing. I agreed with the academics' view of technical analysis. If you look at the record, you see that so many times so and so said you should buy stocks, and the market went straight down. I wish it worked. If someone's stock picks worked consistently, I could have put my feet up on the desk and just bought those stocks. But they didn't. Another issue I have with technicians is that they don't really recommend. They tell you that things like rails are developing an interesting pattern, or you should be very careful about airline stocks. What does that mean? I am very careful about every stock! Don't tell me that something is poised to break through its 50-day moving average on the upside; tell me what to buy and sell.

DEEMER: No, the academics didn't discourage me, because technical analysts are contrarians. We're used to being told we're wrong about the market. When I worked at Putnam, I used to give weekly presentations. If I made a forceful and insightful presentation to a room filled with money managers, saying that the market was going to go up, and the managers all stood up, applauded, hoisted me upon their shoulders and carried me down the hallway yelling, "Hosanna, Hosanna," and then rushed into the trading room with their buy tickets, I would know that I had done something wrong. It was when they did not generally agree with me that I knew I was right. That's the theory of contrary opinion. So when academics don't agree with technical analysis, it makes me think that they haven't looked at technical analysis in the right way, taking into account that there are some terrific limitations on what technical analysis can do. With all due respect to the academics, the fact that they don't accept it simply means that they don't understand it.

DESMOND: I think it's disappointing. I guess I don't understand the academics' side of the thing. To a large extent we are dealing with semantics. Chapter 1 of every economics textbook on every campus in the world is about supply and demand. So we come from that academic starting point. There, technicians and academics are on exactly the same page. More recently, behavioral finance has come along directly from the academic community. Behavioral finance espouses positions that technicians have been espousing for over a hundred years: that investors are responsible for the movements of prices; that they make most of their decisions based on emotional rather than factual considerations; that they therefore make a great deal of mistakes; and that the degree of emotional influence is so pervasive that we ought to be spending our time measuring that emotion rather than measuring the influences that created the emotion in the first place, which are fundamentals — earnings and dividends, corporate and economic developments, and so on. That's precisely what technicians have been saying: we don't know why people are buying or selling. They themselves don't know why they are buying or selling in a lot of cases. But the fact that they are buying and selling does cause prices to change on the exchange, and we can measure those changes with the law of supply and demand. We're preaching the same information that the academic community is preaching, and yet they somehow say that we're doing something entirely different. To a very large extent technicians are their own worst enemy. They tend to talk in a language that academics don't understand. The academics don't like it when we come and talk about the head and shoulders, and pennants, and all of the other arcane language we use. That's a major barrier. We need to talk in more general terms that everybody can understand. I think we are largely responsible for our own position in the world.

DUDACK: No, I was not discouraged. Random walk? Never. I knew it was just a matter of time before the random walk thesis would be discredited. Other "great" theories, such as modern portfolio theory, are still around, but they too are evolving. "Evolving" is a nice way of saying that professional users are finding "it does not always work." Is it not ironic that many of the modern "great theories" did not come from people working in the marketplace? Academic theories don't necessarily work in the real world.

FARRELL: I'd be more concerned if the academics got to the point where they're giving credibility to technical analysis. I don't know how far that's gone. I would like to say that it didn't bother me at all, but I guess it did bother me some, because I would not be as much of an anti-academic as I am. That doesn't mean I don't think academics make great contributions, but they don't live in the real world. In my opinion, the fact that they didn't like technical analysis actually gave it more of a chance to work.

McAVITY: What other people think of my work is their problem, not mine. I love watching what I call the "mainstream technical school people," who work for funds, work for brokers. They get themselves so worked up over the fact that nobody respects what they do, and that some professor somewhere said that something doesn't work. I couldn't care less about what the academic community thinks. It doesn't matter at all to me. But, again, I am not publicly accountable beyond whether my subscribers renew or not. The Wall Street analyst looks at the chartered financial analyst in the research department, and he thinks that the CFA is getting an extra $10,000 a year because he's got the alphabet soup after his name. I am a college dropout. I thought it was a waste of time.

MURPHY: Yes, the lack of credit bothered me probably more than anything. A perfect example was the 2000–2003 bear market. If ever there was an example of the danger of fundamental analysis—and the value of technical analysis—that was it. Markets peaked in early March. I was predicting it, and a lot of other technicians were predicting it as well. We moved out of the market, saved a lot of money. We predicted a recession. It took the economic world six to nine months to spot that something was going wrong. They didn't declare a recession till twelve months later. Yet, how did the media react? Immediately after that, they stopped interviewing technical analysts. I couldn't understand that. They kept interviewing the same people that had been wrong all the way down, rather than those of us who had been right. CNBC now rarely interviews technical analysts. This should have led to the golden age of technical analysis, and yet they're not giving us any credit. That bothers me.

As far as the academic community is concerned, there is a conflict of interest there. The academics teach about the stock market, but none of them makes a living in the stock market. They only teach about it from a textbook and tell us what works and what doesn't work. If you follow the market and follow the charts, a lot of what they teach becomes irrelevant. So why would they look on us favorably? Interestingly, there are at least thirty universities that now teach technical analysis. A lot of them use my textbook. There is a lot of interest in this area.

Also, there is behavioral finance. I've seen articles in the *New York Times* about how professors are now coming up with a new theory that you can beat the market by studying human psychology, but everything they describe is pure technical analysis. So after condemning us for all these years, they're now basically copying what we do, renaming it, and trying to take credit for it. The *New York Times* wrote a front-page article about the values of behavioral finance, but I've never seen them write an article on the values of technical analysis, even though it's essentially the same thing. Behavioral finance is reading the psychology of the market, just as technical analysis is.

As I get older, I don't care that much anymore. It doesn't shake my confidence in technical analysis; it shakes my confidence in the academic community. The academic world is where the economists come from, too. I once wrote a paper when I was getting my master's degree in business back in the '70s. I was at Merrill Lynch at the time. The paper was for a course on market analysis, and I asked the professor if I could write a paper on charts. He said okay, so I took a case study of a prediction I had made, when the market was turning up. Merrill Lynch made a lot of money on this particular trade. He gave me a D on the paper, saying, "That stuff doesn't work." I explained that this was a real-life case study. "I do this for a living," I said. "We saw something happening, made a prediction, bought the market, and made a lot of money." But he insisted that technical analysis didn't work and wouldn't change the grade. So, yes, the lack of credit bothers all of us. That's why there is a movement now to obtain the recognition we deserve.

PRECHTER: Sure, the lack of credit bothered me. I would read the weakest study from academia and wonder why it was considered science, and then I would have to endure comments that technical analysis was magical thinking. There is no magical thinking to compare with the efficient market hypothesis. Academics can be lazy. There is a book out by a professor who defines Elliott waves as "a fifty-five-year cycle." Good grief. But when markets go down or sideways, technical analysis becomes popular. But let's be fair. Technical analysts can be excruciatingly embarrassing to their own profession. I know I have been. Sometimes I get excited about the potential of an idea, so I will apply it as analysis when in fact it is utterly unproved and speculative. When I have to abandon it later, I kick myself for the transgression. It's tough to avoid magical thinking or wishes when you're dealing with something as wild as a financial market. But I get more rigorous as I age.

RASCHKE: What do I care about what the academics think? This is a bottom-line business. You think the guys sitting there with a billion dollars offshore care if the academics give them recognition? The guys at the Renaissance Technologies Medallion Fund are laughing all the way to the bank. I would rather not have this published by the academics; I'd rather not have this taught at universities and colleges. I'm sorry, but I could sum up technical analysis in an hour, and you want to build a whole course off of this? I guess you could get more into things like money flows or sentiment data, but in terms of analyzing price, quantifying retracements, and learning what constitutes momentum, it's all very simple.

TABELL: The lack of credit makes me sad; it doesn't discourage me. I think that the random walk hypothesis did what it was intended to do: it got Eugene Fama a full professorship at the University of Chicago. There was unfortunately almost a personality conflict between the early random walk hypothesis proponents and technicians. That's why I'm interested in seeing a synthesis develop between the academic and the professional technical communities. I just don't think there should be a conflict. Fortunately, the fortress walls between the two disciplines are falling. The pure random walk hypothesis is no longer; it's a question of the degree to which you find yourself drawn in one direction or the other.

WEINSTEIN: The lack of credit bothered me when I was young. Now, I laugh at it. When I was very young, I wanted everybody to know the validity of it, but not anymore. If we can convince everybody to go to one side of the ship, the ship is going to tip over, and we're not going to have a functioning market. Pragmatically, it's good that they don't believe in it. I find it almost amusing now, because I've seen all of these academic types come along and say things, but they don't know what they're talking about, and they're obviously not trading in real markets. Among the people who really trade markets, among the people who've traded commodities, I don't know of any successful traders who don't acknowledge at least to some degree that charts and trends are helpful.

◈ Has a big loss ever made you doubt the validity of technical analysis?

ACAMPORA: Absolutely. It was around 1978. It was a difficult, cyclical environment. I was young and enthusiastic, working for a great guy, Alan Shaw. He was terrific. He caught many major market moves. But there was a period of time—a year or so—when almost everything we said went the other way. It got to the point where I was very frustrated with technical analysis, and I almost left the business. You feel very bad if you make mistakes and lose money for people. It was getting to the point where I couldn't believe the charts.

I loved it so much that, fortunately, I didn't quit. I didn't know what else to do for a living, I guess, so I just hung in there. Being young and having gone through a couple of declines and rallies with Alan, who was so in tune and so accurate, I realized it wasn't all so bad or so hard.

BIRINYI: No, because you can never touch every base. Some of my customers are disappointed that I cannot get it 100 percent right in the market. I've read enough about the market; I've lived it long enough to realize that's impossible.

DEEMER: Sometimes a loss causes me to doubt technical analysis, but mostly I doubt the interpretation. The problem with technical analysis is that you can always build a very bullish case and you can always build a very bearish case for the long term. There are always some indicators that are frightfully bullish, and there are some indicators that are very bearish. So which ones do you listen to? When you're wrong, there are always those indicators that did work, and that's the humbling part of the business. Technicians don't seasonally adjust things. We don't revise data; the price is the ultimate arbiter. There are always reasons, beforehand and afterwards, to explain why it did what it did, but you were listening to something else.

DESMOND: No, because beyond my early learning process, I haven't had a big loss. A big loss occurs when the market is telling you that you need to take some action, and you refuse to take that action because of your emotions. You say, "I am a long-term investor," or "That's too far down now. I'm not going to sell out now," or "I've already got too much of a loss. I'm going to wait till it comes back, and then I'll sell." That's emotion talking. And that's the death penalty in the stock market. I simply don't allow much emotion to come into my investment process. I have had and will always have controlled losses, because we don't have all the answers.

DUDACK: Yes. When you have a big loss, there are always doubts. My biggest public mistake was being bearish on the market too early during the late 1990s bubble. In the bubble, nothing worked for me. Technical stuff didn't work; fundamental stuff didn't work. I had read [Charles] Kindleberger's *Manias, Panics, and Crashes* and had actually mailed the book to our clients in March 1999. I knew I could be wrong for a while by being bearish in a bubble, but I was willing to accept that knowing that a bubble typically lasts one to two years. Our bubble lasted three years, so the last year was very painful and potentially career busting. I did a lot of flow-of-funds work so I could see the money was just cascading in from everywhere. But even after we apparently ran through all of our household savings, all the pension fund cash, and after every investable dollar was invested in equities, it just kept going. In retrospect, it was classic "Kindleberger." People borrowed money from their homes, from their margin accounts, and new forms of credit were created. Day-trading firms created a new (and, as it turned out, illegal) form of margin account, but these borrowings were not reported in the margin debt reports of the NYSE or the National Association of Securities Dealers. So money was found in every corner and crevice, and this kept the bubble going much longer than I would have guessed.

You doubted the validity of technical analysis?

I doubted everything equally. The advance/decline line had topped out in March 1998, and in March 2000 the market still seemed to be going higher. The longer the divergence lasts, the greater the bear market. But in early 2000 it seemed like nothing worked. It was a very challenging three-month period.

FARRELL: Technical analysis is an art. If it doesn't work, it's your fault, not the fault of technical analysis.

McAVITY: I don't doubt the validity of technical analysis in general, but rather the validity of my own applications of it. That happens literally every time a trend changes character. For example, considering pure charts, in a bull market quite often an enthusiastic trend has already started to slope up, and the last gasp will make a new high and everybody will be shouting, "a breakout," and very quickly it will become a fakeout. In other words, the last thing the price will do is poke to a high and then break. And in an accelerated trend, that's actually quite common. The whole market is sort of a living being. It's a psychological thing. When there is enough urgency, quite often the last achievement in terms of a higher high will be the moment at which the market looked its best. And then it fails very quickly. Higher high after an accelerated trend followed by a lower low can be a particularly dangerous moment, because it can really accelerate downward from there. And whether it's a fakeout or a breakout is also one of the hardest calls to make. That's where the art of understanding the trend or having a feel for a trend comes in; that's where the art takes over from the science.

MURPHY: Yes, it did make me doubt technical analysis. I was just starting out in the commodity markets. I stopped trading that particular market. It obviously shook my confidence at that time, but, overall, I had more successes than failures. Fortunately, I was very lucky in those early days of the 1970s, because it was the beginning of a major bull cycle in commodities. So most of the trades or recommendations I made did very well. Over the course of time, the painful memory of that first trade faded.

There have been times when I considered abandoning technical analysis, like when I lost my first job, and stocks went into a bear market for a long time in the early '70s. Also, commodity and futures markets, which were my specialty for about fifteen or sixteen years, are very stressful to trade, because you trade very low margin, but there is tremendous leverage, which means you can make and lose tremendous amounts of money. After about fifteen years—I was in my late thirties—I got very burned out. I literally retired; Merrill Lynch actually threw me a retirement party. I did not stay retired

long. For almost a year, I was looking for a new career. Then, someone said to me: "You don't have to trade. If you have this knowledge,
why don't you teach?" I taught at four or five different schools. I
wasn't making any money, but it was fun. Then someone suggested
I write a book. That launched a whole other career for me. Interestingly, now I am back to trading again, but it's of a very different
type. I enjoy it quite a bit. I am not trading commodities anymore.

PRECHTER: No, I've never lost confidence in it. In fact, my theory
of market impulse, which I talk about in my book *The Wave Principle of Human Social Behavior*, explains losses and simultaneously
validates technical analysis. People don't lose money because the
market is random. They lose money because it *isn't* random. It's
propelled by an unconscious herding impulse that we all have. That
impulse is the basis of technical analysis *and* the reason that losing
money is the norm.

RASCHKE: No, I never have, because technical analysis tells you
where your risk point is. The technicals define where support and
resistance are and how tight you're going to play that. My big losses
come from my own stupidity, not from the technicals failing. There
is no such thing as a technical tool that works 100 percent of the
time. You can't curse yourself because you're an insurance company
and a hurricane hit. The market has risk. You have to ask, what is
the overnight risk? What is the risk that a plane flies into the World
Trade Center? What is the risk that the president gets shot? These
kinds of things are probably not going to change the underlying
technicals, but they can cause large adverse moves. Technical analysis is not going to prevent that kind of risk.

SHAW: Any losses we've taken have been small ones. That is an
asset of the discipline. Marty Zweig (author of *Winning on Wall
Street*) used to say, "Don't fight the tape," and "Don't be afraid to
make mistakes; just don't compound them." That's true. You may be
wrong, but if your discipline tells you you're wrong, don't question
the discipline.

WEINSTEIN: No, I've never lost confidence in technical analysis,
because I'll never ever take a big loss. I'd rather take four or five

small losses. Forty years ago, when I was first starting out, I had a big loss or two, but that didn't make me doubt technical analysis. That made me grow and realize how stupid I was for hoping for a turnaround. Today, I'll quickly sell a losing position, and if I'm wrong, there is always another "street car coming along," and I'll make it up next time. I'm amazed when I see what happens to a lot of these big mutual funds and hedge funds with poor discipline. Often, when I review portfolios, I'll see that a client would have had a terrific year, but he had two or three tremendous losses that wiped out ten or fifteen good things he did. To me, that's silly. I do it the opposite way. One or two big wins will wipe out three or five or six little losses. That approach validates technical analysis because it shows that if you follow the system, it's impossible to have a big loss.

◈ Have you found that your experience with technical analysis contradicts statements made in books? And has that discouraged you?

DESMOND: A lot of books were written on technical analysis in the '30s and '40s. There was an awful lot of progress made in technical analysis during the '20s, '30s, and '40s. People have accepted things, thinking if it's in a book, then it's correct. A lot of books on technical analysis say that when volume expands on a rally or contracts on a decline, that's a very good sign. Well, if you don't know whether the volume is coming from buyers or from sellers, you really can't make that kind of a statement. What if you found that your volume was expanding right near the market top but that the volume expansion was coming from sellers? If the sellers were dumping huge amounts of stock into the market near a top, that would not be bullish. So there are a lot of books that have incorrect information. They were correct at the time at which they were written, but they're simplistic nowadays, when we can measure a lot more information. Technology has helped us get at data we could not get at before.

DEEMER: I wouldn't say my experience contradicted the books, but some indicators are presented as foolproof that are not foolproof. No indicator works all the time; no indicator gives constant information, as John Bollinger [creator of the Bollinger bands] once said. And some things are presented in books that I either don't understand or can't make work, such as the Elliott wave. I can't make the Elliott wave work to forecast. I suppose I could make it work if I wanted to explain something that's happened, but that's not my job. My job is to predict, not to explain what's happened.

DUDACK: There are a variety of technical books out there, and I have read only some basic books, such as those by Edwards and Magee, John Murphy, and William Jiler's *How Charts Can Help You in the Stock Market*. I can't say that I found anything in any of these that contradicted my experiences. The classic book on chart patterns is Edwards and Magee's. If there was anything discouraging there, it was that these patterns, which are so well explained and so clear in the book, happen so rarely in real life. More often than not, you're analyzing a chart that is neither fish nor foul, neither bullish nor bearish, but is somewhere in between. People don't like to hear that a chart is neutral. In other words, they don't like to hear, "I can't help you; it could go either way, or it could do nothing." That's a reality they would rather ignore. There are times when nothing works, and to a young technician that can be disappointing.

FARRELL: The books that I thought were important I largely agreed with. It certainly didn't discourage me if literature did not agree with what I thought, because I tended to emphasize what I thought was important. I always got more nervous when I had more company.

McAVITY: It's a matter of the changing nature of trends. Whenever somebody tries to make it too mechanical, too constrictive, that's an invitation to breaking the parameter. Paint with a broad brush. You can fiddle with the statistics to prove anything you want. And, unfortunately, too many are very good at the fiddle.

MURPHY: Sometimes they contradict each other. I don't agree with everything that's been written. In the early days, I learned my technical work with Edwards and Magee. In their book, they state that this stuff doesn't work in the commodity markets. Well, I applied it to the commodity markets, and it worked extremely well. In my early years, I was always very careful to try to stay within the rules and within what someone said was the right way to do it. Now, I just follow my own thing. I don't worry about the rules too much. If I disagree with something, it doesn't bother me. By the way, I've also disagreed with things that *I* have written in the past. We change. When you write a book, that's the body of your knowledge at that point in time. You're going to evolve, and ten years later you'll know more than you did then.

PRECHTER: I wasn't discouraged when I found contradictions, but I was dismayed, particularly when it led me to the shocking realization that even other technicians don't see markets the way I do. I see them on TV talking about what the Fed chairman is going to say, what the trade deficit numbers are saying, or what the trend of unemployment has been—the *fundamentals*—as if any of that makes a whit of difference in terms of where the stock market is going. I realized I had to write a book about it, so I've written two, in a set called *Socionomics*.

RASCHKE: Probably some of the best writings on technical analysis, which hold up to this day, were written by Richard Schabacker, the grandfather of the science of technical analysis. He wrote his observations on the way price trades around gaps, trends, chart patterns, but he also recognized the human element of it. For example, you can make a lot of money in trends, but most people don't have the patience to stay on that type of time frame.

I like the books written by traders that aren't so much about the technicals, but about the perspective of taking the market one day at a time. For example, there is a book called *The Taylor Trading Technique*, written by George Douglas Taylor in the 1950s. He was a grain trader in the pits. He shows how he does his technicals in there, how he measures the relationship between today's high and the previous day's low, the relationship between yesterday's high and today's low, and various other relationships he calculates by hand every day. His approach is to take it one day at a time: Are we going to have a buy day today, or are we going to look to be short today? Are we in a mark-up period? That type of book reinforced for me the importance of always following my own work, my own road map, and taking one day at a time. If the market gives you a lot, great; if the market gives you a little, you take what it is. If the trade doesn't work out, you get out, and you try again the next day.

TABELL: Richard Schabacker and H. M. Gartley made mistakes, but they were writing in the '30s, when we knew much less. I don't fault Hippocrates for using leeches. Schabacker and Gartley were writing in the early stages of technical analysis. Do you know how Gartley developed the 200-day moving average? He found about thirty women who did not have jobs and sat them down with hand adding machines called "comptometers," and had them figure out moving averages at 5-day intervals, starting from 5 and up to 400. He eventually came up with the idea that the 200-day moving average worked well. That's the kind of tool he had at his disposal at that time.

◈ Does the absence of hard-and-fast rules or proven theories in technical analysis ever bother you?

BIRINYI: Yes, it does. Terribly, because it allows you to pick a stand and then find things that support your stand. If I were a practicing technician working for a Wall Street firm, I would say, "Here is my model. Here are the twenty-five things we're going to look at, and it's always going to be the same twenty-five things. If thirteen of them turn negative, you turn negative." Instead, here's what happens: the market is going up, so technicians say, "Let's be positive," because, after all, you get paid for going along. Nobody wants to be an outcast. What bothers me is that people look sometimes at this and other times at that to justify their case.

DEEMER: No, it doesn't bother me. It's part of the wonderful, fascinating field of technical analysis. There are no rules. Nothing works all the time. When you think you've found a key to the market, somebody changes the lock. There are probabilities, not certainties.

DESMOND: I don't think there are hard-and-fast rules about much of anything. We're measuring human psychology, and I don't think there are any hard-and-fast rules that can be applied to psychology. Are there hard-and-fast rules about how to raise a child? About the law? I don't think so. I think there are some strong general rules, some basic principles that have to be observed, but you don't want to get into a situation that is rigid. You want to have some flexibility to see beyond some rules. Fundamental analysis doesn't provide hard-and-fast rules either, and I don't think it can. Anything that deals with human psychology can't be too rigid. It just doesn't work. Human beings are too arbitrary.

DUDACK: What bothers me most is that there aren't one or two brilliant textbooks. Technical analysis has evolved based on theories that go back to Charles Dow. Technical analysis was born in the workings and writings of some great predecessors of ours and has evolved over time. A whole battery of new, computer generated, fast short-term trading tools is available now. Technical analysis is constantly evolving, but the textbooks have not kept up. I wish there was a basic textbook—even John Murphy's book is more on futures than on equities or bonds—that would trace the history of why the charts and indicators work. You can read ten books on ten different theories within technical analysis. It's very fragmented. And I doubt that many of the theories have been—or can be— back-tested. It becomes confusing as to what it all means and how it all fits together.

FARRELL: No, I think that's a good thing, because if there were hard-and-fast rules, everybody would learn them, and everybody would act in the same way, and nobody would make any money.

McAVITY: There are no hard-and-fast rules, but a successful person will recognize that. Some tools are likely to work better in some periods than in others. For example, within the broad indexes, everyone hates the value line geometric average, because a geometric average apparently has some statistically negative bias. Well, that's fine. For me the value line geometric average is a wonderful tool to use at the bottoms. When I saw it falling at an accelerating rate in 2002, I thought that was pretty impressive. As a net result, I basically turned bullish within two days of the bottom, in October 2002. The value line geometric average fell below its 200-day moving average to a level seen only three times in fifty years. My comment was, "If the world is coming to an end, it doesn't matter, but if the world doesn't end, the market is going up."

MURPHY: There is a body of knowledge. There is a set of rules, which you can program into a computer, and you can do a fairly good job relying on your program. A good analyst sometimes can improve on that. If there is no body of knowledge, there is nothing to it. It's just witchcraft. And it all depends on what you mean by "proven theories." How would you scientifically prove it? You can take many of the indicators and many of the systems we use today—I've done it myself and I've seen others do it—and prove that if you had followed a certain technical system, you would have made a lot of money over the last ten, twenty, thirty years. You can test that historically. You can take track records of technical analysts. If you show academics a winning record, they'll say, "But he is an exception!" So you can never win the argument. We've been managing money for six years; we've never had a losing year, even in the bear market. I am asked if I can prove that technical analysis works, but why isn't anyone asking that question for economic analysis?

PRECHTER: No one has developed a set of rules for precisely predicting aggregate human behavior. But there is a set of rules that applies, and it's called the "wave principle." For example, one rule is that a corrective wave will never take the shape of a motive wave. But this is not the same as buy and sell signals. But please. Does anyone really think that there could be a set of rules to buy and sell at bottoms and tops? If there were, it would be like driving and everyone could do it, in which case the market wouldn't exist. Every software program tries to create rules, but most programmers are too linear and statistics-bound to create truly applicable rules, because what is required are flexible rules, which is almost a contradiction in terms. Look, the market is *alive,* and all one can do is describe the behavior of the beast. There are no hard-and-fast rules about precisely how your friend Charlie will act. But you can assert some soft rules that will apply probabilistically, and that's what technicians do when assessing the market. And, I have to add, compared to what? Does fundamental analysis have hard-and-fast rules? None that I'm aware of.

SHAW: I disagree wholeheartedly that there are no proven theories. Technical analysis can be very rigorous. In a book called *Investment Analysis and Portfolio Management,* by Jerome Cohen and Edward Zinbarg, there is a section on technical analysis in which the authors cite a 1966 *Business Week* article in which I was quoted along with five other technicians. There were six different opinions in that article, and one of them was right. Mine. The conclusion of the article was that technical analysis is not the method; it's the man. They arrived at that conclusion because six technicians supposedly looking at the same stuff arrived at six different opinions. But put a balance sheet in front of five CFAs, and you might find five different opinions.

TABELL: The rules have to be bent a little. So I would agree with the fact that there tend not to be hard-and-fast rules. Why should I be bothered by that? The "perfect" should not be an enemy of the "good."

❖ Do you believe that technical analysis works even when applied to data other than the market-action data—for example, the weather or river flow data?

BIRINYI: No. The truth is technical analysis doesn't work in the market, so I see no reason for it to work in these other contexts. I think technical analysis would work with something like foreign exchange. One of the things about the market is that you have different people doing different things: Some people are hedging, some people are buying short term, some people are buying long term, some people are buying income. In foreign exchange, everybody is doing the same thing. Everybody is trading in the same place; all the information is captured. In Forex and in some of the commodity markets, technical analysis is much more useful, because there is consistency, and it's all charts. In the stock market, I think there is no question that it doesn't work. If you go to a major brokerage firm that has significant technical operations, the traders in those firms do not depend on the technical groups, which to me is pretty indicative of something.

Technical groups are for the benefit of the public. Technical analysts are like fortune-tellers who say something good and make people feel better. You feel good when someone tells you you'll meet a handsome man who is rich.

DESMOND: There are a lot of tools used in technical analysis that don't necessarily belong to technical analysis. For example, the moving average is a basic mathematical concept that could be applied to anything: changes in corporate earnings, weather, or anything else. But other tools are designed to deal specifically with human psychology, where there is a consistency in the human behavior. For example, toward the end of a major market advance, buying enthusiasm narrows. That is unique to human behavior. It wouldn't apply to weather, to farm production, and so on. You really need to separate the tools that are just mathematical computations and aren't exclusive to technical analysis at all from those that help to measure investor psychology, the uniqueness of the mass psychology, and the human mind.

Continuation and reversal patterns specifically designed to measure human psychology include things like head and shoulders, which probably apply only to human behavior because they reflect human emotion and human psychology. In its simplest form, head and shoulders is a series of attempts to rise to a peak. When any trend ends, it ends by simply not being able to exceed the previous peak. That's what creates a head-and-shoulders pattern. But head and shoulders applies only to human nature, because the minute the market sells off from its high, there are investors who say that it's an opportunity to buy back in again. That's what completes the head-and-shoulders pattern.

I am a very strong believer that technical analysis doesn't forecast much of anything. There is a big difference between measuring and forecasting. If you say that, based upon whatever, the weather in three weeks will be such and such, I am very skeptical about that, because you're predicting the future. I've never seen that anyone anywhere in life could accurately predict the future with any consistency. Therefore, I think anyone who says that they're predicting the future is a fool or a liar. This is one of the places where academia may find fault with technicians, because many technicians like to give the impression that they can forecast the future. Therefore, academics see it as fakery.

But you *can* measure situations as they exist. Let's say everybody is running in one direction. When are they going to stop? I
have no idea. But when they stop, I will see it, and I can react to it,
and I can act on it. I can say they stopped. And if they all turn
around and face in the opposite direction, I can say they're not
going in the original direction any more, and therefore I am able to
expect a different type of behavior from them. There is a very
important distinction there. One is measurement, and the other is
prediction. If you follow technical analysis in a very disciplined
manner, the net effect is that, except for the totally unexpected, it
dramatically reduces the chances of your being blindsided and
taking a dramatic loss. That's the whole point of technical analysis.
The likelihood of an experienced, well-trained, disciplined, objective technical analyst taking a large loss is rather low. The market
leaves tracks behind when it goes from a high point to a low point.
And those tracks tell technical analysts that the market is weakening and they need to take appropriate action.

PRECHTER: Technical analysis is the analysis of collective human
behavior, not wind and water. On a much broader level, it reveals
patterns of life forms. I suspect that the number of species through
time follows the wave principle, although I have limited data. The
only technical tools that might be useful with respect to inanimate
objects or processes are momentum indicators. But that's probably
why they are the least useful in the stock market.

RASCHKE: Some indicators are only for the markets. Volatility
indicators—range expansion, range contraction, that type of
thing—can show that there is a cyclicality of volatility in the market that is more regular than the cyclicality in the price or in the
direction. Everything moves, then it has to take a breather; then
once again everything moves, then it has to take a breather. So it's
always this dynamic model that most of the time is checking back
and forth as it processes new information. That process might not
be applicable to other data series in the same way. With the
weather, it's not going to absorb this new information and check
back and consolidate, then again absorb new information. That
volatility, that physicality between the movement and then the
rest isn't there.

WEINSTEIN: I always use the analogy of a doctor: even without ever meeting you, I can say, "Okay, I am going to run a cardiogram on you, and I want to do blood tests." I can do tests without having met you or spoken to you, and after I get test results, I can have a good idea of your health, or lack thereof, and people won't think that I am strange or that I am using magic or astrology. Similarly, with technical analysis, I am measuring how strong or how healthy the buyers are versus the sellers. There is always a tug of war going on in the marketplace. And I am measuring which side is healthier or stronger—the buyers or the sellers. Technical analysis works best in measuring supply and demand. You can do trend analysis or run moving averages on other kinds of data, and you'll be able to detect certain trend changes, but I don't think you'll get as high a correlation of success as you will with the stock market or the commodity market data.

◈ What do you believe is the best proof of the validity of technical analysis?

ACAMPORA: The fact that folks like me are still in the business. That's proof enough. Alan Shaw spent his whole business career doing it; Bob Farrell at Merrill Lynch is another example. They're the proof that it's valid. Many people have made major commitments on their market calls over the years.

BIRINYI: The proof is our record.

DEEMER: The proof is that I am not on Debtors' Row, that I am not standing on the street corner begging for food—just the fact that it works. I know some people want to see track records. But when your analysis is long term, it gets difficult to do track records. Let's say the market is coming into a bottom and I think that my clients should be turning more bullish. I can't turn an out-and-out bear into an out-and-out bull overnight. Nobody can. What I can do, if I'm lucky and if I do my job properly, is turn that person into a little less of a bear and then, the next week or the next month, into a little bit less of a bear still. In other words, I'm working at the margin. Unfortunately, if I really do my job well, the money managers will think that it's their ideas rather than mine.

DESMOND: Avoiding bear markets is the most dramatic evidence of its validity. Using fundamental analysis, people generally are left to suffer the full ravages of a bear market. They rarely get out of a bear market because fundamentals are telling them to get out. More often, it's because they abandon fundamentals and react to fear and sell out, regardless of the fundamentals. You'll generally find that corporate earnings are improving all through the bear markets. If there is anything that proves the value of technical analysis, it's the ability to avoid large parts of the major market declines that occur from time to time.

DUDACK: The evidence is my portfolio. The best *proof* of technical analysis is that among the analysts who have been working in our business for thirty years or more and who are still viewed as credible you find a disproportionate number of technicians. We've outlived a lot of other analysts. Wall Street is not an easy place; it's very cruel, actually. So if you can survive Wall Street for that length of time, there has to be something there. You cannot survive it if you are not adding value for your clients.

FARRELL: If you can make money using technical analysis, that's the best proof that it has some validity. I think the fact that there are cycles in markets and in nature says there are forces to look at other than just whether the economy is good or bad or if interest rates are going up or down. In the 1990s, economists started becoming experts on the stock market. But they didn't become experts until near the end of the boom. It was the kiss of death when the economists saw that the economy was going up and the stock market was going up. "The economy is going up, so the stock market will keep going up," they said. They really thought they had the answer. Of course, when the market goes up faster than the fundamentals, you get an expansion in the P/E multiples and over-valuation. And eventually you reach a clearing price, and back down the market comes even without the fundamentals crumbling.

MURPHY: The best proof is our track records and the fact that most of us have survived in very difficult environments. Those of us who manage money or make recommendations have track records, and we've done very well. We outperformed the market dramatically during the bear market. For proof, you just need to look at the record. What else is there?

PRECHTER: The evidence is that some short-term traders make lots of money, month after month, year after year.

RASCHKE: I prove theories every day with my bottom line. My theories work. Or let's take the Renaissance Medallion Fund, a nice offshore hedge fund. I think it was started by five guys out in Berkeley, all with PhDs in math. It's 100 percent mechanical. There is no human guessing or decision making involved, and they've achieved a 40–60 percent return a year on between $500 million and $1 billion. What more proof do you need? Anybody who demands proof is silly. It's sour grapes. They just couldn't figure out how to execute it themselves, that's all. I don't want to sound flippant on this stuff either. What's most important is to recognize that there is an edge. It's a very small edge, and that edge can easily be lost through friction, the execution, the commissions, and things like that. But there is definitely an edge, and the people who have been able to harness that edge and do it in a really good way that manages the risk have extremely sophisticated set-ups. They are working a thousand different patterns, twenty-four hours, around the clock, around fifty markets.

SHAW: How would I have had a successful career if I were constantly advising people about things that went wrong? The great success of our model, if followed with discipline over time, shows that the application of our technical discipline allows one to significantly outperform the S&P 500. Looking at historical data, we're able to show our clients which sectors we were overweighted in and which sectors we were underweighted in at any given point. That gives our clients an understanding of how the technical discipline might fit in with the fundamental advice they're receiving.

TABELL: Technical analysis improved the performance of money managers.

WEINSTEIN: The best proof is in the batting average. Over the past four decades, we've caught every major bull and bear market top within a matter of sometimes a day, sometimes weeks. In mid-March 2003, for example, we turned bullish on that bottom day, after having been long-term bearish for three years. Again, nothing is infallible, but the fact that we've had so many good market calls and that so many individual stocks have worked must be more than random.

15

The Evolution of
Technical Analysis

People ask, with things moving so quickly, is technical analysis still relevant? Has it changed? It's still the same. It's as if they speeded up the records from 33 rpm to 78 rpm. Everything develops faster. Charts are still valid for the simple reason that what we're measuring is supply and demand, which is never going to change, and human nature is never going to change. Fear and greed are always the same.

— S. Weinstein

❖ How has the craft evolved since you first started this work?

ACAMPORA: The biggest thing that happened to technical analysis is the Market Technicians Association. In 1975 we started the MTA library, the first of its kind. The MTA provides a forum, and, as an organization, it is very proactive. We do a lot of things for people. Mike Epstein, for example, who is both part of MIT and part of the MTA Educational Foundation, is doing things that have never been done before, such as providing education on college campuses. We have sister societies all around the world now.

BIRINYI: Technical analysis has become more publicized because there is more media. You now have *SmartMoney* magazine, *Money* magazine, CNBC, etc., but there is a need for input and content. There have been some dramatic developments that have brought technicians to the fore. I don't think the practice is any better. I think that people practicing technical analysis twenty or thirty years ago were probably more diligent. Joe Granville did some very good work; James Dines's book *How the Average Investor Can Use Technical Analysis for Stock Profits* is pretty good. But you could be good in those days, because if a stock opened up half a point, the chances are that by the end of the day it would be up a quarter or three quarters, whereas now you have all this intraday activity going on.

The odd-lot indicator was useful in those days, because the odd lots constituted 10 percent of volume. As far as the odd lots are concerned, in those days we were not talking just about sentiment; we were talking about the actual supply and demand. So the indicators reflected what happened. When I came into the business, the market opened at 10 a.m. and closed at 2 p.m. News was very limited. For a long time, there was no news on the floor of the NYSE and no quote machines.

DEEMER: Technical analysis has evolved in many ways. One important change, from a practitioner's standpoint, is that the formation of the Market Technicians Association fostered sharing of information. In the old days you heard the terms *proprietary indicator* or *my work* all the time, which didn't help. If I went to MIT with the perfect indicator, but I gave you only the signals without telling you what it was, it wouldn't help you a whole lot. If I went to MIT and told you what was behind it, then you could take it apart and find out whether it was just random luck or something more. The MTA encouraged the sharing of information, so technical analysis is a lot more open. The other change is the information age. When I first started in business on my own in 1980, my main data source was a VCR hooked to a television set that recorded the stock market channel. I don't need to do that anymore, because now, with the Internet, all the information is available for free and instantaneously.

DESMOND: Technical analysis hasn't evolved nearly as much as it should have. We still tend to do a lot of things today the same way we did them thirty-five to forty years ago. For example, a lot of people used 10-day moving averages because you could add up a column of numbers by hand and move the decimal place over along the line, and that divided it by 10. And even though we now have all these super-fast computers, people are still using 10-day moving averages.

And if you ask them why they're using them, they'll tell you it's because they've just always done it that way, not that 10 days is a good time period to measure. It's *not* a good time period to measure.

Then there's the concept of segmentation, which is not a popular theory at this point, but we hope it will be in the future. So many investors want to view the market as one huge market. That just isn't true. It's like saying all Americans are the same. They are dramatically different from one another, and unless you recognize those differences, you're missing out on some wonderful opportunities.

Some new investment vehicles have helped technical analysis greatly. For example, exchange-traded funds are going to be an extremely important factor in money management and in technical analysis in the years ahead. You can't apply fundamentals to them, so if you're going to be successful with ETFs, you're probably going to be successful because of technical analysis. The more we have computers available to us, the more we see how much information is buried down inside the numbers. So I think there are going to be dramatic changes in technical analysis in the years ahead, and I hope people will understand more thoroughly what they're doing with technical analysis than they do today.

DUDACK: So much has changed. Sentiment indicators, for example, which could be very effective, are less effective now because of changes in the markets and markets that disappeared. Sentiment can be measured in some other areas. For example, the options market seems to be a place to look at sentiment, but now so much hedging takes place that you cannot be sure what real sentiment is when you look at option premiums and volumes. When I got into the business in the 1970s, it was the end of the cycle when average investors had an impact on the market. There was a shift, and the market became professionally driven. Then came the 1990s, and again the market was driven by the public. Now, I sense that we're going into a new cycle, in which the market will be driven by professionals. These are important shifts.

As technicians, we have to be alert to the fact that the actual execution of a trade has changed. Trading used to be done either on the New York and American stock exchanges or on the over-the-counter market. Today, volume is found on the Nasdaq Composite

Index, on multiple electronic communication networks, in global twenty-four-hour trading, and on upstairs desks that never hit the system. This change means we can *no longer* define volume. If we're talking about an NYSE stock, volume could be defined as exchange-only volume or exchange plus after-hours volume, or it could be composite volume. If I'm trying to get one consistent series of volumes on five hundred stocks, it can be a nightmare. For each individual stock, I have three different sets of volumes and three different sets of numbers. Why? The trading structure has changed. Trading no longer starts at 9:30 a.m. on the New York Stock Exchange and ends at 4:00 p.m. Volume is a very important ingredient since it is a measure of conviction.

Thirty years ago the market structure was simple, and we did not have these questions. When I'm buying a volume series, I have too many choices to make. I have to ask myself if after-hours trading is relevant to my project because a different kind of trader is involved there. Is using only the NYSE volume good enough, or do I really want composite volume? How about ECN volume? Some trading takes place today that is not measured, and we never see or hear about it. Since the charts are looking at price and volume, these choices are important. You can come to a wrong conclusion if you inadvertently chose the volume series that doesn't relate to your study. You *must* understand your data to make good decisions. It's better to use a smaller number of indicators, use them really well, and really understand them.

MURPHY: There is a lot more written on technical analysis now. Many more indicators have been developed over the years. Technical analysis is more widely used now. One of the major changes has been in the intermarket area. When I first wrote my book fifteen years ago on the intermarket, most stock market analysts did not pay much attention to the price of gold or the price of oil. Whenever the price of oil moves up close to $40 a barrel, the stock market always goes down. That has happened every time over the last thirty years. So, oil becomes a tremendous factor. Every recession we've had has been caused by a rise in oil prices. Fifteen years ago nobody paid any attention to that, but now you turn on CNBC, and they talk about the impact of the dollar on interest rates, and technical analysts talk about these things.

Technical work has broadened in that we look at global markets, commodity prices, oil, etc. I'd like to see the technical community get away from the use of a lot of technical jargon, words such as *head and shoulders*. That's a very hard sell when you're talking to a nontechnical audience. But if you could tell them we see a head-and-shoulders bottom in the energy group as the price of oil is going up and that on a relative strength basis, oil and energy stocks are beginning to outperform the rest of the market, then they understand. If you talk to them in language that they can understand, there is a lot more credibility.

Technical analysis is just beginning to move forward. I manage a mutual fund now, and we're doing asset allocation. In other words, we're allocating how much goes into stocks, how much into bonds, how much is in cash, how much goes into global markets, and this is all technical. Then we decide which asset classes we want to be in. Commodities have done very well in the last couple of years. Within the stock market, we consider sector rotations. That's all technical. I know that the TV and the print media have a very narrow view of what technical work is. I experience this all the time when I get calls from CNN or other TV stations. All they want us to talk about is a trendline or a moving average. If I start talking about inflation and interest rates, they say, "No, no, no! You're just a technical analyst; you shouldn't be talking about these things!"

Technical analysis is being recognized as a much broader field. Let's compare it to economic analysis, for example. Geoffrey Moore was the leading business cycle expert in this country. He created a system of leading economic indicators. He passed away a few years ago, but he worked well into his eighties. He wrote a book called *Leading Indicators for the 1990s.* He compared commodities, bonds, and stocks, and went back and showed that there was a very predictable chronological relationship. At the end of an economic expansion, for example, bonds always turn down first. That's because of inflation. Then, after a while, stocks turn down, and a while after that, commodities turn down. At the bottom it's just the opposite. So by studying the three of them, you can tell where you are in the economic cycle. Moore did it quantitatively. He calculated leads, lags, and everything else. Very often, I write pieces on where the economy is. By knowing where we are in stocks, bonds, and commodities, we are actually doing economic analysis. These markets are leading indicators. The stock market is the leading indicator of the economy. So, technical analysts are actually moving into economic analysis.

PRECHTER: Technical analysis has mostly *de*volved. In bear market decades, such as the 1930s, 1940s, and 1970s, there is technical analysis innovation going on all the time. In bull markets, most investors pay no attention to it. They revert to exogenous-cause thinking, which is our mental default. Computers have helped a lot because they save so much time in plotting.

RASCHKE: I have no idea how technical analysis has evolved, because I really don't see much of what other people are doing. I've noticed a proliferation of books in the last seven or eight years, but I don't read any of them. I think a lot of them are written for marketing purposes. I haven't seen very much good published research. I thought James O'Shaughnessy's book *What Works on Wall Street,* which I think came out in the mid-'90s, was a nice study, an examination of the different strategies out there. Whether it's right or wrong and how thorough it is is a totally different issue. That's the type of book that might have value to me because at least it's backed up by some numbers. Perry Kaufman wrote some excellent books, and at least he has quantifiable data behind them. Whether you agree with his thesis or not is a different story, but at least he presented it in a good format.

So technical analysis has seen a proliferation of a lot more junk out there. What can you say about technical analysis? There's nothing new to say about it. You're testing a previous high or a low, you're buying a retracement and a trend, or you're following a breakout strategy. It's really simple. If you want to be successful, it's all about risk, the money management, and the leverage. At least now we have computers, so it's easier to crunch numbers and calculate probabilities.

SHAW: When I retired, I had to clean out my office. I came across a transcript of a panel that I was on for the very first annual Institutional Investor Conference, in the late '60s. There were over a thousand people in the room, and my guess is that a lot of them came to be entertained. They probably thought that they were going to see four people with pointed hats arriving on a broom. I think a lot of them probably left with the understanding that technical analysis was not witchcraft, that this was not sorcery, and that there was something legitimate to it.

Means of communication are more readily available today than ever before. When I was starting out in the business, it used to take me twenty minutes to get a quote. We had ticker tapes that went across the wall, of course, but to get a quote you had to call down to the floor. You couldn't press a machine and get an instant quote. Alvin Toffler wrote a book called *Future Shock* in which he talked about the acceleration of the rate of change. In my view, nowhere has the acceleration of the rate of change appeared more dramatically than in the stock market. To a degree, Toffler's book prepared me for the future, and for how to accept the computer, e-mail, the instantaneous communication. We send out a "tech fax," and all the brokers and all the clients see it immediately; it goes right to their computers. We recognize how that has possibly affected our indicators as time has passed. Market movements could appear faster; times might get more volatile. So we recognize that, and we go with that flow as it happens.

TABELL: The evolvement is the development of the computer. Technical analysis is measuring an incredible amount of data. It's measuring every single transaction that takes place. Moreover, the number of operations that can be performed on this data is infinite. You could not do one thousandth of them prior to the advent of the computer. The field itself has expanded; it has become broader and more complex. More resources had to be devoted to it. The principles of technical analysis have stayed the same as they've always been, but now we're able to implement these principles more accurately than before.

WEINSTEIN: In my book, *Secrets for Profiting in Bull and Bear Markets,* I wrote about some of the things that have changed in technical analysis. We used to see many more saucer bottoms. Over a six-month period, the mutual funds and a lot of individual investors would slowly accumulate stock. You had much more time to round out your positions. "So," people ask, "with things moving so quickly, is technical analysis still relevant? Has it changed?" It's still the same. It's as if they speeded up the records from 33 rpm to 78 rpm. Everything develops faster. Certain things used to develop over six-month periods, and you almost never see that anymore. Now, changes develop over six weeks, so the accumulation and distribution are much faster. It's become like a commodity market. Patterns work faster in commodities, and you have to use short-term moving averages. This is why I advise people to look at 50-day moving averages. Charts are still valid for the simple reason that what we're measuring is supply and demand, which is never going to change, and human nature is never going to change. Fear and greed are always the same.

◈ As the field evolves, new indicators and patterns are being introduced. Do you try to stay on top by familiarizing yourself with the new inventions?

ACAMPORA: Yes, that's why we go to all these seminars. But I don't have the luxury of doing as much original research as I used to. Every year or so, I'll do a major "think piece" that requires me to take time out and go back into the history of the markets. That's the thing I believe I do best. I know there are new indicators, but most of the newer indicators are more sensitive to the trading aspect of technical analysis. They're very short-term oriented, and I think they make too much out of the market noise.

BIRINYI: Over the years I've been subscribed to numerous technical analysis and financial publications, and I've found that one cannot substitute mathematics for experience. A lot of the things that I've seen are very cumbersome and impractical; it's obvious that they're not being done by practitioners. These financial publications authors want to prove something, so they keep messing around with numbers until they prove it. Basically, they know what the answer is, so they devise the formula that yields the desired answer. By being a good consumer, I found out that much of this stuff doesn't work. It's one thing to do something in theory, and it's another thing to do it in real-world situations.

DEEMER: I update my own strategies. I'm always trying to get the best feel for the market no matter what tools I can use. Take Rydex Investments, for example, which has a whole bunch of mutual funds, many of which are indexed to the market, and some of which are indexed inversely to the market. So Rydex has an index fund that moves with the S&P 500 and an index fund that moves inversely to the S&P 500. And Rydex is nice enough to report the assets in each of its funds at about midnight every night. So by comparing the change in assets with the change in the net asset value you can find out how much money came into and out of those funds every single day. That's very different from opinion polls or sentiment. With Rydex, you're looking at what people are actually doing with their money, rather than what people think about the market. I'm convinced that these 6 or 7 billion dollars of assets in Rydex reflect the general hedge fund trading activity, which is the driving force in the market. So this is something we've been doing a lot of work with, getting these numbers every single day from Rydex, figuring out what the flows are, and trying to find out how best to measure them. This is one new indicator that's come along to replace the many that have fallen by the wayside. So we're always looking, but it's kind of tough. Because so much arbitrage goes on in the market now, it's very difficult to find out where a short sale is just hedging something and where it's a reflection of somebody thinking that the market is about to crash.

DESMOND: Sure, we like to be aware of what other people are doing. Some of the best ideas you ever come up with come from just talking with other people in the field. Sometimes a little hint or a germ of an idea can bring out a whole new thought. For example, I'd been struggling with how to measure divergences, in which the price of a stock is rising, but the buying enthusiasm for that stock, the internal strength of that stock, is weakening. I was trying to figure out how to program that into a computer. I know how to see it on a chart. When I see it, I know what it is, but to be able to define that is tough. Then I saw something that gave me a germ of an idea, and I ended up figuring out how to program a divergence.

I don't think that there are that many new indicators. It really comes down to saying you can find ways of measuring changes in prices, changes in volume, or changes in momentum. But that becomes a pretty scarce territory after a while. There isn't much else to work with. A lot of indicators that have been developed really don't have much substance. People are often creating them for commercial value, rather than market analysis value.

DUDACK: I find that most of the new inventions in technical analysis have evolved from the futures markets, and they are very short-term oriented—things like the relative strength index and the true strength index. To some people, these might be ancient; to me, they're new. I look at them, but I don't put much emphasis on them. My clients invest a lot of money, and it takes a long time for them to move in and out of a position. They're not day traders. This is not to say that I don't talk to hedge funds. When they ask me day-trading type questions, I answer. But I'm not focused on day-trading, nor do I plan to be. I look for inventions in the strategic area.

Nevertheless, I look at everything. I have not seen anything terribly creative. I've seen variations of a theme, and I've tried them, but I always go back to basics. For example, I follow the RSI. These are nothing more than overbought/oversold oscillators based on price and volume and the combination thereof. I prefer to use my old overbought/oversold oscillators, the ones I inherited when I started doing Peter Ruggles's charts. These are 25-day nets. They talk to me. I see no reason to add the RSI indicators since they cut off the extreme readings at the top and the bottom of the oscillator. So I go back to my old basic oscillators because I love to find those extreme readings. I want to see how extreme it goes. I want to see if it's an all-time overbought reading or not.

When I look at something new, I find it's just a variation of something old, some old indicator tweaked in a different way. Most of the time, it doesn't add much. I would be interested in new tweakings to account for the way the New York Stock Exchange has changed, because the data from there (up/down volume, advance/declines, new highs/lows) have also changed. For example, many closed-end funds are fixed-income oriented and trade as stocks on the New York Stock Exchange. These are not "stocks," and yet they're advancing and declining; they're adding or subtracting to the volume. So if I were going to tweak some old indicator, it would be to make that old indicator better, more refined, and more suitable for the current environment.

MURPHY: One of the most fertile areas for technical work is the intermarket area. I am always very interested in the linkages. For example, emerging markets are very closely tied to commodity prices. That's the kind of thing that gets me excited. Or, when the Fed raises interest rates, I'm interested to see what effect that has on the dollar and on the gold market. I'm looking at the markets, at relationships, and I'm trying to understand why one group goes up. For example, when the Fed is about to start raising interest rates, I want to know which market sectors do better in a climate of rising rates. I can see that on my charts, but I like to know if there is an economic justification for it. There has to be an economic reason for something to happen. We're just doing short-cut fundamental and economic analysis, so I always want to understand whether whatever is happening makes sense from an economic standpoint. Relationships between sectors constitute a very fertile area for investigation. And, by the way, determining which sectors are in the lead tells us a lot about the economic cycle. For example, when energy stocks take over market leadership, that's an early sign that the economic cycle is coming to an end. When financial or transportation stocks take over leadership, that's usually a sign that an economic cycle is beginning. So, by studying sector rotations, we can also tell where we are in the business cycle. Those are the areas I find interesting. It's not so much technical indicators; it's more the understanding of economic relationships that concerns me.

There is only so much you can do with the numbers. Every now and then, I'll run across an interesting idea, but generally speaking, I don't see a lot of future in new technical indicators. It's all been done. All we have is price and volume data, and there is only so much you can do with that.

PRECHTER: Most of what I see in terms of innovation is the nth derivative of a momentum oscillator or the presumptive application of Fibonacci retracements—without a shred of evidence to indicate their value. I know of no new chart patterns since George Lindsay's "3 peaks and a domed house" from the '60s. Candlesticks are new to me but not to the field. I haven't learned them and probably won't, because you have to draw the line somewhere. Too many approaches will cause you to go into data overload and hurt your success rate.

◈ To what extent has the introduction of the variety of computer software aided the craft?

ACAMPORA: Computers have exponentially aided the craft. They've put technical analysis in front of everybody—traders and all kinds of nontechnicians alike. It's easier to do technical analysis with a computer. You pump in numbers, and it gives you back pictures (charts). It's almost as if the computer was made for us. That's the good news. The bad news is that computers make everything look so simple. People think they can read a chart, but they don't realize that it's not that easy. That's my biggest fear.

Computers have enabled people to do the back-testing, which is wonderful. More and more academics are starting to realize that there is value here. Technical analysis provides them with a completely new field to investigate. Fundamental analysis has been overrun; the academics have done so much with it. They've turned over that ground so many times, but they haven't done that with technical analysis yet. They will do that, and much will come out of it. First we have to get the establishment to accept us; then the academics will be coming on board more and more.

BIRINYI: Computers often become a substitute for experience. I am not anticomputers—in fact, my first job was as a programmer—but for individuals who have a portfolio of ten stocks, I recommend tracking the portfolio daily or weekly by hand. Write those numbers using a red pen and a blue pen. You get a sense of what's going on by actually doing it. We don't realize the potential weakness of data when we're getting it off of a machine. If you do it by hand, you start to get a much better understanding of the data.

There was a story in the *Wall Street Journal* on corporate buybacks. It argued that corporate buybacks were at something like $270 billion in 2004. The reporter got that number from Thomson Financial [now Thomson Reuters], which probably got it from a computer. I am sure the computer searched an index or a bibliography, looked up buybacks, and added them all up, and that came to $270 billion. We started in 1985 to keep track of buybacks, and we still do it today. And the way we do it is this: every day when I read the *Wall Street Journal*, I circle buybacks, and we look at a couple of other places as well. We do it by hand, daily, and we keep track of it. The number that the *Wall Street Journal* printed ($270 billion) was off by $80 billion. I can give you a list of corporate buybacks in 2004, which totals $350 billion. So you have to do it by hand, daily. You can't substitute computerized data for that.

DESMOND: Computers have been critical to everything we do. Most of the programs we use are homegrown. We don't use too many canned programs, other than word processing and things of that sort. All of the statistical programs we use we create ourselves. But with all the advantages come the disadvantages. One disadvantage for a lot of the novice investors is that the industry has created software that makes it so easy to generate numbers, graphs, or indicators. Most of the software packages today have literally hundreds of different indicators that you can program in an instant. So you find people using indicators without having any idea what these indicators are trying to measure and what their historical records are. People are risking their money with that. That's a shame.

People can invest their money today with less knowledge than ever before and feel more confident about what they are doing than they could have ever felt before. They're not stopping to learn. They think a software package gives them all they need, and they really don't understand basic principles involved in successful investing—about knowing yourself and your limitations, knowing when you're in over your head. That success lasts just long enough to set them up, before they get knocked down.

DUDACK: I used to keep my indicators by hand on spreadsheets. I did all the numbers, and I had all my hand-drawn charts up on the wall. It was time consuming. Now all my numbers and all my data are in Microsoft Excel spreadsheets, and I can link the files to each other and to data sources to quickly update everything. Charts come up in an instant. The ability to add or delete indicators and back-test them is wonderful. But having been part of the old generation, I can tell you that you lose touch by having everything computerized. When I was plugging the numbers into a spreadsheet myself every day, I would get a feel for the market that was much deeper. But I would not be able to do all my indicators if I did not have a computer. It's less personal, but it's faster.

The advantages outweigh the disadvantages, but one of the biggest disadvantages is that if you compare these computer charts to hand-drawn charts, the trendlines do not match. No printer in the world can be as precise as a piece of graph paper. You'd be off by half a point, three-quarters of a point, or a couple of points, but if you're using that dollar number as a trigger level for a reversal, it can matter. As a result, I give myself a little more leeway on my analysis of computer trendlines—a margin of error you could say— because I know they're not exact.

MURPHY: The computer has become very useful in allowing us to look at a lot of different things at the same time. Another great use of the computer is easy implementation of filtering devices. For example, you can program a computer to tell you which stocks are moving above their 50-day moving average. If you have five thousand stocks, you can't look at them all. You can program a computer to alert you, at the end of the day or during the day, if certain things are happening. A computer will rank which sectors are the strongest today. And then I'll take it a step further, and it will tell me which stocks are the strongest. I can look at two screens, and with two clicks the computer will show me a chart of the strongest sector of that day, as well as a chart of the strongest stock. Within twenty seconds, I can be looking at the five best-performing stocks in the best sector. The downside is that sometimes the computer gives you too much information, and you have to learn how to use it. Some software programs have eighty indicators in them. I don't know what someone can do with that much information.

PRECHTER: The best thing a computer does is save plotting time. I don't think much of the analytical software programs I've seen. The market is so complex to model that you can't use equations and statistics to do it. You can only model aspects of it. I think the future will be in getting computers to recognize patterns and forms despite quantitative variation. We're working on it, but it isn't easy.

RASCHKE: Computers have definitely speeded things up. Everybody is looking at the same levels, the same points. People are getting very good at technical analysis, and you've got very smart money out there. You've got the total automation of market-maker functions, with which you can work the spread between the bid and the ask a thousand times, all day long. Longer-term trend-following systems are automated. Information processing is done a lot more quickly, and often the window of opportunity is not as big as it used to be.

SHAW: Both professional and nonprofessional investors have at their disposal a variety of technical software, and with it they're now able to see more clearly what [technical analysts] do. You can subscribe to MetaStock and make your own charts, draw your own trendlines, put on your own moving averages, create your own relative strength numbers, do your own momentum calculations. You can use the same TC2000 software I use and subscribe to the same chart services. The problem is that some of this software lacks in certain respects. Sometimes I get into debates on the use of software in point and figure analysis. People today accept some of the more commercially available studies of Xs going up and Os going down, thinking that that's basic point and figure. It's not. It's a variation of basic point and figure. I try my best to educate people on this. The way the discipline got its name is that every time a stock goes up or down a point, you put in a figure. They don't call it "three box and figure"; they call it "point and figure." And you make three-box reversal charts after you've made your one-point reversal chart. No computer software out there does basic point and figure. It's latched onto what they think is the more consumer-friendly three-box reversal method.

❖ To what extent do you rely on computer-generated signals? And what are the advantages and disadvantages of doing so?

ACAMPORA: I don't use the computer to give me any signals. I have to see things evolve myself. The computer looks for things that I want to see, but I don't rely on computer-made decisions. People stop thinking for themselves when they think computers have all the answers.

BIRINYI: I look at signals, but what a lot of this work does is help me focus my attention. My overbought work tells me which stocks are overbought, but I don't buy them as a basket. I look for reasons for what's going on. For example, when Apple computer was grossly overbought one week, I asked myself, "Do I really want to sell Apple just because it's overbought? Maybe something good is going to come out. The company may have good earnings." So a lot of the indicators are useful to me in that they help me segregate my thinking. Computer-generated signals help you narrow down the pile: of all of the S&P 500 stocks, you can find twenty that you really ought to be paying attention to. The main disadvantage of computer-generated signals is that they are not adjusting for the dynamics of the market.

DEEMER: We don't rely on computer-generated signals; we just look at indicators. There is no magic to it. Computers just provide a much easier way to follow and test the data. We don't have a buy signal today and a sell signal tomorrow, or anything like that. It's all subjective analysis, rather than objective analysis. If I think that the Nasdaq is vulnerable to a decline, I don't have some red light that's going to go off at the precise moment when it starts declining.

DUDACK: I would never rely purely on one computer-generated formula. The market is a summation of all investors' thoughts on the market. Price and volume are very important, but I don't think we're able to quantify them to the extent that we can create a model that would work in all circumstances. I always put my overlay on it; I don't rely only on computer-generated signals.

The best example of a computer-generated model that went wrong is Long-Term Capital Management. Too often a model is based on regression to the mean. But the actual *mean* occurs perhaps once (for a nanosecond) every ten years. If you're relying on the mean to take place, you can be wrong for a long time. I would, however, rely on a model if it were a combination of what I think are the ten most important indicators at that time. If they all worked in the same way, it would be a good signal. That is, in fact, how I work, except I don't have a black box. It's all in my head. I look at what I think is most relevant at the time, put all those pieces together, and then come to a judgment. I always allow my judgment to override my indicators if I believe that's necessary.

Relying solely on computer-generated signals has created some problems. Ten or fifteen years ago there was at least one quantitative analyst in every single brokerage firm. There would be a strategist, a technician, a quant, and an economist. There are few if any quants left at most brokerage firms. Why? They created brilliant models that analyzed the past to predict the future. Now, to be honest, that is what all of us—technicians, fundamentalists, and economists—do; we analyze the past to predict the future. A quantitative model needs some kind of judgmental overlay to make it work. That overlay is a seasoned analyst. Quantitative models are fantastic *tools*, but they are tools that do not always have the answer. They can direct you toward the answer, as long as you understand the weaknesses of your model. You have to understand how today's data inputs differ from the data used in that model's creation twenty years ago. If you understand all this, then you can work that model very successfully. Otherwise you will end up hitting a wall, and the model will just blow up. Why do the models blow up? Because people who use them do not know what the models really are. They do not anticipate what might happen to change the model down the road.

McAVITY: In terms of signals, I don't let the computer tell me to do anything. I use the computer in pretty much the same way I use a typewriter or an adding machine. It generates data; I interpret.

MURPHY: A lot of our signals are computer generated. We use a trading model in our money-management work. The real value there is the discipline. You can't possibly see everything that's going on everywhere, but having a printout, at the end of the day or in the morning, which ranks various stock market sectors and shows you where strengths and weaknesses are, is useful. We set certain criteria that have to be met in order for us to buy something. I may not totally agree with the decision brought about by these criteria, and I may feel uncomfortable doing it. If we have a position in something that slips below a certain rank, the computer will tell us to sell some of it, and I may not always agree with that. And I am very often wrong, and the system is right.

I don't believe, however, in following a computer system slavishly. I am not a pure system trader, because there is always a little art involved. I never want to deviate too far from the discipline, but there are times when you can anticipate something. Most trading systems are trend-following systems, and they may not always work well. As an analyst, if you see that the market is in a trading range, that has to influence you. You can't just continue to buy and sell, buy and sell, and just lose money all the time. There is a certain element of judgment required. Even if you follow the signals, you may have to decide how much weight you want to put on them. You may put a little weight on some signals, more on others. You have to blend the two—computer-generated signals on the one hand and your judgment on the other.

PRECHTER: I don't use them at all. Black boxes don't interest me. They're usually programmed by people who use only a certain market history—usually the recent past—as data. If computers could get stressed, the future would do it!

RASCHKE: I do a lot of systems and a lot of modeling, and I use systems as an indicator. The key is to know when to turn them off. If I'm in a certain type of market environment, I'm not going to follow a certain system. The only systems that I would ever dream of doing on a 100 percent mechanical basis would be strictly range-based systems, volatility breakout type stuff, some filters—that's about it.

SHAW: We rely on computer-generated signals 40 to 60 percent of the time, because we've had the ability to back-test those signals at other points. Remember, those signals may be based on the same calculation, but the first one will come based on daily data, the second one on weekly data, and the third one on monthly data, allowing us to look at things from short-, intermediate-, and long-term perspectives. And some of these studies are incredible. Our indicators have been able to detect the bottoms and the tops almost at their peaks. That's a very effective discipline. We give a particular mechanical signal a 40 percent weight if other indicators are nonsupportive, and we give it 60 percent weight if our subjective work is supporting it. The advantage of computer-generated signals is the ability to do the back-testing, period. The fact that you can see that some of your gains are precisely at the points they should have been gives you more confidence in this signal going forward.

The advantages of technical computer software far outweigh the disadvantages. You have to be confident of what goes into the makeup of the signal and what the batting average of the signal has been when applied to past data. And as with anything else, you have to know what you're doing. If you want to ride a bicycle, you have to have some instruction. In a Barnes & Noble the other day, I saw a book called *Technical Analysis for Dummies*. And I bought it. It's actually a good book, and maybe some people who aren't dummies will buy it.

TABELL: It was not that long ago that computerized data became easily available. I relied on computer-generated signals to an increasing extent, as more computerized data became available, first on the general market and then, as time went on, on the individual stocks. With individual stocks, there is more complexity, because you are dealing with five thousand different names.

The advantage of computer-generated signals is that the computer is a trillion times faster than I am; the disadvantage is that it's not as smart. But it depends on what you're doing. Because I was dealing with longer-term-oriented money managers, I never paid a lot of attention to short-term trading. Computer-generated signals would be a necessity for short-term stuff. How else could you do it? If you're long-term oriented, some of that advantage disappears. You're taking computerized output and you're trying to intuitively reason from it. In short-term trading you have many decisions to make, so you've got to have some kind of computerized input.

WEINSTEIN: I don't use computer-generated signals at all. I'm old fashioned. My wife says I've only recently joined the nineteenth century. I switched over to computer-generated charts only about ten years ago. The staff in the office hated it, but we used to keep up two thousand charts a night by hand. I like the feel of looking at charts on paper. We are now past that, so now I look at the charts on the screen, and go over all the blues and greens and reds, but I don't use computer-generated signals at all. I don't care how you move down the field, whether you're running or passing, whatever works for you, as long as you get across the goal line. If investors can make a lot of money using computer-generated signals, God bless them. I don't go by any computer-generated stuff. I go strictly by my feel and by my signals.

❖ Would you recommend that people construct their own charts by hand? And should they do so throughout their careers?

ACAMPORA: For thirty-four years I've been teaching it the same way: "Do it yourself." You should start that way. Later you can expand to computers. I'll admit that maybe I'm stuck in my old ways, but there is a certain amount of it that you have to do yourself. I now keep very few charts by hand. Most of them are printed from the machine. But the machine doesn't just make the charts; it helps identify patterns, etc.

BIRINYI: I think it's a good idea. I don't do it, because I'm dealing with one hundred thousand pieces of information every day. But it helps you get a sense of the price and of what happened that day. When I started out, I kept blue books, and every day I would mark what the Dow did, where it closed, what the advance/decline line was, etc. The physical act of writing down something like "the market is down 20 but the advance/decline line is positive" makes you pay attention to that information. Today, I let the computer make the chart for me, but I don't think a chart is very useful, because it does not capture much of the intraday fluctuation. It is mostly useful for looking at things such as moving averages.

DEEMER: You get more information when you construct charts by hand because you're forced to look at it. The problem is that it takes so much time to follow. If you do a chart of each of the S&P 500 and each of the Nasdaq 100 stocks by hand, that's six hundred daily charts. If you can do one in every ten seconds, that's six a minute, so if you're lucky, it's going to take you a hundred minutes to do that. So you've taken almost two hours to do this, before you've even started doing any other work. When the computer draws the charts, you can review them much more quickly. You can also set up parameters for the things you're looking for and have the computer flag them.

DESMOND: You develop more of a feel for the charts when you're doing them by hand, though nobody has time to do it. The more you get acquainted with the chart, the better an understanding you have of what's on the chart. When you look at a chart that someone else has created, you tend to just glance at it; you don't get involved with all the little details.

DUDACK: If I could, I would do all the charts by hand for two reasons: First of all, you're living through the whole day as you plot a chart by hand. You evolve with the chart. You understand the trend better than anyone. Secondly, your chart is going to be more precise if it's done on graph paper. I don't have the time to keep my charts by hand; it's too big of a luxury. The gain for me is not large enough to offset the time involved.

I don't know whether my analysis would be any different if I were to do my charts by hand. I might be a better technician if I did that because I would be closer to everything. If we were honest about it, we'd probably say that we all loved the old days better. Some of the other people you're interviewing, who have been around for a long time and who now have their own businesses, have the luxury of doing handmade charts. Their time is more their own and they spend it where they see it best used. But when you're in a big organization where you have calls, meetings, trips, and media and management obligations, you need to find the most efficient way to get the most out of your indicators and still get everything done. For me, the computer is the most efficient way. I can work with that "handicap," because I understand it.

MURPHY: I don't keep charts by hand anymore, because I just look at too many different things, but I used to do it for many years. There is a certain discipline involved in sitting down at the end of the day and plotting the chart and looking at it, because while you're looking at it, you're analyzing it. When you're trading or doing technical analysis, you have to be disciplined. You have to be on top of everything. Very often, if you make a mistake, it's because you didn't see something or you just didn't pay attention to it. Charting is discipline; it forces you to look into things. But I don't know how you could do them by hand anymore. And, besides, the charts that I am looking at have three or four preselected indicators on them, and they're being updated all the time. If I were doing charts by hand, that couldn't happen.

PRECHTER: Having the computer do the plots saves so much time that you can do other useful things. I would never go back to hand plotting, but I would definitely recommend it for beginners. Doing indicators by hand forces you to think about them. It takes time to do, and your mind is occupied thinking about them, and your memories of previous plots are very valuable. You think, "Hey, when was the last time this 10-day oscillator jumped this much in three days?" Or, "What's my drop-off number for tomorrow?" When you see it only on the screen, you tend not to think about such things. But if you've plotted by hand before, you can translate what you learned to what's on the screen. For example, I don't need momentum oscillators anymore because I can tell if there is a divergence—and at what degree—just by looking at the slopes and extents of price.

RASCHKE: If you really want to get an understanding of the markets and of price behavior, there is no better way to do it than by doing stuff by hand. You will process information differently if you are writing stuff down rather than looking at the screen. And that's why at night I make it a point to write things down. On the computer I can pull a page, and the numbers are all right there. But if I write them down, it goes to a different part of my brain, and I do get a different feel.

SHAW: Yes, do some by hand if you can. It's like with anything else: the more you do it yourself, the more it will mean to you. If you're doing a chart by hand day after day after day, you're watching a trend unfold right in front of your eyes, instead of once a week opening up something and maybe finding a trend there.

TABELL: For a long time I agreed with charting by hand, but I became less convinced of it as time went on. For years, out of a series of over five thousand stocks, I kept a set of about five hundred stocks that I posted myself by hand. I was a senior guy with a big corner office, but I was sitting there and making marks on charts because I thought it was useful. I thought it brought you closer to the chart. Later on in my career I went more in the direction of programming the computer myself to create new indicators. That became my hands-on involvement, rather than posting the charts. If there were forty-eight hours in a day instead of twenty-four, I would still post five hundred charts by hand.

WEINSTEIN: I think it's nice to chart by hand. And I still get a little bit of a better feel, but I think it's a question of what you're used to. It's not realistic for most people, unless you're just keeping a handful of charts a night. I used to plot them, but in the real world most people are not going to find time for that. There is a tradeoff of time versus getting used to looking at the computer-generated chart. Even I, an old-fashioned kind of guy, use computer-generated charts today.

Doing the charts by hand makes you focus more because you have to physically plot the day's action. Hand charting probably just makes you more aware. I look at the computer screen, and it all looks a little bit like a blur. You see the big picture, but you don't feel today's action as clearly and as cleanly as you would had you charted it yourself. But what is the bang for a buck? It's a little marginal extra you get off of it, but I don't think you get that much of an extra that's worth all that time. We're advising clients, and we need to construct more than two thousand charts a night. There is no way on earth we're going to do it by hand anymore.

16

Luck, Astrology, and Other Unsanctioned Signs

You make your luck. There are certain factors that tend to encourage luck, and part of that is discipline, objectivity, sticking to the numbers, letting the market tell you the story.

—P. Desmond

◆ **What is the role of luck in technical analysis?**

ACAMPORA: One of the smartest men I've known in this business is Bill Maloney. He was a hard man, a tough guy. One day he asked me a question: "Would you rather be right or lucky?" Stupid kid that I was, I immediately answered, "I want to be right." As soon as the word got out of my mouth, I knew I was wrong. He said, "I'm not paying you to be right; I'm paying you to be lucky." I'll take luck any time. But you don't invest because you're lucky. You invest because you think you have knowledge and discipline. It has to start out that way. But when knowledge and discipline don't work, I like to have a little luck. But even when they don't work, I have to use them. I have to know enough to cut my losses short. That's what technical analysis really is: it's risk management. So managing risk is making sure that you don't take a big loss, but luck comes in when you catch one good stock and it doubles or triples on you.

BIRINYI: I would hope the role of luck is very small. I like to think that we certainly do not depend on luck. I don't ever count on it or hope for it. When you're running money, it's different from when you are giving advice.

DEEMER: It shouldn't be much of a role, should it? But it always seems to be, doesn't it? And maybe even your artificial intelligence model will have a little luck in it. In other words, sometimes the model may get the market right because of luck, rather than thanks to all the variables and weights you put in.

DESMOND: You make your luck. There are certain factors that tend to encourage luck, and part of that is discipline, objectivity, sticking to the numbers, and letting the market tell you the story. By the same token, ignoring those kinds of things will guarantee that you will be unlucky.

DUDACK: I think it does play a role. If all the indicators line up on one side of the road, it's fairly easy to decide whether the trend is bullish or bearish. Assume you're in a bear market. The market is down twenty percent; it has been down all year. With this as background you know that the odds are in favor of a bullish turn at some point. When many of your indicators move into line as well, you can make an intelligent and timely decision to be bullish based on experience and science. But when markets are more neutral or mixed and most indicators appear to be in the middle of the road, it's far more difficult to analyze and predict the market or stocks. However, you may see something subtle in your indicators or in stocks, which, in your opinion, might be the *beginning* of a trend. Suppose that because of these subtleties you make a call to buy a stock. It's possible for the market to turn around the next day and the stock to go up, because—as you correctly recognized—the environment is very mixed. But in this particular case, you might feel there was luck in your call because the path of the market was not clear. You could look at a chart and say, "What are the odds of this being the beginning of a new trend?" You know full well that the odds are only slightly in favor of a new trend beginning, but you must decide whether or not to make the call. If you're right, is it luck or science or judgment or creativity? Sometimes you just feel lucky. So I think there is some luck. But I would like to underscore that you create your luck in this career because you're making intelligent decisions. You make decisions to take risk knowing what your odds are.

FARRELL: Luck plays a part. You could buy a stock because you thought a lot of things fit together—for example, it's in the right group, it's a leadership stock, and it came out of an accumulation pattern—but then a merger could be announced causing the stock to go up, and you could suddenly be lucky to be the person who picked that stock. They say it's better to be lucky than to be good, but I'd rather have a basis for my conclusions. If luck comes in addition to that, fine.

McAVITY: I think luck is ever present, but it's certainly not dominant. I've often heard Mike Epstein say he would rather bet on a lucky guy in terms of short-term trading, and I think he is very right. All of the guys he is working with are going to be qualified to some degree, very good at what they do, but every once in a while, one is going to be a little better than the others. And it's not because suddenly he got up one morning smarter. It's because he got a little luckier.

You've mentioned how certain people go through periods of being tremendously precise [cf. Chapter 17]. How is that possible? Is that luck?

No, it's the adherence to a specific discipline, Elliott wave theory and Gann analysis being but two examples. According to the Elliott wave theory, there are stages of five waves, each of which is subdivided. At certain stages there may be more predictability than at other stages (in my opinion), depending on where in the trending process you are and on the nature of the trend at that point. In the 1970s, there were periods when the interest rates were in the late stages of the Elliott wave, probably leg four or leg five. There were periods when Prechter's market opinion would be "next Thursday, X will be the optimal number," and the market would do it. There may have been a slight element of self-fulfillment, because of traders watching it. There are a lot of ingredients that go into it, but I would never dismiss it as just luck.

So these techniques work very well over certain short periods of time. What exactly makes them fail other times?

Different trend conditions. Bottoms are made by urgent fear. Tops are made by greed, but greed lingers over longer periods of time. Think about it this way: you're likely to have higher velocity around the bottoms and lower velocity on the highs. So we're not only going from low price to high price, we're also going through velocity-changing characteristics. Elliott waves would be one way of trying to quantify those characteristics. I am a simple chartist; for me, a higher high continues the trend, a higher low says the trend is still intact, and I throw a moving average on it. Now, the trend is going to be changing its character all the way from the bottom to the top. What worked in the first leg may be quite different from what would be optimal in the last leg. If we have a trend that's three waves up and two waves down, the first wave and the fifth wave are likely to be very different. The trend is imprecise, may be choppy, and is varying as we go, so to try to specify precisely what is right or wrong will not always work. And this is the problem in the case of Elliott. I am not an Elliott person at all. I respect Prechter, and I am aware of a lot of the research that he has done. I think it's a marvelous attempt at trying to quantify the nature of trend, but since the trend is imprecise, the theory will not always be precise, in my opinion.

MURPHY: After years of working and competing with fundamental analysts, I can honestly say I think I've been right more often than I've been wrong, and they've been wrong more often than they've been right. But I'm often told, "You were lucky. If there hadn't been a war, this wouldn't have happened, or if there hadn't been a recession, this wouldn't have happened." Sometimes they'll say, "You were right, but for the wrong reason." I say to them, "But you were wrong for the right reason; I'd rather have it my way." Maybe some people are lucky; I don't know. But ultimately there is a big difference between gambling and investing. In gambling, you may win in the short term, but you'll always lose in the long term. In investing, you may lose in the short term, but if you follow the rules, you should win in the long term. That's the big difference. But I think you make your own luck. Certain people who are "lucky" work a little harder. They have a little more skill. And who are the ones calling them lucky? The guys who are making all the mistakes.

PRECHTER: The good kind or the bad kind? Comparatively speaking, luck plays less of a role in technical analysis than it does in fundamental analysis. Think of all the people in the latter half of the 1990s who said that stocks would go up as long as earnings per share increased each quarter. They utterly disregarded the relationships between the level of earnings and the stock price. It was stupidity at its worst. Yet they appeared correct *for years*. Of course, they never sold at the top because their logic was wrong, but they were lucky for a while. Then there was the "New Economy" crowd, which looked right for a few years even though their premise was false.

RASCHKE: Luck is the residue of effort. That's what luck is.

SHAW: How do you define luck? I've never been able to define it. I had a good day the other day, even though a black cat walked in front of me five times. Is that luck or is it randomness? Newmont Mining went from 20 to 40 or 50 that day, and we were long in the stock. Is that luck or is it talent? I don't know. I certainly would not think of luck as playing a role in my success, although it might have been partly that.

TABELL: Luck plays no more or less a role than it does in anything that involves uncertainty. What determines whether a baseball player makes a successful hit? What determines whether a soccer player scores a goal or not? To a great extent, it's that person's skill, but there is also something that goes beyond the skill. So there is luck in there, but it comes in the individual cases, and it cancels out over the long term.

WEINSTEIN: I kid around and say the harder I work, the luckier I get. True, on any one trade—when the stock breaks out and looks terrific—it may be likely to go up, but you wouldn't know in advance that it's going to be a really big winner (such as in a takeover situation). That has a little bit of luck involved in it. But over time, good luck and bad luck will even out. So luck to me plays no part in technical analysis. On any one trade there could be a little element of good luck or bad luck, but not over time, say, over a year, over five years. Football greats Joe Montana and Dan Marino may have been lucky on one play where the guy didn't intercept the ball, but that did not make their careers.

❖ Do you think that the inclusion of astrology in technical analysis undermines the credibility of the craft?

ACAMPORA: I have been frustrated throughout the thirty-eight years I've been involved with technical analysis, because people who were critical of it really didn't know what they were talking about. If I were to be critical of financial astrologers, I would be doing the same thing, because I don't really understand what they do. That doesn't mean I accept their conclusions. But the inclusion of astrology certainly doesn't help the technicians. You'll say, "Gee, these guys look at stars." It doesn't play well. This goes back to knowing your audience. You can't tell them, "I'm going to look at Jupiter and tell you when to buy."

Having said that, the gravitational pull of the Earth is a physical phenomenon that keeps the bodies in balance, and it does have a powerful effect on life on the planet. Some doctors tell me that when there is a full moon, women are more likely to give birth. Since technical analysis is basically studying the psychology of investors, do full moons have an effect on one's trading? I guess so. Could astrology in some offhand way be beneficial or instructive? I'm going to say yes. But in the long-term scheme of things, it has a negative impact on people's perception of technical analysis. We technicians have a tough enough time. I can't cloak my work in astrology. That would be the worst thing for our credibility.

BIRINYI: Yes, absolutely. Astrology undermines credibility, as do some of the other indicators, such as the hemline indicator. One summer, we sent an intern to the Fashion Institute of Technology to find out how hemlines change with time and if there was some kind of telling pattern. It didn't exist. The astrology is the same way. People have to remember that the stock market goes up or down, and just because two things happen at the same time doesn't mean they are causally related. If you were somehow able to get huge amounts of data, you would probably find some indicator that has 100 percent correlation with the market. It might be baby birth in Latvia or new red car sales in California. The correlation could be absolutely perfect, but it doesn't mean that the two things are linked.

DEEMER: Yes, it does hurt credibility, because technical analysis basically is looking at the market internals. As a technical analyst, I analyze the price of a stock. My fundamental colleagues analyze the value of a stock, which really depends on the value of a company. The problem is that, as an investor, you're not buying the company, you are buying a little piece of paper that represents part ownership of the company. The value of that little piece of paper goes up and down for all sorts of reasons, not all of which have to do with what the company is doing. Sometimes the value of the little piece of paper will go up and down because a fund manager has a hangover and decides to do some selling of a bunch of stocks and this is one of them, and that has nothing to do with the fundamentals. Technical analysts analyze the price of that little piece of paper, and, in aggregate, we're analyzing the stock market rather than the economy.

Many things play a role in that analysis: for example, money supply, because money makes the world go around and causes the stock prices to go up and down. Foreign policy also plays a role because it influences some people's buy and sell decisions. As a technical analyst, you're trying to measure the impact that the stimulus has on the market and quantify the unquantifiable. In a bear market, no amount of good news will make the market go up, and in a bull market, hardly any amount of bearish news will make the market go down. So if you have something bearish happen and the market ignores it, you know it's a bull market. Astrology tries to put a cause and effect on something that really cannot be understood in terms of cause and effect. Linking astrology to the stock market, saying that by observing something in the heavens you can automatically infer what is going on in the stock market, is a mistake.

DESMOND: Absolutely. It hurts credibility. We're learning more about life all the time. I think over time we'll find that electric impulses, gravitational forces, and all kinds of other things have an effect on our lives. We know that the moon has an effect on our lives. We can see it in the tides. If it can pull oceans up and down, it most certainly must have an effect on us. We're affected by day and night, by the seasons of the year, and by a lot of other cycles that exist in nature. So I am not saying that my mind is closed. I am simply saying that some aspects of astrology to me are purely fraudulent, and some aspects of it are beyond our current comprehension. Until they become a part of our comprehension, they have to be put aside. They have to be statistically proven before they can be used, and I have never seen valid statistical proof of them. I have had astrologers tell me that when Mars is in some aspect, it will affect war. When I asked them why is it that Mars should have more of an effect on war than Jupiter or some other planet, the answer that I got was because Mars is the god of war. That's fraudulent to me. So I don't mean that the Earth is flat and that it will always be flat, but I do think that it's important that anyone presenting information that they want you to use to manage your investment portfolio ought to be able to provide a statistical proof of its ability to produce good answers. I've never seen that come out of astrology.

DUDACK: I would be willing to look at anything if it made me money. But I have not been personally successful in using astrology to analyze the market. Once a year I enjoy receiving a report that uses the Chinese lunar calendar and Chinese astrology to predict the Hong Kong market. All these things are fascinating, but I know that, for more than half of the population, relating astrology to technical analysis is not seen as a positive. Many people relate astrology to the "Read your fortune for $5" sign that they see as they walk down 36th Street. The technicians who do use astrology look at the scientific aspects of astrology and include technical indicators to come to their decisions. I'm not going to put it down. The fact that I do not use it does not mean others cannot be successful using it. But astrology forecasters do not help our image.

FARRELL: I don't think inclusion of astrology does much for technical analysis. Astrology is like the black box. If you're right enough times, people will listen. It's very hard to keep their attention once you're wrong. Arch Crawford, who publicized astrology as his tool, has a pretty good record. However, I think he is a good technician, and he uses astrology as a marketing device, because everybody is interested in some kind of fortune-telling. I think he does well more because he is good technician than because he is a good astrologer.

McAVITY: Astrology is bad for technical analysis only in the eyes of closed minds. I actually published a paper in the early 1980s on the impact of the full moon on the stock market. When they first launched the listed option and futures trading, I thought it was marvelous. I could finally trade stocks on a 1 percent margin. In those days, there were 50 percent margins. On a 1 percent margin, if I can get a 3 percent move, I'm rich. So I asked a friend of mine to get me the dates of all the full moons and new moons. I took fifteen years of "this is the night of the full moon, this is the night of the new moon" data, and I approached it on the premise that if the full moon does one thing, the new moon should offset it, because we start another cycle. Then I measured the changes in the market; that is, I listed the daily change for each of the ten days before and after the full moon—I used the Dow. And I did exactly the same thing on either side of the new moon. I did this by hand. I found that I could take a position from the night before the full moon till the third day after the full moon—I could sell short, cover the third day after—and on that short sale win more points than I lost on that short sale. It worked a little over 50 percent of the time, but when it worked, it substantially exceeded the costs of when it didn't work. So a statistician would say it works only half the time. My reaction as a market person is this: when it works, it pays; when it doesn't work, it doesn't cost me much.

I used to do a lot of television commentary. I was always outspoken, and I never took myself or the business too seriously. There was a talk show in Canada called *The Shulman File*. Morty Shulman had an opinion of himself that was difficult to share. He was very arrogant. He loved attacking anybody who thought he knew what was going on. I was one of the few guests who would go back regularly, because I challenged him on the air. When I told him I had published this full moon paper, he thought I had gone right over the deep end. So I proposed a bet. I said, I'll bet you a thousand dollars that over six lunar cycles, it will work. I will short the market the night before and cover the third day after the full moon. And I'll go long five days before the new moon, sell five days after, and I'll give you a one-point transaction cost on each trade. And I won. He claimed I got lucky, because Mr. Volcker cut interest rates, and this happened or that happened, and sure enough, of the twelve trades, I probably made most of my money on three or four. But I didn't lose big. I did a second and third bet with him and won all three of them. To this day, when I'm active in the markets, I'm always looking at the count—full moon, new moon. I'm not sure that I would completely change a trade based on it, but it would be an influence. I stopped tracking it closely about a year after the S&P futures got going. In those early days, the premium levels over spot were highly variable, before that market became "smarter." I found that my model would work on the cash indexes but lose money in the futures because of premium to spot variability around the full moon!

MURPHY: It very definitely affects credibility. I don't know what to think about astrology. Maybe it works; I don't know. But technical analysis is the study of markets based on tangible evidence. A market is going up or it's going down. What the position of Mars and Venus has to do with the market, I don't understand. That's not technical analysis. You're looking at something outside the market, out in the universe. I don't see how that comes under the heading of technical analysis, because you're not studying the market; you're studying the stars. It really bothers me when some of these astrologists are identified as technical analysts, because the average person is going to laugh at that and say, "These technical analysts are all lunatics!" What we do is serious work; it's sound economic analysis. It has nothing to do with the stars. Now, some of these astrologists have pretty good track records, so I don't want to disparage astrology. I just don't think it should be called "technical analysis." Call it "astrology."

PRECHTER: It depends on the type of astrology you're talking about. To my mind, the traditional kind—reading charts based on a company's date of incorporation, for example—is bogus. On the other hand, there is some physical evidence that phases of the moon alter electrical potentials in plants, and from that possible explanation has developed an area called astro-economics, under which it is asserted that planetary alignments trigger changes in electrical and magnetic energy reaching the Earth and thereby changes in the mental states of populations. Because it addresses primarily the psychological state of the market irrespective of anything else, it's technical analysis. I don't know of any conclusive studies, but I would encourage testing any plausible idea that might advance our knowledge of market behavior. If the claims are true, then it would be an explanation for why technical analysis works. My own opinion is that mood states are endogenously, not exogenously, formed, but I would be remiss in failing to point out that some astro-economists have consistently excellent records at market forecasting. They're a hundred times better than economists are. As one of them likes to say, "Economics was invented to make astrologers look good."

RASCHKE: No, I don't think astrology affects the credibility of technical analysis, not at all. I don't consider astrology to be part of technical analysis. I guess you can measure things like an increase in the ion activity, see if there are solar flares, and maybe you'll have a corresponding increase in volatility, because people are all wild and edgy. I don't know; maybe there is some validity to that. I don't think people consider astrology as part of technical analysis; if anything, it's an amusement factor. If it makes you watch the market a little more closely around a certain window of time, what's the harm?

SHAW: The fact that astrology is akin to hocus-pocus in people's minds is probably something that does discredit the craft a bit. But, by the same token, I am not an astrologer. Maybe if I knew more about it, I'd think differently. I realize that the Gann analysis applies some concepts of astrology in its work. I've seen some copies of the Gann work, and I walked away completely astonished. I am a student of Nostradamus, and I know he relied on astrology a bit when he made his prophecies. But, of course, astrology is a discrediting factor just because in other people's minds it's akin to witchcraft and palm reading. But, again, if all of us who discredit it learned more about it, we would possibly see that there is a fit somewhere. Would I take it on as my main input? Probably not.

TABELL: Yes, it's a credibility problem, because astrology is a fraud. Nobody has been able to prove the validity of astrology, and to a degree it has even been proven to be a fraud. If you were to ask Eugene Fama, he would tell you that the idea that you can get any meaningful information whatsoever from stock prices is a fraud. So while I may think that Arch Crawford is a fraud, Eugene Fama may think that I am a fraud.

WEINSTEIN: On the one hand, from a public relations point of view, I think astrology does have a negative effect. On the other hand, I've seen some people make some very good calls using astrology. I am the ultimate pragmatist. When I used to do my *Professional Tape Reader*, in the back of each issue I would list fifty indicators, which comprised my weight of the evidence. I used to kid around and say that if I could drop a pin onto the *Wall Street Journal* and it gave me a good answer eight out of ten times, I would add it to my weight of the evidence. The same thing is true for astrology. If it gives enough good calls and it seems to work, then why not? But from a public relations point of view, even if it does pragmatically work, I think there is no doubt that it does undermine credibility.

◈ **Some prominent technicians believe that structures, such as the Elliott wave, Gann's natural order postulates, Fibonacci numbers, etc., are the laws that underlie market action. What is your opinion?**

ACAMPORA: I think there are kernels of truth in each of these theories, but to embrace them solely or to make any one of those philosophies a dogma is absolutely wrong. I tell my students, "You don't hang your hat on one hook." That caution applies especially to Elliott wave. I've seen too many good people lose credibility for staying too negative too long. I put more credence in Fibonacci because part of what I do follows the retracement philosophy, and I am very happy with it. I am not a Gann theorist; to me, Gann theory is like astrology. Is there some truth or some basis to them? Yes, there is. Is there some basis to the Elliott wave? There are plenty of useful parts in the Elliott wave. But to take it and become completely indoctrinated by it is a mistake. The only thing I'm going to be 100 percent tied to is price.

DEEMER: I don't use any of those approaches. I wish that my colleagues didn't use them a lot either. Call me an old fuddy-duddy, but I can't get them to work. I think Elliott wave is wonderful in hindsight, but I'm living today, not in hindsight. When you get a ten-page paper, the first five pages of which give you an Elliott wave count, and the last five pages of which give you an alternate wave count, that doesn't really help much.

Do you believe that these structures underlie the market action, that they are the governing principles?

The governing principles? I don't think so. I think there are long-term generational cycles—you go through a boom-bust cycle over a period of a generation. Then you have shorter-term cycles. For example, a presidential cycle is well documented as having an effect. I find it fascinating that there is a four-year cycle in Great Britain, which does not have presidential elections every four years, and that the cycle existed before the British and the U.S. economies were linked nearly as closely as they are today. So I think there are some long-term psychological cycles, but I am not sure that they are quantifiable enough to be useful except in a very broad sense. For example, according to the Kondratieff cycle, there is supposed to be a horrible decline every fifty or sixty years. Some people say that it is somewhere ahead of us. Some people say the Kondratieff cycle did indeed occur and that it was in Japan rather than the United States this time—that is, that the Japanese stock market and the economy went through a true Kondratieff bust cycle. So, there is some long-term evidence, but whether there's an underlying structure that explains everything in the market is another question. Nobody has proven it to my satisfaction yet. There is too much irrationality to make it that rational.

DESMOND: I think a lot of these theories are religions. People who advocate those approaches speak of them almost as a religion. They say the theory is right and the market is wrong. Any approach that takes a position like that is just fallacious. The market is always right. We're trying to take profits out of the market. To take a position saying the market is wrong and I am correct is just beyond understanding for me. If we were to say there are cycles and pressures that affect us, that may well be true. If we took the position that people are not in as positive a mood in the winter as they are in the summer, psychologists would say that that's recognizable and that it can almost be statistically proven. So the general idea of that is perfectly acceptable to me. But when you say it is winter, therefore it is cold, that's wrong. You could say it is winter, therefore it is more likely to be cold than warm. But to say that it is December, and, therefore, I am going to wear a parka no matter what, and I am not even going to bother to put my hand out of the window to see what it is like out there doesn't make any sense. Most of these "religions," as I've called them, break down because they are placed in front of the reality. The reality is what's going on: investors are buying, investors are selling, the market today is up strongly. To say no, it isn't up strongly because my cycle says it should have turned down a week ago is just flat out wrong. I consider those theories to be background indicators.

DUDACK: I am fascinated by fractals, Fibonacci numbers, and the fact that these numerical patterns and mathematical equations appear again and again throughout nature and life. I do believe that there is, in fact, something to it. My background is economics, not science or math. As a result, I'm more interested in measuring supply and demand than in measuring patterns in nature. But since we're all part of nature and since markets are governed by human psychology, I do believe that there is something there. How does this help you to decide whether energy stocks will outperform the S&P 500 Index? I don't see how fractals help you do that, although I may be wrong.

FARRELL: I think there are cycles and waves in stock market behavior. There is definite validity to some of these studies. The Elliott wave is based on the Fibonacci numbers. I have found that the Elliott wave always had an alternative outcome, so if it didn't work out as it should have, there was always an alternate count, always some way you could say, "Well, I read that wrong, and it's something else." But people have done very well using the Elliott wave. Bob Prechter has had a significant degree of success with it. Walter Murphy is also one of the best Elliott wave people. It's not something to use by itself, though; it's something to use as a guide, in my opinion.

McAVITY: It's not so much that these adherents have an enormous faith in these theories; I would say they are specialists, and they seem to be able to utilize them much better than other people can. Sadly, sometimes the best advertiser is not the best practitioner. That's the nature of the financial industry. Over thirty years I've seen more than my share of illegitimate practitioners come and go. To me, what Prechter does with the Elliott wave is highly legitimate. I disagree with him a lot, but I have a lot of respect for his discipline. And I'm amazed sometimes, when he is in phase. I think of it as being in gear or in tune with the market. I am not quite as impressed by Gann, but it seemed to work in shorter-term commodity trading over the years, particularly in the '80s, when we had sufficient volatility. A lot of this stuff will work better in a volatile market. As for Gann, I've seen periods in which some people would literally pick time and price levels, which would then materialize. I don't grasp it; I don't track it. I've done very little work with Gann. But from time to time, I meet "Gann people" in whom I get interested. I'm completely open. I don't want to be rigid. I do believe that there are some underlying cycles that are reflected in price and volume. And Gann, Elliott, astrology, those are all methods for trying to pinpoint price with time. But time within markets, to my mind, is an artistic judgment, not a mechanical judgment. These are people who use their own mechanics, sometimes with great success. I am very impressed with it. I don't use it nor rely on it. But I want to know what they're saying, in case I am at a point at which I can be persuaded one way or the other and I'm looking for one more piece of evidence.

MURPHY: I've studied the Elliott wave; the theory behind it is fascinating, and I am sure that there is some truth in it. Now the Fibonacci numbers are part of the Elliott wave, and I use that quite a bit in my work. I've seen it work many times. It's very commonly used in the markets. In fact, it's used by most traders. For example, if the market has been going up for a while, and it comes down, it tends to retrace about 38 percent or 62 percent. I don't know why those things work, but they do work, and we pay a lot of attention to them. Maybe it's a self-fulfilling prophecy. I do use the Elliott wave sometimes in my work, if I find it very clear. I just find that the margin of error is high. I've seen Elliott wave people get on the wrong side of the market and stay on the wrong side. My attitude is that it is not our job to predict or outsmart the market. Our job is to read the market's message and be in tune with the market. More and more I find that in my money-management work, all I want to know is whether or not the market is going up, because if it is, then we want to participate. We don't consider ourselves to be overly smart, but we track what the smart money is doing. By seeing which stocks or groups are going up and where the volume is going, you can tell where the money is going and what it's coming out of. We just want to follow it, be in the right place at the right time. I don't think this has to be that complicated. I'm a believer in simplicity. Using esoteric, complicated theories is unnecessary.

When Elliott wave or Gann theories confirm what my own interpretations tell me, that makes me even more confident. I do have an eye for the Elliott wave patterns, because I've been doing it for a long time. For example, I see the market going up in five waves. Normally, if the market is peaking and then goes down, it will go down only in five waves; then it will rally and go back down again. That suggests to me that this is corrective in nature. If I see five very clear up waves, I become very cautious. If the market shows me the pattern, then I pay attention to it, but if I don't see it, then I don't look for it. So I do use some of it in my work; I just try not to force it.

RASCHKE: I don't believe in any of these theories; I don't subscribe to any of them. They might be tools. For example, the Fibonacci numbers might be a tool in tape reading, which tells you to watch when the price action reaches a certain number relative to another number. Is there any statistical significance to it? Zero. In my opinion, there is zero statistical significance to that stuff.

SHAW: I respect Elliott wave and Gann analyses. Do I practice them wholly? Of course not. It's a thought process that might come into the final opinion. I knew Bob Prechter when he worked for Bob Farrell and started emphasizing the Elliott wave work in his writings at Merrill Lynch. He went out on his own and became a millionaire with the *Elliott Wave Theorist* newsletter. He was right for a good period with his calls. He was dead wrong with a few of them, too. I don't think he really admitted when he was wrong, which is bad. But I have indeed studied the spiral and I studied the angle of the pyramids, and I'm very much taken aback by the number 0.618. In technical analysis, based on some of the classic theories, we have one-third and two-thirds retracements that are acceptable for a major move. Now, those theories had been put in place long before the Elliott wave and Fibonacci sequences. But what is a two-thirds reversal? It's a 66 percent move. It's close enough to 0.618, isn't it? So as the Elliott wave method became more understandable to us, we found that we were already applying some of its principles with

Charles Dow's work, accepting a one-third to a two-thirds retracement or a 50 percent move as a normal retracement of a move. The Elliott wave theory does pivot off of the discovery, the belief, and the greed phases and then tries to subject them to subminuettes, minuettes, cycles, grand supercycles, etc. Having at least the knowledge of that is helpful. We created certain filter charts of the market, which allow us to look at the market on a longer-term basis. One is a filter chart of the Dow Jones Industrial Average, from its inception in 1885 right up to the present. Only moves that are 10 percent or more are represented on this graph. So, given that a secular bull market did begin in 1932, you can count the legs—1, 2, 3, 4, 5—they're so prominent. This is why Prechter is looking for a significant down still to come. Isn't it interesting how we can overlay the Elliott wave work onto that big picture, because we have this study at our disposal?

Are you convinced that these theories are the underlying laws of the market?

It's there. It's not a 100 percent governing principle, because I don't know what the governing principle is, except that there is greed and fear at each end of the equation and that it's human psychology that takes us there.

TABELL: I can prove that Gann angles are false. I have relatively little faith in the Elliott wave. But there are some very brilliant people who firmly believe in the Elliott wave and Fibonacci numbers, such as Bob Prechter, and A. Hamilton Bolton before him. But I personally haven't found them that useful. I've been led into more bad calls by the Elliott wave than I've been led into good ones. I still look at it out of pure interest, but I don't take it that seriously.

WEINSTEIN: I am not an expert on Gann, and I am certainly not an expert on the Elliott wave, even though I know the wave counts. I don't use these techniques, but I'm not going to put them down. I don't think their inclusion in technical analysis undermines anything. If something works for you, use it. I don't use it. I try to stick to what I know.

17

Creativity, Talent, and
the Art of the Craft

*Technical analysis attracts people with a certain mindset: someone
who is unconventional, willing to take chances, creative, a bit of
a maverick, a little crazy. It attracts a certain type of person, a
risk taker.*

—J. Murphy

⸺◦꘏◦⸺

◈ What role does creativity play in technical analysis? Can this creativity be learned?

ACAMPORA: Creativity plays a great role. But there is a difference between creating new tools and creating new ideas. I don't
need new tools to create new ideas. Whatever is happening during the day—it might be technology stocks going down or utilities going up—creates ideas and starts all sorts of bells ringing
for me. Maybe the tenor of the market has changed, and you need
to find out why. Maybe interest rates are going up. Do I need new
indicators to get these ideas? Absolutely not. You can't change
the basics of supply and demand; it is what it is. Up is good and
down is bad, and I don't care how you want to slice and dice it;
that doesn't change. It's the understanding of the subject that's
important.

BIRINYI: For most of the work being done in technical analysis,
creativity is a nonissue. There is a lot of marketing being done. The
newsletters today are very similar to the newsletters from twenty or
thirty years ago. They still talk about volume, breakouts, and chart

patterns. Practitioners today have no creativity. If you go to a major firm, they have these chart rooms with charts going back to 1940 or 1960. They don't want to throw them away, and they don't recognize that things have changed.

DEEMER: Creativity plays a great role, and I don't think it can really be learned. I don't think Rembrandt learned to be creative.

DESMOND: As a general rule, traders are much more interested in "doing" things, so they tend to rely on analysts to be the creative ones. The analysts are usually the ones who will spend hours and hours poring over piles of statistics, looking at charts, analyzing, and doing back-record studies. Most traders don't have a spirit for that kind of thing. They say, "Let's get down to it. Should I buy or should I sell?" My experience has been that most creativity comes from analysts, not from traders and not from portfolio managers.

DUDACK: The craft and the discipline of technical analysis clearly can be taught and learned, but the creative part is like the icing on a cake. What is creativity? You can't really describe it. It's like singing on key. Some people can do it; others can't. I don't know if creativity in technical analysis can be learned. I am primarily visual. That is how I analyze everything. Charts are the way I see things. Accounting, which I've taken, doesn't speak to me the way charts do, even though charts are nothing more than numbers in picture form. Charts are a wonderful shortcut for assimilating a whole lot of information very quickly. That's how I create new models, too.

FARRELL: Creativity is realizing interrelationships of markets and the relationships between the technicals and the fundamental, economic, political, and other backgrounds. But creativity is 5 percent inspiration and 95 percent perspiration, like anything else in life. Can creativity be learned? I don't think so. You either have a creative bent or you don't. More people are mechanics.

MURPHY: Technical analysis is a surprisingly broad field. There is a creative element to it. If you talk to three or four different technical analysts, each one will have a different way of doing it. We are always connecting dots, and I think there is a creative element in how you put everything together. You may have two things—one thing may be giving you a buy signal and the other a sell signal—and you have to decide how much weight to give to each one.

I don't think you can teach that creativity to somebody. When I used to teach classes, I would first teach students the rules, and then I would give them examples of trades. We usually looked at live markets. Every once in a while we would come across an example where everything looked good, and I would say, "Yes, but I sold it today." Students would ask me why, and I couldn't totally explain it. Something just didn't look right to me.

PRECHTER: Creativity is crucial. A noncreative person can learn to read in another language, but it takes a creative person to decipher a language he's never seen. The market's language is complex, and you have to be creative to discover its hidden regularities. I don't know if it can be learned—but I doubt it—although it can be encouraged.

RASCHKE: Everybody has a different way of processing data. Some people are very good at processing data just by looking at the numbers, quantifying things. Other people process data from the visuals, like bar charts. One fellow that worked for me loved reading the *Wall Street Journal* and all these news stories. Somehow that stuff messes me up, but that was his way of processing data. Ultimately, in the marketplace, you have to find something that's going to work for you. And that's where you have to be creative. It's a willingness to be independent, a willingness to do your own analysis and develop your own model. If you don't do that, it's not that you're not creative, it's just that you're lazy. I am sorry, but you just don't want to work. Everybody, even the most boring mathematician or engineer, can be creative in coming up with some model that works for him.

SHAW: On a scale of 1 to 10, creativity is a 10. You've got to be creative in many ways, and you've got to be accepting, have an open mind. You have to be able to discern that something could be changing. The attributes of a good technician are intelligence, open-mindedness, willingness to be a student of history, and of course willingness to accept change, because that's what it's all about. Ron Daino, a colleague of mine at Smith Barney, is a good technician because he's really an artist. He studied technical analysis while he was a creative art director for Avon Products. The fact that he has that artistic creativity makes him a much better technician.

TABELL: I don't think creativity can be learned. Good technicians are simply all creative. That is the definition of a good technician.

WEINSTEIN: Sometimes I'll get into a more creative state. Things will suddenly hit me, and I'll come up with a new indicator. I'll be thinking, "Let's try this; let's see how that works." That's okay when what I'm doing is theoretical. Obviously, I've developed a lot of new things in technical analysis. But when it comes to being a practitioner, creativity can actually be a hindrance. In executing, you want to be pragmatic and robotic, not creative. When I am trading, there is no creativity; it's all cut-and-dried. It's about following the game plan.

◈ Is there such a thing as a talent for technical analysis? And can you define it?

ACAMPORA: Yes, there is such a talent. First of all, there has to be the love for technical analysis. I tell my students, "You are going to love it or hate it." It's like a game of chess. You're making moves and analyzing things, and you can do that in a number of ways. As you get older, you develop a set of indicators that you feel very comfortable with. And you know that they don't all work 100 percent of the time, but you've worked with them enough to understand them and to know that they're reliable. After thirty-eight years in business, I've gotten to that point. The young people working around me have new things that they use and new ways of looking at things, and I say, "Fine, that's good." The talent is the skill of using and interpreting the technicals.

DEEMER: Some people have a knack for technical analysis. I think the psychological element also has something to do with it—the fact that you have to be unemotional, especially if you're a trader.

A technician is usually a contrarian, because the market usually goes against the crowd. You have to be bullish when people are bearish, and you have to be bearish when people are bullish. I am not just talking about the masses on the street; I'm talking about the money managers too. You have to be very strong-willed to stand up to these people and say, "Precisely because everybody in America says that things look bad, you should be buying stocks."

DUDACK: There is such a thing as a talent for technical analysis. When I came into the business, there were fascinating traders called "tape readers." In those days, there was a ticker tape machine in every office, which printed out the tape that you see now on the bottom of the screen on CNBC. In my office, there were many wonderful gentlemen who would come by to read that tape, watch the prices go by, and tell you all sorts of things about the market. They were very talented people who understood many things about the market and its environment. There are still some people who can look at computer printouts and do something similar—the "nouveau tape readers." Some are really talented; others can look at all the numbers, draw the lines, come to very good decisions, but they're not quite as good. How do you explain it? I don't know, but I see it.

McAVITY: I'm certainly not one of the most talented. I think of myself as a graphic, visual artist and a storyteller. I'm a storyteller of the markets. I've seen a number of technical people go through periods of being tremendously precise. Bob Prechter of the Elliott wave has had periods of several years with extraordinary calls, within one thirty-second (one tick) in the bond market. He would pick the day and the price, and Mr. Market would say, "Okay, Bob." And then, all of a sudden, it turned upside down. You can find yourself not being able to hit the broad side of a barn. But it's wonderful to watch a short-term forecaster when he's hot.

MURPHY: You can look at any field—whether it's fundamental analysis, economic analysis, or technical analysis—there are always going to be some people who are better than others, even though we're dealing with the same information. So, obviously, there is a talent there and creativity. I can't define that talent; some people apply the tools better. It may be due to a better understanding, better grasp, better intuition, or better temperament.

Do people drawn to technical analysis tend to have a more developed analytical side or a stronger creative side?

I've often thought that an economist is an example of someone who has no creativity whatsoever. We follow markets. I often get into debates with economists because I talk a lot about the economy. In June 2004, we entered a phase during which the Fed was about to start raising interest rates. For months, in the beginning of the year, the economists were saying that there was no sign of inflation anywhere, because all the old indicators they were using showed no inflation. But all the indicators that we looked at—like the fall in the dollar or the rise in commodity prices—suggested that inflation was becoming a problem. So we look into the future, we see things, we put our necks on the line, we predict. Economists, it seems to me, never predict. They're always looking at old numbers, such as the consumer price index or the producer price index. It's the nature of their craft; they're always stuck in a box, always looking backwards. They don't seem to be able to project anything into the future. Technical analysis—and only a small minority of people in our business are technical analysts who devote their life to it—attracts a certain mindset: someone who is unconventional, willing to take chances, a creative thinker, a bit of a maverick, out there in left field, a little crazy. Another trait is an affinity for numbers and charts. It attracts a certain type of person, a risk taker. On the other hand, a lot of security analysts or economists strike me as being non–risk takers. They always play it safe. They always have consensus views. Technical analysts are more willing to think outside the box.

PRECHTER: Sure there is. A good technical analyst has a talent for turning data into pictures, and pictures into conclusions.

RASCHKE: Absolutely, there is such a talent. One fellow who works for me has an amazing eye for the bar charts. He doesn't trade; he just does the technicals. He doesn't look at indicators, he doesn't do the research, he doesn't do anything except look at bar charts in several different time frames. And this guy is amazing. He never went to college. He had a construction company for a while in New York, made a million dollars by the time he was twenty-six, and lost a million getting overleveraged. So he is definitely an independent person. Call it intuition or whatever, but the bar chart will speak to him. When people talk about bar charts or the technicals "speaking" to them, they mean they have a feel for spotting a supply-and-demand imbalance in the chart, if there is momentum, etc.—all these things show up in the visuals. It's about being able to take the ego out of it and follow the market, rather than thinking you know better or that you can forecast something. It's the ability to follow what the market is telling you.

◈ What personality traits characterize a highly successful trader?

BIRINYI: You have to be disciplined and you have to have some breadth in your life. One of the great influences on my thinking over the years was a gentleman by the name of Marshall McLuhan. His point was that technology and structural changes have ripple effects, and you don't know where they end up. That has happened in the market. For example, who knows what the effect of exchange-traded funds is? I am terribly concerned about what's happening with ETFs and ECNs [electronic communications networks]. What happens if we have a billion-dollar fund that decides, "I don't want to own any drug stocks, but I'll buy a drug ETF"? You have a billion-dollar pool that owns no stocks but is 100 percent in the market. What does that do to everything?

RASCHKE: First of all, confidence. You have to be confident in your own analysis, you have to believe in your own work, you have to believe in the model that you're trading. And second, independent thinking. You have to do the research that supports the model you're using. You can't be listening to what the consensus is or what this person says or that person says, or allow doubts in. It also takes a lot of patience.

TABELL: There has to be a willingness to be guided by facts rather than by myth. As we've improved standard statistical testing, the ability to pay attention to the facts has improved.

WEINSTEIN: Having a facility with numbers certainly helps. It's also important to have a certain kind of personality. Somebody who is straight down the middle of the road is going to follow the tried-and-true conventional wisdom, rather than advocate technical analysis. They say, how could squiggles and wiggles on a chart be as good as getting an economics degree? I think it's a matter of a talent, but it's also a matter of a personality type. Those who have the talent, but have a different kind of a personality, will probably end up being bankers or fundamentalists.

◈ Can the absence of talent or favorable personality traits be compensated by hard work and dedication?

ACAMPORA: You can learn the rules. And you can develop the ability to recognize a trend and a good-looking chart. Will you like doing it? Not necessarily. I have two fellows who work for me. One comes in very early in the morning. I live twelve minutes from here, and he is here before I am, even though he lives in New Jersey. The other gentleman leaves later than I do, and he lives way out on Long Island. Are they talented? Yes. Do they know the rules? Yes. But what's important is that they love the work. They find it fun and challenging. Technicians are like that. I'm convinced sometimes that we would play for marbles instead of money. It's a passion. Everybody can read the same books and learn the same rules, but if you don't have that passion, it can be the most boring thing in the world.

BIRINYI: Yes, I think you can compensate. This is a very straightforward business. If you recommend stocks that go up, the world is very efficient in finding a way to your door. Most people really don't do the work. I heard someone three weeks ago refer to forecaster Edson Gould's "three steps and a stumble." If they had done the research, they would have found out that he himself said it didn't work.

DESMOND: If you don't have the basic traits, if you don't have the ability to control your emotions, you're doomed from day one. That's what destroys investors more than anything else. Typical investors tend to buy at the top and sell at the bottom, because that's what their emotions are telling them to do. It's easy to do it that way. You buy when everyone else is buying, because that makes it comfortable. Well, that's the way to lose. The trick is to have the discipline, the emotional control, and the objectivity to be able to buy when no one else wants to buy, and to be able to sell when nobody else wants to sell. That's the way to be successful; without that, nothing else matters.

DUDACK: I think you can compensate. Creative people find indicators where none existed before. But other people learn by rote, make mistakes, learn from them, look at millions of stocks, and do it over and over again until they get better. With a lot of hard work, you can become a good technician and develop this talent. Maybe a way of looking at this question is by thinking about how most traders on a large institutional trading desk end up being technicians—or amateur technicians. They live in a world of price and volume and look at charts of price and volume a lot. They live it and breathe it. Are the traders that do well and survive gifted? Are those who work on a desk but can't take it after a year or two and leave not gifted? By sitting at a desk and being exposed to tons of information and learning day after day, you *can* become quite good. There is a dividing line that separates those who do *not* get it and can't take the pressure of a trading desk from those who can take the pressure and do learn. These traders often become very talented and very successful. The same can be true of technical analysts. But some technicians should get honorable mention because they're truly special and creative. These are the pioneers who may not have sat in the middle of a trading desk or amid the chaos of the markets, but they developed new ideas. People like Edson Gould, for example, were creative and special.

MURPHY: Any field you go into, you have to have a feel or a flair for it. Everyone has a talent; everyone is a genius at something. Most of us who were drawn to technical analysis came into it by accident. None of us wrote in our college yearbook, "I want to be a technical analyst." I try to teach some people technical analysis, and they just don't get it. You know when you're drawn to something, because you enjoy it.

PRECHTER: You can overcome unfavorable traits to a degree and perhaps even succeed. But you can never be at the top of the profession if you have them. If you are skinny, you can't overcome it to be a lineman in football. If you're short, you can't overcome it to be Michael Jordan. You might play a mean game of football or basketball, but you won't be the best. If you're a plodding thinker, you might make a great accountant, but you'll never make a great technical analyst. So pick a profession that suits you.

RASCHKE: It's a matter of finding a style or methodology that's suitable for that person's temperament. For example, I could mentor somebody to learn to trade a basic trend-following system. I'd say, "These are the numbers; look for this pattern. When it takes a high, you're going to buy. This is how to manage the risk, etc." But ultimately, they would fail if they got bored or if they didn't believe in it. With some people there is no way; you could never teach them anything about the market in that respect.

◈ If technical analysis is partly art, then it's subject to many interpretations. Does that validate the idea that "technical analysis is what you want it to be"?

ACAMPORA: Science is a body of knowledge with its own language and its own axioms. Technical analysis has its own language and its own axioms. So it's a science. Is it an art? Absolutely. Think of an x-ray. Why is it that one radiologist sees something in it that's different from what another one sees, but they're both educated in the best schools? It's a science that really needs an interpretation, and that interpretation is artistic. The art involves intuition, experience, some innate knowledge.

BIRINYI: Applying technical analysis should have a very healthy dose of science, but it should have some art in it as well. Sometimes indicators have to be adjusted for circumstances. For example, stocks can show up in our work as very positive, but we may find that they are hugely overbought, so we have to make adjustments. Market analysis is fluid because the market is that way. The worst thing you could do to the market is to have three-decimal-point numbers, because the market will change and bite you. So the art comes into the picture as you adapt your strategies to the new environments.

The analysis is also an art in that it's subject to interpretation. Many times I've found technicians saying, "The market is going up, so let's be positive." Too often, a stock has good earnings and all of a sudden everybody is positive the day after. Most technicians are not leading, but lagging in their opinions. Very few technical indicators are leading indicators. If you look at the advance/decline line, every advance/decline line of the bear market has bottomed on the last day. So when the market turns up, people get bullish. The stock market itself is not a leading indicator of the economy. The stock market, the bond market, and the economy are in sync about 41 percent of the time. When these indicators are lagging, you make predictions about the future through money flows, sentiment, and some guessing.

What do you mean by guessing?

Just reading the paper and coming to a conclusion. When I read the papers in the fall of 1990 when everyone on Wall Street was bearish, or at the end of 2000 when everybody was bullish, or at the end of 1994 when everybody was bearish, that told me something. More important, when you interrogate the rationale, you find that behind the newspaper articles there are weak arguments. In 1995, one analyst came up with a very dramatic forecast that the market was going to appreciate significantly, and that analyst got a lot of publicity for it, but I thought the arguments were not very compelling. One was that the United States was a good and strong country and a leader in technology. That's not the kind of thing that I want to put money on. People publishing these reports use random pieces of information to prove their case.

DEEMER: Technical analysis is an art. The science is developing the argument; the art is deciding which argument to embrace, and that's the tough thing.

DESMOND: Technical analysis is a study of human psychology, as measured by the law of supply and demand. It's an art to the extent that psychology is an art. Of course, psychologists will say that their subject is a science. But there is an awful lot that you can't quantify statistically, so I personally think that psychology is largely art. Then there is a math side to technical analysis, which comes from the law of supply and demand, where you watch investors and measure what they do in statistical terms. Statistics is very much a science, but the human emotion that's involved, which is what we're ulti-mately getting to, is very much an art. So, technical analysis con-tains both the statistical side and the artistic side. But is it anything you want it to be? I don't think so. I think it's confined to measuring what human beings are doing with their money and measuring that in terms of the law of supply and demand.

DUDACK: Technical analysis is both an art and a science. It's a steady string of information that's interpreted in a certain way. There are rules that can be quantified; therefore, it's a science. In technical analysis, we're studying the psychology of investors when put into action, which creates supply and demand. What we're reading in the charts is supply and demand. But a part of it is art, and that part can't be quantified. Similarly, psychology—the analysis of "people"—is a science, but it's also an art. Let's say you're a psychologist and you have a model for certain types of personalities. Suppose a person comes to you for help. You can't just blindly apply the "model" of that personality type to help this person. Although he may have a clear personality type, he is also an individual. I would think you would customize your model to fit him if you are a good psychologist. In the same way, a good technician needs to customize the interpretation of the market to this *particular* market. First you should learn everything you can about this market, before you customize your analysis. This is where art begins. I think that someone who approaches technical analysis as pure science might not make as much money as some-one who combines science and art, especially in a market domi-nated by hedge funds going for short-term gains. The potential for false signals is greater. Without an understanding of the bigger picture, you would be prone to chasing signals that do not have any follow-thorough.

MURPHY: There is some art to technical analysis, although *skill* would be a better word. In the technical world, there are so many different things we're looking at, and things can be seen in differ-ent ways. If you turn on the TV on any given day, you may see two or three technical analysts whose views may differ on certain things. So there is a body of rules, otherwise we have nothing, but there is a lot of subjectivity involved in how you apply and interpret those rules. Again, some people are better than others. There is always room for disagreement, but that's true with anything.

PRECHTER: The truth is that *fundamental* analysis is what you want it to be. I sometimes demonstrate this by declaring, for example, that as interest rates rise, stocks go up, and people have no trouble explaining it: "Sure, as the economy heats up in a boom, lending goes up." Then I tell them I lied, that actually, as interest rates fall, stocks go up, and people say, "Sure, as interest payouts fall, stocks become more attractive to investors." You can "explain" either side of *every* fundamentalist argument. What do you think financial media commentators do all day long? They rationalize market behavior with this nonsense. Anyone who says that technical analysis is open to interpretation has to answer the question, *compared to what?* And they don't have an answer. The answer can't be "science," because until very recently, science has not addressed the task of financial market forecasting except to say it can't be done. Market analysis is in a prescientific era. That's not to say that brilliant work isn't being done; it is. But most people use it to make money, not to get tenure. Fundamental analysis is way worse off; it's in a mystical era. People believe it because they believe it.

The statement "technical analysis is what you want it to be" is improper because it seems to equate facts and performance, which are different. Technical analysis is properly a science of probabilities, and at best right now it's a young science. But whether a person can *predict* markets well is not only a matter of science. The study of facts and the talent to apply facts are different things. Physics is a science, but does that mean anyone can be a great theoretical physicist? No, it requires such sublime thought that it becomes an art. You could determine *scientifically* how to win at chess, but you can't make someone win. You have to be talented to win. Market analysis is likewise performed in an emotional setting, which complicates matters. I say that performing technical analysis is a *craft*, which requires both science and artistry.

RASCHKE: Nowadays technical analysis is probably half science and half art. The art is the subjective interpretation of the indicator. The science is that buy or sell signal based on the back-testing you've done. The art comes down to which relationships you choose to focus on. For example, if you're analyzing the stock market, the art is going to come from the experience in knowing that you need to look at the relationships between the small caps or different sectors, or perhaps look at the global markets, macro–money flows, seasonal tendencies, or different things along those lines. You can't put all these variables into a mechanical model; there are just so many different relationships that can affect the price.

SHAW: Technical analysis is subject to many interpretations. But so are fundamental analysis and economic analysis. If economic analysis is a science, how can there be five economists in a room with five different opinions? Give me a break. Let's make a common platform for all forms of analysis. It's all educated guesswork, and the degree of your success is based on the degree of your education. That's the bottom line. How can all these economic interpretations of gross domestic product, unemployment, or CPI be all over the place if economics is a science?

TABELL: The last market letter that I wrote prior to my retirement was on the difference between art and science. Science is the continual building of knowledge; you build on what has been done before. When you get into art, it's too easy to be a charlatan; it's too easy to say, "I am an artist and the rules don't apply." I think this is the case with a great deal of what is called "modern art" today, which in my view truly should not be considered art. If it can be duplicated by a five-year-old, it's not art. So on the one hand you have art, where there are no true answers and where there is room for all kinds of different opinions, and on the other hand you have science, which is continually developing and discovering truth. Technical analysis is a little bit of both. I would say it's fifty-fifty. To the extent that the technician intuits, there is an element of art to it. It's also a science; it's something provable. With the use of a computer, I can prove that certain principles work.

18

The Challenge of Emotions

No one assessing or trading markets is unemotional about it. This job is not like building cars. It's like trying to outwit a pack of murderous inmates in an insane asylum. You can't do it calmly because you don't know what they're capable of, and they don't have to use reason.

—R. Prechter

◈ **How did you feel when you first lost a lot of money? Did it become easier to lose as you became more experienced?**

ACAMPORA: Throughout my professional life on the Street, I haven't committed much personal money to my stock ideas. I knew that if I became too involved with my own money and my own ideas, I would lose objectivity. So I divorced myself from it. Instead, I would put my money in a fund, and I would adjust the fund periodically. I can't say I lost a lot of money. I didn't get out of everything in the crash of 2000, 2001, 2002. So I lost some money, but it wasn't heck of a lot.

I learned a lot from my market calls, because I feel just as concerned if I'm wrong and someone else's money is lost as I would if it were my own money. In fact, I feel worse. For example, the crash of 1987 was very hard for me. I saw something coming, but I did not foresee the magnitude of what happened. I took a lot of people down with me, and people were angry. In hindsight, everybody said, "Who could have expected it?" But there were some technicians who got out. I didn't do as thorough a job as I could have. That incident made me very conscious of major risk. I understood risk, but I did not understand it could be as bad as that. Since then, I run a little scared, which is good. I am always looking over my shoulder to find out where I could be wrong, where I could limit my losses and get quickly out of a situation. But it's never easy to lose money. I don't care who tells you that it is. It's easier for me to understand my mistakes because now I don't make big mistakes. I might not get in early enough, but I am not going to miss a major market move. I won't allow it, because I'll change. You have to change fast.

BIRINYI: I felt very disappointed when we lost a lot of money. I was disappointed that we lost sight of our discipline. I have learned how decimalization affects trading and how the whole marketplace has changed. Fast trading has brought havoc to old approaches. But it has not become easier to lose, and I still feel bad.

DEEMER: I'm not masochistic. I didn't feel good; I felt that the gods had failed me. And how do I feel when I still lose money? I still feel bad, especially as I get older, because I don't have as many chances to make it back. Sometimes I get a little more conservative.

DESMOND: Who is your enemy? Whom are you competing against? Who is trying to take your money away from you? Who is trying to ruin you? And the answer is *you* are. You are your own worst enemy. You are the one who gets emotional. You are the one who starts making decisions based upon what you think you'd like the answer to be, rather than on what the answer really is. You are the one who allows greed or fear to get into the picture. The first objective in being a good investor is to control those factors. If you don't, nothing else counts. And if you reach the point where you can say, "I don't need to look at my indicators anymore because I already know the answer," then you're reduced to the level of a novice. And novices lose money. So, part of being a professional is to never let down your guard, never give in to those emotions, never surrender that discipline. If you do that, you are finished. The famous analyst Joe Granville let down his guard and let his emotions and ego take over. He'd say, "I know more than the market does." And he caused thousands and thousands of people to lose enormous amounts of money, because he was not disciplined.

DUDACK: When I first lost money, it was painful. Luckily it was not a lot of money, but I felt so stupid. It was difficult to figure out why I was wrong. Of course, I was young and trying to figure out the "whole" market. I write a public market letter that's very visible. Some people can get my views by reading newspapers. Being wrong may not necessarily be financially destructive, but it's embarrassing. It always feels bad. As I've gained experience, my losses have been cut sooner, and financially I haven't suffered big losses. The embarrassment of being wrong is something I've learned to step up to, admit, analyze, explain, and move beyond. And as they say, the most successful people are the ones who make the most mistakes. The important thing is to learn with each mistake so that you don't make it again.

FARRELL: It's never easy to lose, but it depends on the bets you make. If you think something should be bought and you don't buy enough of it, George Soros would think you're wrong even if you're right. Yet if you're more conservative, you may not make that full bet. A very good test of your emotional stamina is how much you can stand to have the market go against you. I try not to let it go too far against me. One of the first stocks I ever bought was Raytheon. This was in 1958 or 1959. The chart was okay and then it broke down. I did not get out of it. I got killed. It taught me a lesson. And I couldn't afford to lose money at that point. That's the other issue: what can you afford to lose?

MURPHY: When I first lost a lot of money back in the '70s, I felt very stupid and very embarrassed, because I was working in a very public position at the time. In one of the first trades I made, I recommended a particular commodity, and it just fell out of bed for a full week. That could have ended my career, and it almost did. But I've learned that you're always going to be wrong on occasion. With that in mind, you're always testing the market. You think that a certain market is beginning to turn up, whether it's a stock, a sector, or a commodity, and you put a little bit of money into it. Then, if it starts to get better, you put a little more in. You do it gradually. But if things start to go wrong, you abort it; you get out very quickly. In the long run, everybody is going to make money when the market goes up. You have to try not to lose too much of it when you're wrong.

Losing is easier as you gain experience only in the sense that you accept it. You have to accept losing as part of trading. You can't be right all the time, but you have to be comfortable with yourself and able to say afterward, "Yes, I knew what I was doing, I had good reasons for doing this, and I would do it again, but it just didn't work this time."

PRECHTER: When I started investing, I made money for six years straight, the last four trading in options. Then in early October 1979 I took a weekend off and was talked into staying another day. I returned to find that the market was in a "massacre" that began on the Monday that I was visiting relatives instead of watching the market. I lost my whole account in two weeks. It was probably the most valuable experience of my life because I knew I had to decide right then whether I was going to be a full-time trader or a full-time analyst, and I chose the latter. Frankly, a trader's life mostly stinks. A trader friend of mine sums it up as "hours and hours of boredom punctuated by moments of sheer terror." That may not be scientifically precise, but people who think it's glamorous are wrong.

RASCHKE: My first loss was very depressing. I knew it was going to take a long time to make back the money. You really try not to think about it; you just take one day at a time. And the older you get, the more you know that you don't know anything. I go in under that assumption. When you have more experience, it's not hard losing at all. I don't care if I lose if I'm playing by the rules. I know that what I do has a good edge. It has worked for twenty years; it's not going to change. I can always make money with it. What's harder is, if I know I've made an error and I don't fix the error on a timely basis.

SHAW: No, it never gets easier to lose. Hopefully, as you become more experienced, you don't lose as often. Remember, it's that big loss that we want to avoid, so sometimes we may sell prematurely. The stock may go up a little bit more after we've sold it, and the client might get mad at us, but if it goes down big after that, we feel good.

◈ To what extent, if any, do your emotions interfere with your craft?

ACAMPORA: First of all, you have to identify the range of your emotions. Sometimes you think you're being emotional when you're really not. Because I'm not as short-term oriented as other people, my tendency to become extremely emotional is lessened. Part of the reason is that I don't trade. If I had to make four or five very short-term decisions every couple of hours, I would be a basket case. I can go home and think about something, plan my market letters, and plan my outlook for the year. And I do it with tools that help me look beyond the noise and take a longer-term view.

BIRINYI: Emotions do interfere because of the clients, but hopefully it's become less so over time. One of my best-performing accounts is one of my biggest, because we know that the gentleman has an awful lot of money and that if he loses a couple of million dollars, he is not even going to notice it. Then we have other clients whose individual retirement account represents 85 percent of their net wealth, so we are a little more cautious and hesitant with those people, but unfortunately that's sometimes detrimental. I may not buy a particular stock for some clients, because the multiple is too high and industry is not doing well, so it's a little bit out there on the risk curve. But for the rich gentleman, if we lose, it would not bother him too much. So to the extent that I feel responsibility to my clients, the emotions interfere with my practice.

DEEMER: Emotions always interfere. That's part of the problem. I don't trade because I get too emotional. If I start trading something like stock index futures, I end up looking at every trade on them. I get upset every tick that goes against me, and I get excited every tick that goes for me. Some people are just not emotionally suited to trading. That's why I've chosen to be a long-term market analyst.

DESMOND: I am no less human today than I was when I was twenty. But improving your discipline is a constant process. It's something that needs constant work. The more you work on it, the more trained you become, and the more you automatically react in a disciplined way, without having to think about it.

DUDACK: Our emotions are often our biggest handicap. That's why quantitative or technical analysis is a tremendous discipline. In both cases, numbers are pushing you in some direction. Technical analysis will tell you whether you're right or wrong fairly quickly. You cannot stay wrong forever. Technical analysis has a discipline to it.

I trained in a vacuum of opinions so I am very independent in my thought process. I can distinguish between what I want to happen and what is the likely event. When I want something to happen, I am aware of my bias and that's very important. I'm good at separating my emotions from the signals. We all have a lot invested in our market calls. When you write on the market, your reputation is on the line; you want your view to be accurate. But I'm able to control the emotional side of forecasting.

FARRELL: The emotions are significant in many ways. We don't like to admit a mistake, but being able to do that is very important, or you're going to compound that mistake. For example, analysts recommend a stock, the stock goes down, they recommend it again, and the stock goes down further. The analysts wind up digging a hole because emotionally they get caught up in not wanting to admit a mistake. It's important to analyze the analyst as well as the stock that he's talking about.

The most successful people are insecure. As soon as you think you have all the answers, that's when you get in the most trouble. So I was always reexamining my premises. But there were times I would have in my mind a pattern, such as a final washout or selling climax to a decline. Then instead of having a selling climax, the market turns around from a soft bottom. Can I admit, "Gee, that's a good turn, but it didn't fit with what I thought was going to happen"? I wasn't always able to admit that right away. You have to have discipline to admit that you were not right and adjust your thinking.

McAVITY: When I was young my emotions interfered with my craft about 95 percent of the time, because of the "I am right, the chart must be wrong" mentality. Thirty years later, it's the opposite. The older I got, the more cynical I got, although there is always a little bit of emotion. When I first started, I was trying to tell the market what to do. Once I formed a hypothesis, I thought that was what would happen. The first thing you learn in the business of publishing investment opinions is never to use the words *will, for sure,* and *never.* The minute somebody says something can't happen, the only absolute law of the markets, which was written by Edward Murphy, will manifest itself: if anything can go wrong, it will.

MURPHY: We all get emotional. I do, though I try not to. Sometimes you're watching CNBC or you're watching your computer screen, and something happens. There is a lot of noise, markets are jumping, and you start feeling like you don't own enough of it. Or if the market suddenly drops sharply, you start feeling like you own too much of it. Even when your system is telling you to not do anything, it's very tempting to sell some here or buy some there. I've learned that you're better off not making decisions during the trading day. That may sound crazy, but it's true. We determine beforehand, very often before the market opens, what we want to do that day. If we decide to take a certain position if something happens during the day, we may wait for that something to happen. We know exactly what we're looking for, so that if the market suddenly starts to do something unusual, we don't just jump around wondering what to do. We try to follow the rules very closely. Whenever I make decisions during the day based on sudden market moves, I am usually making mistakes. Sometimes it's better to just turn the machine off once your positions are put in.

In the old days, the markets I was trading—the commodity markets—were very volatile. Now the way we trade is much more disciplined. I'm also part of a team, so I don't have a total say in everything we do. We have parameters that tell us how much money we should have in the market at any given point. I have a little bit of leverage there. I may go a little bit above or a little below what the system tells us to do, but I don't deviate too far from it. The system keeps me honest, and it keeps me from getting too emotional. You're better off being disciplined, and once you decide what you want to do, it's better to give the instructions to somebody else, as opposed to executing them yourself. For example, if you decide in the morning that you are going to buy such and such a position if such and such happens, write down the instructions and let somebody else handle it, because when the time comes, you might change your mind. Let somebody else implement the strategies, so that you are removed from them. Then there is no need for you to watch the market.

PRECHTER: The market itself is naked emotion on the rampage. When your job is to assess degrees of insanity, how can you remain unemotional? This job is not like building cars. It's like trying to outwit a pack of murderous inmates in an insane asylum. You can't do it calmly because you don't know what they're capable of, and they don't have to use reason. A situation like that makes using your own reason a complex task, to say the least, and we are not built to handle some aspects of the markets. No one assessing or trading markets is unemotional about it.

RASCHKE: I am very good about controlling my emotions. I've got a really thick skin. That's because I had a really big loss when I first started trading, that very first year. And nothing can ever be as bad as that big first loss. The bigger problem for me is making sure that I am well rested. That's a far bigger problem than my emotions.

SHAW: Separating emotions from technical analysis is something I've learned. It comes with experience. Technical analysis takes the emotion out of the equation. Joe Granville once was giving a speech, and a lady got up in the back of the room and talked about how her husband, who had passed away, owned General Motors and how that was his favorite stock. The stock wasn't acting well, so she asked, "What would you do, Mr. Granville, with this investment?" He said, "Madam, I am very sorry to hear of your husband's passing, but I will tell you this: the stock couldn't care less that your husband is dead. If you don't like the way the stock is performing, don't hold onto it just because your husband liked it. Sell it. Don't let your emotions get in the way."

At Smith Barney, the difficult times have been when our views were negative, because no one likes to hear negative messages. We were simply trying to explain that the environment was in the process of changing. Unfortunately, some of our colleagues who lean more toward fundamentals or economics were not able to accept that, and our clients suffered because some of them stayed bullish while we were bearish. The firm permitted us to voice these two points of view, and it was up to the clients to select which one to go with. Of course, we were right and our nontechnical colleagues were wrong, so our discipline was very much in demand during the difficult periods.

TABELL: Emotions do interfere, and I don't think it's changed very much. We can never keep our emotions completely out of the picture. Most of the time I've been able to have the attitude, "Okay, this is what I do, I'm going to make decisions, I'm not going to be devastated by the bad call that I made the day before yesterday." I've had any number of emotional problems, but dealing with the stock market was never one of them.

WEINSTEIN: Some people say analysts learn to control emotions. As far as I'm concerned, we're human beings and we're always going to be emotional. This is the way my system evolved. I'm a very emotional person, and I used to call it a problem. Now I've learned that it's important to accept what we are, to accept our emotions. Each problem should be incorporated into the system and turned into a positive. That's how I developed my stop-loss system. When I'm getting into a stock, I decide where I'm going to take a loss and get out, and when I'm going to buy more. It's all diagrammed for me, so even though I can be as emotional as the next person, my system separates the emotions from my decision-making process. The decision-making is automatic.

◈ Is the ability to separate emotions from the work of technical analysis an inherent trait, or can it be learned?

ACAMPORA: People tell me that they learn to do that. There are certain breathing exercises that they do. I myself never went that route. In the late '70s, when I was getting whipsawed so much, I realized that the Street expects you to make mistakes. When I first came into the business, I thought that everything had to be correct. That's why I had so much difficulty during that time and thought that technical analysis was terrible and wrong. But the Street expects you to be wrong sometimes. What it wants, though, is honesty, and it doesn't want you to stay wrong. I learned to duck. If I'm buying, I know exactly the reasons why I'm buying, and I know exactly where I'm going to get out in case I'm wrong.

BIRINYI: I don't think separating emotions from the work can be learned, especially when you're running individual accounts as opposed to a fund. We know these clients, and we can't segregate that emotional factor. Other issues come into the picture as well. You do get depressed about the market.

DEEMER: I think it can be learned, but it's very difficult to do it. Mike Epstein has been able to do it over the years, and I admire him for it. I could not do what he does.

DESMOND: It can be learned. All discipline is eventually learned. We are really victims of our emotions to a very large extent. The whole field of behavioral finance is discovering this finally. Technical analysis has known for a hundred years that most people make their decisions heavily influenced by emotions, and not by logic. When it comes to making or losing money, it's much better to be highly disciplined and highly objective. That's something you have to commit yourself to, and practice and practice and practice.

DUDACK: I think it can be learned. It begins with a desire and the ability to know oneself. Second, you must define what it means to be wrong in a particular situation. Everybody can do this. If you're an average investor and you're considering buying a stock, you would be wise to think about what would define your position as "wrong." Decide this before you even buy a stock. Then if the scenario takes place, the emotional content is removed from the equation. You'll sell, and you won't lose as much money as you might otherwise. The same is true with professionals. If they set some parameters ahead of time, they won't be caught up in the emotions that might lead them to make excuses and mistakes. They won't be caught up in thinking, "The stock is down 10 percent, but it's even cheaper now," or "The volume is low so it doesn't matter."

Are there people who just cannot conquer their emotions and reverse their positions when the time comes, no matter how much advance planning they do?
Yes. Professionals who have been in the business for a long time are successful because they have dealt with their emotions fairly successfully. They're less likely to fall into traps; though every once in a while you will see professionals succumbing to their emotions. It happened to me early on. I bought Occidental Petroleum because of a technical pattern, made some money, and fell in love with this stock. I bought it right, held it, and I remember telling people, "I am never going to sell this stock." Sure enough, I kept my word and did *not* sell the stock until the price round-tripped up and back down. It was a very stupid thing to say and do, but I learned a lot.

MURPHY: I think it's learned. As you trade, as you mature, you see that the discipline is the right way to go. It's something that comes with experience. Maybe it comes with old age. Besides, not only are your trading results better if you're disciplined, it's also much less of a strain. If I'm following a system, I may be using judgment here or there, but I know there is a backbone, there is a system there. That takes a lot of the burden off of me, so I don't get a heart attack every time the market goes down. As you get older, you don't want to live and die by the stock market every day. In the beginning you're trying to learn your craft and trying to prove yourself, so sometimes you take chances. As you get older, it's not so much an ego thing; it's not a personal thing. You just go about your business and, hopefully, you beat the market.

PRECHTER: You can identify and deal with your emotions *only* if you've had experience. Book learning or paper trading alone won't cut it. But some minds are equipped better for this task than others. There are many hopeless cases. There are people who cannot help regarding news as the motivator of markets and people who cannot help getting bullish at tops and bearish at bottoms. I meet them all the time, and when I figure out that a person is hopeless, I change the subject.

19

The Path to Success

Sometimes too much formal education is a big hindrance, because education centers around models and the way things should work, but the markets aren't that way. The markets do things that the models don't predict.

— L. Raschke

◈ **What kind of formal education is the best preparation for the profession of technical analysis?**

ACAMPORA: You have to like the subject and the markets. You have to be analytical. You could be an English, history, or French major, and still be a great technical analyst. I don't think there is any one subject that has to be studied. To be an analyst, you have to be able to write. A trader doesn't need to write, so you're talking about two different animals. I don't think any particular formal background is necessary, but you have to take a technical analysis class like the one I teach. At the end of that class, you'll know whether you like the subject or not. And if you're already wound up, you'll study as hard as you can. But you have to be exposed to it first. A strong quantitative background is not necessary at all to be a good technician.

BIRINYI: Somebody said to me twenty to twenty-five years ago that 25 percent of money managers in the United States were art history majors. That's not the case anymore; they're all MBAs now. But I think you have to be well rounded. History is my background, and I found that a lot of our work encompasses history. Any discipline that is rigorous—mathematics, computer science, engineering—is more favorable than art. People who are successful have discipline. When the market is going up and people have buy ideas, it's very hard to stand up and say that according to your indicators the market is about to go down. The choice of major is not as crucial as the discipline and the well roundedness. Some people get too limited in their scope, and they take it personally when their charts don't work. I recognize that our analysis isn't going to work all the time. If you recognize that, you won't try to come up with three- or four-decimal-point accuracy.

I was fortunate to have been exposed to computers while in college. That helped me a great deal. In the early days of computing—and I'm talking about the 1970s and 1980s—all the computer people were geeks. There was this huge gulf between the computer department and all the other departments. One of the reasons Michael Bloomberg hired me at Salomon Brothers [for the trading desk] is that I could talk to the computer people. I could tell them what we needed to develop and, at least to some degree, how it could be done. They could not snow me with technical terms.

A background in computer science is not as important anymore, because everybody knows enough computer science today. Back in my day, computers were this huge black hole in which only MIT graduates and few others dared to venture. It's worth having some knowledge of economics and finance. Although I have an MBA, for all it's worth, I feel I've never used it. I don't think it helped me very much. *State of Fear* by Michael Crichton describes the scientific process, how we look at things, how we investigate and do research. I think those things are helpful. One of the great ingredients in my whole background is that I probably spent more time in my last two years of college playing poker than going to class.

What do you look for in people when hiring?
I look for someone who is hungry, ambitious, innovative, and who wants to be successful. I look more for character skills than for background skills. I've had a lot of success over the years at Salomon Brothers hiring English or history majors. Those were the people who couldn't get into business, so once they got into the business, they were really hungry. Having worked so hard to get their foot in the door, they appreciated it. They did not think it was

their right to have a job on Wall Street, as MBAs do. They worked harder; they were more productive and industrious.

Does being aggressive and pushy help in this business?

Being aggressive and pushy helps to a very, very limited extent. I like to think that I made very few enemies. People who succeed are people who are ambitious and intelligent about it. Very few people are successful in the business just by doing their job well; it's the people who go beyond their job and who want to grow who are successful. Michael Bloomberg was a good trader, but not great. What made him successful was realizing that the quote machine could also be a computer terminal that could put a database at people's fingertips. Michael Bloomberg has an engineering degree, so after trading all day long, he stayed at night to work with the computer department for four or five hours a night, four days a week, to create the database he envisioned, which later became the Bloomberg terminal. No one told Michael that that was part of his job.

DEEMER: Experience is the best teacher. Whatever experience you can get in academia, get it. I was very lucky at Penn State. We had in the early 1960s an IBM 70 or 74, one of the five biggest computers in the country. It was doing Department of Defense work. Because I was in the honors program, I was allowed to program that thing. At the same time, I was getting a bit into technical analysis.

Ultimately, experience is the only way you learn. Somebody can show you something, but you've got to find out for yourself that that's not going to work all the time. I've seen the wheel go around and into the mud and come back out again. You've got to live through it a couple of times to realize that things at the bottom really do look ugly. You can't get an idea out of a book of how ugly it can be. And you can't get out of a book how euphoric it can be at the top.

DESMOND: I think that a mathematical background would be a big help, but it doesn't necessarily have to be directly related. I find that a lot of engineers or mathematicians tend to be drawn to technical analysis, more because of the discipline of numbers than from anything else. Also, some accounting background or maybe some military background might be helpful for the discipline required.

DUDACK: I have seen many different people—some with music backgrounds—become very successful technicians. My background is in math and economics. I also had a course or two in psychology. I think that is a perfect combination. I do not think anyone in college plans a career in technical analysis. But I do think my academic background provided a very good foundation to become an analyst. It explains my approach in many ways, which is very supply-and-demand oriented, which comes from the economics background. Having a psychology input is great. Math is wonderful because technical analysis is all about number crunching and formulas. But I may have learned as much from my senior year black-and-white art class as I did from anything else. It was there that I started to look at forms and patterns, and that's what charts are about.

MURPHY: In the early days, we used to pride ourselves on not knowing anything about anything; all we did was read the charts. I actually have a bachelor's degree in economics, which, interestingly, I didn't use for a long time. It's only in the last five or ten years, when I've gotten into the intermarket work, that I've found myself going back and reading more about economic theory. I also have a master's degree in business administration, which I don't think ever had much of an impact on what I do. Quantitative skills are very important today. Some of the older guys are considered the experts only because we've been at it the longest, but most of us probably couldn't get a job today in this field because we don't have the quantitative skills. Some of these young people coming in—my son, who is studying computer engineering, is an example—can do amazing stuff with the computer.

Can formal education enhance the creativity required in the practice of technical analysis?

The creative part isn't something that's taught to you. It's something you pick up over time. There is an artistic element to technical analysis—colors, symmetry, etc. I was doing an interview for a magazine, and they asked me why I would be interested in painting, which I recently took up, and I said, "I've been drawing pictures all my life." Whenever we talk about something, we always show a picture. We're always working on color schemes, always trying to make the picture look attractive. It seems to me painting is a natural extension of that.

Are verbal skills and communication skills important to work on?

Very important. I was lucky, because when I retired from trading in my midthirties, I taught technical analysis for a few years, so I got very comfortable talking in front of audiences and explaining this stuff. Later on I worked on television for several years. That's even more challenging, because you have only a few minutes to make your point. You have to be very much to the point and very clear. You can't use technical jargon, and your pictures have to be crystal clear.

I would give two pieces of advice to technical analysis students. Number one, avoid using technical jargon. If you're talking to a technical audience, that's fine, but most people we talk to are nontechnical. For example, I have to think about why whatever I'm telling this audience makes sense from an economic standpoint, as opposed to telling them, "You have to buy this because we have a head-and-shoulders bottom." That just doesn't work. Number two, don't overwhelm people with information. When I worked on TV, technical people would send in charts with fifteen lines on them. Most of the time you can't use more than two lines on a chart. People see it for five seconds.

PRECHTER: The best preparation is psychology, sociology, and history, no question about it. You can combine all these with what I think is a new field: socionomics. Economics has to be unlearned, so avoid that.

RASCHKE: I don't think formal education matters. It certainly doesn't matter for a trader. If you want to do research and be a good practitioner of technical analysis, you should be able to do quantitative research, so having a good understanding of statistics is important. One fellow who works for me in New York has zero formal education, but if he said, "Buy this market now," I would do it without even looking at it. That's how much confidence I have in him. He doesn't have any background or education in statistics. He is just very, very experienced in doing charts. Temperament is more of a factor than education. You have to have a very open mind and be flexible. There is really no room for the ego in the markets. You have to be able to say that this is the approach now, I underestimated this; this variable is more important than I thought it was, etc. You can't get married to an opinion or a market. You have to learn to stretch and be open to all different kinds of opportunities. Sometimes I think that too much formal education is a big hindrance, because a lot of the education centers around models and the way things should work, but the markets aren't that way. The markets do a lot of things that the models don't predict. And models change. You have to be very open-minded and not get caught trying to fit the market into a little equation.

SHAW: I flunked out of college. I went to a school called Susquehanna University for one year, and I didn't do very well. So they told my parents they thought I'd be better off doing something else rather than wasting their money. I did that something else. I went to school at night, which was very difficult, and I almost got enough credits to get a degree. However, as a recognition of my accomplishments in life, Susquehanna University awarded me an honorary Doctor of Arts degree two years ago, which I am very proud of, as I am sure it took a lot of investigation on their part to see whether or not I was worthy of that honor. So you can correctly call me Dr. Shaw.

If you have a flair for figures, that's going to be important, and I do have that, even though I didn't prove it in my accounting class. You have to be mathematically inclined, and you have to be somewhat historically inclined, because knowledge of market history is so important. And, of course, you have to take classes in English, in writing, and maybe in speaking, but a lot of that just came naturally to me. I was always a ham. I've appeared in front of audiences of thousands of people. I used to love it.

In terms of formal education, what would be the best subject to major in?

Major in investments, if there is such a major. Certainly, accounting would be helpful. Getting an MBA or the equivalent is also important. Nowadays, that's mandatory to get any job in the brokerage business. My chapter in *The Financial Analyst's Handbook* discusses all the things that are involved.

TABELL: The way the industry is going, I think formal education for technical analysis has to include some in-depth statistical training—math through the calculus level and three or four levels of statistics. I did not have that; nor did most of the technicians my age, but if you're going to start out now, that is the direction you should be going.

WEINSTEIN: This may be why a lot of people look down their noses at technical analysis, but I don't think it takes a whole lot of formal education; it takes studying it and, more important, doing it. This is a silly analogy, but what kind of formal education does it take to become a good tennis player? It takes going out and practicing it. First you need a good teacher to teach you the basics, and then it's up to you. I could teach you all the different disciplines I know and get you to a certain point, but then it's up to you to develop your feel, like the "Aha, now I know what he's talking about!"

It doesn't take an economics degree to be successful in the marketplace. I can think of several very prominent, very famous economists, who have made disastrous market calls, because they're talking about the economy, which we know is supposed to be a discounting mechanism, as we all learn in Econ 101. So they'll be talking about the present state of the economy—how the unemployment rate is still high—and they won't realize that when the market turns up, it is looking ahead. It's a very interesting game, and that's why I love it. It's amazing; even people who should know better often don't know better.

You mentioned the importance of a good teacher when you're studying technical analysis. When you were studying, did you have a teacher or a mentor?

I had no mentor. I wish I had. It would have been easier; I could have gotten where I got faster. My dad loved the market, but he was a typical fundamentalist, and he got me interested in the market. I had to learn everything myself. I started out going down the traditional path. I remember looking at very famous fundamental services that are still around today, taking their recommendations, and I lost a lot of money. And that's where the negative turned into a positive for me. I went to a college library, got the Edwards and Magee book, and started reading it. Nobody mentored me. What I've learned, I've learned over many, many years, doing it for a long, long time, and the system has evolved. And I feel good that I have mentored so many people.

❖ Do you believe artificial intelligence will ever be sophisticated enough to replace a human technical analyst?

ACAMPORA: I hope not because then I would be out of a job. I am sure they have programs that can pick stocks, but I don't know how good they are. You can't put a human being into that little box. A human can sense a change. I have a home in Minnesota, and the roads are long and straight as an arrow. One day I put my car on cruise control at 75 mph. But suddenly there was a little curve in the road, and the car was still doing 75 mph. I hit the brakes. The car would have kept going at 75 mph, even though there was a turn too sharp for that speed. The same is true for computer boxes. You have to have a human sensing the road.

BIRINYI: I would hope not. I would hope that experience has some value. But I will admit that more and more firms are trading stocks using algorithms, which are apparently much more successful than the traders.

DEEMER: The stock market is the result of an infinite number of factors and variables, with an infinitely varying number of weightings on them. One day the market will be excited about something that's going on concerning Washington's foreign policy; another day it might not be interested at all. There are all sorts of variables, and the artificial intelligence model first has to be big enough to encompass every single variable including, say, astrology: if any single person ever buys or sells a single share of stock based on something astrological, then astrology is, by definition, a market factor. You have to put that in your artificial intelligence model. On some days astrology may have tremendous weight; other days fear may have tremendous weight. It's just an infinitely varying degree of weights. I think the human brain can probably cope with this a little better than artificial models.

DESMOND: You have to program the machine first, and the person who is programming the machine has to be a really good analyst. I don't think there is any way to teach one computer to program another computer. But can the programmer do a really effective job of programming a computer, and then have the computer carry out the thought process? Probably so. And the evidence of that is the amount of programmed trading that exists on the floor of the exchanges now. The majority of the volume on the exchanges is created by programmed traders, and they wouldn't be doing that if it wasn't successful. Can computers be programmed to produce a profitable trading program? Apparently so. Could a computer ever figure that out for itself? No.

DUDACK: You can put a vast amount of technical knowledge into a model. As technicians we're dealing with a steady stream of decisions that can be quantified numerically. But there is another part of the analysis in which you put the chart or indicator into a bigger context. The event you're watching may have a meaning today that's different from what it meant historically. The model is based on a historical perspective, not on today. Changes in the environment and how they affect technical interpretation are difficult things to model. To generate the numbers we study, it takes a lot of people deciding unilaterally and in unison to buy or to sell stocks. That in itself is information. We try to understand why the crowd made the decision it did and to factor that into our analysis. Computers can't answer why. They can tell you whether this pattern ever happened in the past and what usually followed when it did. But the past environment is different from today's. I don't think you can program a computer to adjust itself to an environment it has never seen and still produce accurate results. If we get that part, then we can all be robots.

McAVITY: Artificial intelligence essentially is doomed to not work, because a market is an ever self-correcting process. That approach will work for a while. I see a lot of chaos theory, people developing their fractals, which they get to fine-tune so that they might get five great calls in a row. But the market will change its behavior unpredictably. That's the fun of the market. If you can develop an artificial intelligence model that beats the market, be assured there is somebody right behind you who is going to do the same thing. That would take all the volatility out of the market, and trading would become as exciting as owning Treasury bills. If there is no volatility, what's the point? Artificial intelligence will never control the market. It will have an influence on the market, but no more than George Soros does for a while, when he is getting a lot of publicity, but only for a while. The machines can do a great deal more than any human can when it comes to searching for optimal moving-average combinations or screening for signals that have varying predictability. But I am not sure I would be comfortable with an

IBM computer that said, "go buy" or "go sell." Somebody will put some money on it, but it won't be me.

MURPHY: The creativity of a human being cannot be replaced by artificial intelligence. Take a chart pattern, for example. We developed a chart-pattern-recognition package, which recognizes double tops, triple tops, and that kind of stuff. When we sat down to teach the computer how to read chart patterns, I was astounded. Something that a human can see so easily can be so hard to program. There are things that the human eye can see that the computer can't see. Also, there's the ability to put pieces together and to weigh things; that cannot be replaced. A computer may be better than a bad analyst. Anything would be better than a bad analyst!

But I will say this about a computer: back in the days when I was trading futures markets more actively, I traded more intuitively, based more on my own style, but I worked with traders who just traded blindly off of a system. On any given day or any given week, I could beat them, but over the long run I think they would beat me for a simple reason: a computer doesn't get tired, it doesn't take a vacation, it doesn't get discouraged. If I make five losing trades in a row, the sixth time around I may get another buy signal, but I can't act because my confidence is shattered. I am afraid to act, so maybe I pass up a profitable trade. A computer could have eighteen losses in a row, and it wouldn't care. Come the nineteenth one, it's just as confident as it was before.

PRECHTER: Computers someday might be able to mimic a talented person. After all, computer programmers can be creative, too. Computers' one big advantage for market analysis is their utter lack of emotion, which gives them a huge edge. Their current—perhaps insurmountable—drawback is that they are not adaptive or creative.

RASCHKE: The '70s was a totally different type of economic environment than the '80s, when bonds and equities were highly correlated. Then in the '90s you got the deflationary fears, and the model flipped to the inverse. When the relationship is changing, I don't think artificial intelligence can recognize as quickly as a sophisticated analyst or a trader can. That's what makes a trader or an analyst exceptionally good: the ability to recognize when a relationship is changing faster than the models. Also hard to quantify is when a relationship starts trading beyond its historical norm. It could be implied volatility, it could be yield curve, it could be price-to-earnings ratios, it could be any type of relationship. When a relationship deviates from its norm, makes new highs or new lows, that's the market providing you a very powerful piece of information. And you can't train an artificial-intelligence-based model to recognize that, because it does not have any experience in dealing with it. You just don't have a large enough sample size of these occurrences to program anything well enough to give it a high enough confidence factor.

TABELL: Computers are tremendously faster than I am, but the problem is, they are not as smart. Read *The Emperor's New Mind* by Roger Penrose, which basically says that artificial intelligence is never going to exist. I am a very strong advocate of the use of the computer, but I don't think that artificial intelligence is going to replace people in any field.

WEINSTEIN: Until someone shows me that artificial intelligence can have a consistent batting average, I would be dubious. I know it can be helpful, but I would be doubtful, because there is a bit of a "feel" in the practice of technical analysis, and systems are so cut-and-dried. Given the intuitive side of technical analysis, I don't think artificial intelligence can ever replace a human analyst. I guess it can be a starting point, but I don't use it. That's not me.

◈ What advice would you give to students of technical analysis? What is the key to success?

ACAMPORA: Decide right up front whether you're an investor or a trader, and then apply technical principles to the timeline most appropriate for your style of investing. Take a class on the subject. Read as many books as you can, and join an organization that promotes the subject. By associating yourself with those who use technical analysis, it will be easier for you to learn from other people's experiences.

BIRINYI: First of all, learn the craft. Before you can do what I do, which is to criticize technical analysis and come up with new indicators, study the old indicators and understand why they don't work. It's not enough to say that the advance/decline line doesn't work; you have to find out the reasons. It's because it's an unweighted measure, and the S&P 500 is a weighted measure. You have to understand the language that technicians speak before you can deviate from it.

The second thing is, literally, work. Even when I was a vice president at Salomon Brothers, I was reading the newspaper every day and clipping out stories. It helped that I was somewhat cynical. The more I listened to what people were saying, the more I asked myself, "How does *he* know?" So I would ask them, and the response would be, "Everybody knows that." So I would research these things, and I would find out that no one really knew. For example, in the 1980s there were a lot of leveraged buyout funds. If you read the newspapers in 1983 or 1984, every story said that LBO funds had raised $25.2 billion for investments. Deals would come, new funds would be raised, and yet every story said $25 billion. I said, "Wait a minute, it can't still be $25 billion three years later!"

Because I questioned everything, we did huge studies on market cycles. Everybody is always talking about rotation, but how do you know that small stocks do well in the first part of the rally? "Everybody knows that," people on Wall Street will say. If you go back, you find that in half of the bull markets small stocks outperformed and in the other half they didn't. So we got all the data, analyzed it, and we now have the most complete study of group rotation and movements in the market, just because we asked questions.

DEEMER: The keys to success are experience, open-mindedness, realizing that the market is bigger than you are, realizing that no matter how smart you think you are, the market is going to make you look like an idiot every once in a while, and realizing that it's all a matter of probabilities. In baseball, if you've got four out of ten right, you could be a national champion, but in the stock market four out of ten right is not very good.

DESMOND: Knowing yourself is the real key to success. The indicators don't mean a thing. If you don't know who you are, if you don't know what your strengths are, and, most important of all, what your weaknesses are, you haven't got a chance. Any student of technical analysis—any student of much of anything, but particularly of the stock market, because there you can lose money so fast—has to understand that *he* is the enemy, and unless he learns how to control that enemy, it will conquer him.

DUDACK: The first key to success is to understand that your first few successes with technical analysis were luck and that you should keep working harder. Second, look at tons of individual stock charts, look at all the indicators you can, and try to back-test some of them to understand them better. Third, try many things. The biggest mistake many people make with technical analysis is that they learn a few theories, always use the same ones, and never go any further. It's important to look at everything when you're still learning. You never know when you might discover some tool that really clicks with you. Last, focus on what works for you and understand why it works. Understand the psychology behind a chart pattern or an indicator. Don't just memorize the rules. Memorizing the rules is like the tip of the iceberg; it's 10 percent of the answer. The other 90 percent is the understanding of the data and how that data can change over time. That understanding is what truly makes a good technical analyst.

FARRELL: Figure out what your strength is, whether you're right-brained or left-brained. Simple things work best. Look at technical analysis as a way to long-term investing rather than short-term investing. Look at it from a sector standpoint rather than trying to call the general market. Try to identify extremes in behavior so that you can be prepared for reversals. Have an exit strategy, and constantly review what the consensus is so that you have something against which to take a valid contrary view.

McAVITY: The key to success is to always have an open mind. Don't try to tell the market what to do. I don't care what statistical test you've made to prove that something does or doesn't work. At any point in time, there are all kinds of influences, and I would defy anybody who says that they know all of the possible influences that have an effect on price. The biggest hazard would be what I call the "arrogance of youth." If you're going to be sufficiently arrogant to say that you've quantified every variable, I'll bet against you. The market is a tableau that's in constant motion; appreciate it as such. Develop edges, techniques for identifying trends, characteristics of trend, relative volatility. Some people don't have a strong stomach. Well, don't play options on junior gold stocks if you don't. If you have a weak stomach, then buy Treasury bills.

Risk is tremendously varied; study it. And don't ever believe that somehow this time is different. It's always different, but it has a remarkable number of similarities to comparable conditions before. Fear and greed are very basic. Markets have changed because margin requirements are higher or lower, which may enable more or less volatility. Don't try to put a color on the market. It's a breathing beast. It's a good horse; ride it. Anyone who thinks that a horse going around the track three times is a mechanical measurement doesn't understand it. The horse's heart has a lot to do with it. And there is no way that you can plug a computer into that horse's heart to figure out why that horse was that little bit faster to win. Recognize that, accept it, respect it. Play to the best of your ability. Perfection will never be achieved.

MURPHY: First of all, you have to learn the field. There are courses taught at universities. Join the Market Technicians Association and attend meetings. There are chapters all over the country now. You should also take the three-year CMT program because it forces you to learn the subject. Before you can become creative, you have to know the rules, so you have to put a few years into learning them. Read the books. It's like anything else; you have to learn the basics. Also, you have to learn the quantitative skills. But don't get too caught up in the really complicated stuff. There is a tendency among younger people, especially with computers now, to come up with really fancy and complicated stuff. If there is a shortcut I could offer to them, it would be to appreciate the simplicity, but maybe that's a process you have to go through yourself. The older guys tend to eventually come back to the simplicity of it, but I am not sure that's a place you can get to without going through the complexity of it first.

PRECHTER: The key to success is to love what you do.

RASCHKE: The key to success is ultimately to do 100 percent of your own work and rely on yourself and not look at other people's work. Of course, learn from other people's ideas and their ways of looking at things, but a technician has to be self-reliant. You also don't want to overcomplicate it. If you learn a basic simple model and stick with that, over time you'll understand the little intricacies and nuances of it. But it's not going to work if you clutter up your model with too many variables and too many indicators, and if you don't allow enough room for the model to adapt to changing conditions.

SHAW: The ability to first recognize mistakes and then understand why the mistakes were made so that you don't make them again is important. Keeping an open mind has to do with this mistake recognition. Just because it's your research or your report doesn't mean that the market can't prove you wrong. We have a saying that the stock market is man's creation that humbles him the most. The market will always humble you, but try not to let it humiliate you. There is a difference.

TABELL: The key is to have a good time. Enjoy it. If you're a student of technical analysis, it almost goes without saying that this business turns you on somehow. You have to like what you're doing. I made a fair amount of money from technical analysis, but that was never the reason I did it.

WEINSTEIN: The key to success in technical analysis consists of two things: "can do" and "will do." That means first make sure you have an aptitude for it. If you have an aptitude for numbers and patterns, that's a start. That's the "can do." The "will do" is the passion. You have to have a bit of a passion for it. I'm sure someone for whom it's just a job can reach a certain level of success, but that's not going to be the same level as that of somebody who is a little "nutty," like me. You also need to learn the discipline. I used to keep a diary; that's how my system evolved. I used to write down the trades that didn't work and the ones that did work, and I started to see patterns form in the things I was doing right or doing wrong. You must say to yourself, "I'm going to use this game plan, and I'm going to spend some serious time on it." You're going against the best brains and the best computers on Wall Street. If you think, "I'm going to spend fifteen minutes on a weekend looking at a couple of charts," you're not going to be a serious player.

20

Favorite Patterns
and Indicators

*For the first thirty years of my career, one of the most accurate
market top indicators was the measurement of total volume and
upside volume. Invariably, all markets topped down in exactly
the same way—by volume declining, and that volume decline
would be totally caused by a decline in upside volume, and all
this took place with something like a six-month lead time. This
happened with every major top. Then it stopped. It didn't work
anymore. It doesn't work to this day. The markets now top on
increasing volume, not on decreasing volume.*

—A. Tabell

◈ **Which technical indicators do you consider to be the most
and the least reliable?**

ACAMPORA: You must start with market breadth (the direction of
the majority of stocks) because the Dow and the S&P 500 are flawed
averages; they're distorted by weighted components. To assess "the
market," I first find out what the stocks are doing. I look at different
kinds of breadth measurements. That's important. As for which
technical approaches I use least, I don't do Gann analysis because
the old-timers say that Gann is not the kind of analysis you should
base a lot of your conclusions on. I have questions regarding Elliott
wave, only because even the people who are supposed to be good
at it and who have quite a reputation have made huge mistakes.
There's something wrong there. What I think really works is trend

analysis. Keep it simple. Up is good, and down is bad. It really comes down to identifying trends.

BIRINYI: The advance/decline line is a hugely overdone technical indicator. If you plot the advance/decline line cumulatively, you'll see that it peaked in 1957 or so, long ago, and that peak was not surpassed until the last six months. So from 1957 to 2002, this indicator was still below its high-level mark, therefore suggesting that you should stay out of the market.

In 1999, one of the great issues was market breadth. Every technician, every quantitative analyst, and anyone with access to a computer calculated the seven stocks that were accounting for the majority of the game in Nasdaq, and the ten stocks accounting for 60 percent of the game in the S&P 500. I wrote a piece called "Market Breadth" back then in which I argued that it doesn't matter how many stocks are going up, it matters *which* stocks are going up, because the S&P is a weighted index. So you could have fifty stocks up and 450 down, and have a flat number. That showed me how little people really understand about how the market works. You have to realize that Wal-Mart is twice as big as all the other stores combined.

You have to distinguish between indicators that are descriptive and indicators that are indicative. The advance/decline line is descriptive. For example, in 2004 we had a strong advance/decline line, which basically said that you ought to buy a lot of stocks. It was not a good stock-picker's market. In fact, almost twenty-five years ago there was the fourth strongest S&P advance/decline line, but only the seventh strongest S&P gain. So the averages actually understated what happened in the marketplace. It basically says that it wasn't a stock-picker's market; it was an asset-allocation market. So the advance/decline line is a descriptive indicator versus an indicative indicator, which tells you that something is going to happen tomorrow.

The indicators that I consider most useful are probably the moving averages. We're doing some work now testing the golden cross and the iron cross ideas, and we're getting some respectable results. More and more, stocks with rising 200-day and rising 50-day moving averages are okay. I would not buy them on that basis; I would validate them on that basis.

Are the indicative indicators generally more useful than the descriptive ones? Is there a particular indicative indicator that you like to use?

Most of the indicators are descriptive; very few indicators are indicative. Even the golden cross rule has to trade through something that's happened. Very few things tell you something is going to happen. Even the moving averages don't tell you that something is going to happen, except perhaps that nothing bad is going to happen. If you have a stock with positive 50-day and 200-day moving averages, nothing bad is going to happen; the opportunity for surprise is limited. That's really about the only one that I give a lot of credence to, as far as traditional things go. But then you also have the things that we have done.

Money flows is the best indicative indicator that exists. Going back to my days with Salomon Brothers, because of our success with money flows—especially when they were not known and when they were limited to us because we were calculating them ourselves—we were able to make a lot of money because we were able to tell the trader, "You want to be short on this and long on that." We helped the trading desk to know where the action was. For example, our first version of what we call the "block monitor," which was the printout of the ticker tape every day, would point out that Gulf Oil usually trades three blocks a week and that last week it traded ten, where eight of those ten trades were upticks. So you could see that someone was buying the stock. If a lot of institutions came looking for an offering, you knew not to sell short close to the last sale. As a result, I was given a lot more leeway, a lot more flexibility, and a lot more money.

Are there indicators that are completely useless both from the descriptive and indicative standpoints?

I think volume is a hugely useless indicator. It's even useless as a confirming factor. In *Market Cycles II*, a thousand-page publication, we looked at a number of indicators. There are two theories about volume in bear markets. One is that heavy volume tells you that you're at the end of a bear market, because heavy volume means everybody is giving up, selling, and getting out of there. The other theory is that there is low volume at the end of the bear market because everybody is out; no one is there to sell anymore. It's only buyers. So we looked at it, and we found that sometimes bear markets end on heavy volume, and other times they end on very light volume. The only indicator we found that tells you the bear market is about to end (it doesn't give you the time and the day, it just tells you it's near) is when public shorting exceeds professional shorting.

DESMOND: Short-term traders would like to recognize the evidence of the approaching change in trend before that change actually takes place. I think that makes a very limited amount of sense, but that's what they want. So they use momentum indicators. They're saying that if they see a stock declining in price, they will watch very closely for that stock to lose momentum, to come to the point where it's not dropping as fast as it was before. And the trader assumes that a change in momentum will translate into a change of trend. Sometimes that's true, but an awful lot of times it isn't true. But for a short-term trader that's fine, because he thinks if he simply has a clue whether there might be a turn in the next day or so and acts before the turn comes, he's willing to accept all of the other times when it doesn't work out. When he thinks it's going to turn, he'll buy, but if it doesn't work, he'll quickly reverse himself and get out. But for a longer-term investor, that's a frustrating experience. There are indicators like stochastics that produce a huge, uncomfortable number of whipsaws, which cause you to buy or sell, and then you quickly have to turn around and reverse yourself again. Those are the most frustrating types of indicators. There are indicators based upon theories—for example, the Gann theory and the Elliott wave theory. What their proponents are saying is our theory is right, and the stock market, if it's not doing what our theory says it should be doing, is wrong. I just don't have any patience for that kind of thinking.

I firmly believe that the most useful indicators are supply and demand, or the money flow, which you analyze through price action and volume. Those are the real keys to the stock market. I don't know of anything that works better or that's more basic. The mistake investors tend to make is to try to simplify the process too much. A bunch of different things help to measure the health of the stock market. Volume, for example, is extremely important, because it's a direct indicator of investor confidence. If the volume is expanding on the upside, that means investors are confident enough about the future that they're willing to take more money out of their wallets and invest in the stock market. If you see volume contracting, that's a strong indication that they're not taking money out of their wallets. In fact, they're probably putting money back into their wallets.

Price action itself is, obviously, a huge part of the process, as is the market breadth, which measures how broad the buying enthusiasm is. Are investors buying a large number of stocks, or are they simply buying a narrow sector of stocks? We know clearly that in the last stages of an uptrend, buying enthusiasm generally narrows dramatically, which is what happened with the nifty fifty in 1972–1973, or the tech stocks and the dot-coms that we had at the top in 2000. That's very common, and you can trace it all the way back through history. So market breadth is an important part of the process. Momentum is a big part of it, too, which is also related to breadth. We look at the percentage of stocks that are above 10-day, 30-day, 10-week, and 30-week moving averages. That shows us, again, whether the buying enthusiasm is broadening or narrowing, whether stocks have failed to participate in an uptrend or are actually improving as they reach the bottom of the decline. So we're applying a series of tests to try to measure the health of the stock market. One indicator just doesn't do.

DUDACK: The most reliable indicator is the combination of price moves and volume. I go back to basics and to my background, which is economics and math. A chart is nothing more than a graphic description of supply and demand. Looking at price movement and adding volume (volume constitutes conviction in the price movement) is one of the best tools. In today's environment, the worst tools are the sentiment indicators. It's not that I don't believe in sentiment indicators, because I do. I just think that the world has changed in such a way that we don't have good sentiment indicators to look at. In the 1970s a great sentiment tool was the American Stock Exchange volume divided by the New York Stock Exchange volume. It was a proxy for activity in low-priced stocks versus high-priced stocks: speculative activity versus blue chip activity. Well, the American Stock Exchange has completely changed. It does not represent small-capitalization stocks or small-cap volume anymore. You can't use Nasdaq volume (although I tried), because the Nasdaq is not all small-cap volume. Given the trading taking place in puts, calls, and derivatives, there are many potential sources for sentiment indicators. But at the same time so much hedging is going on that it is not easy to measure real sentiment in these markets. There are surveys of sentiment, but if you study them, these surveys have huge flaws. Very often they're sampling different people every week. To me that's not a very good survey. So I don't believe there are good sentiment indicators today. This is a big hole in the technical arsenal. One sentiment indicator is the one created by Ed Hyman (an economist), which is a survey of hedge funds. Because I'm interested in hedge funds, I like having a measure of sentiment in this arena. This survey is one of the most interesting I've seen in a long time.

FARRELL: The most useful indicators to me are the sentiment indicators, with which I analyze where the consensus is and what the contrary might be. The least reliable are the short-term chart patterns. My belief on chart patterns is as simple as can be: umbrellas are bearish; saucers are bullish. It does not take a lot of intellectual skill to figure that out. If you look at a long-term chart and you see these big umbrellas forming, you'll know something is getting in trouble.

McAVITY: I wouldn't rely on anything that purports to pick time and price in a short time frame. If there is random behavior in the market, short-term price forecasting or precise price forecasting becomes meaningless. I'll talk about a range of 10 percent over a period of a few months being the probable direction. That's an easy target to hit. But to try to say that the S&P will hit 1,142 on August the third at four o'clock is unreliable. If somebody gets it right, he probably should have bought a lottery ticket that day.

MURPHY: It's hard to say what the least reliable indicators are because there are so many indicators out there. I've worked with many over the years. A lot of what I use is just simple charts. Because I look at so many different things—the stock market, all the sectors and industry groups—I don't have time to analyze each one minutely. I'm always looking for stocks and industry groups, and I have screening techniques to see what's outperforming and what's underperforming the market. I look at a lot of charts using trend-lines, moving averages, relative strength analysis, volume—very simple classical stuff. I just look for what's going up and avoid what's going down. Looking at too many indicators is a mistake that's often made, particularly among younger analysts I've worked with. I've given a lot of seminars, and I've taught a lot of classes; I still talk to some of the students, and they just look at too many indicators. They look at some very fancy, esoteric indicators, but I'm not sure they understand what they mean.

One of my favorite indicators is called MACD (moving average convergence divergence). I also use things like the relative strength index (RSI) and stochastics. There are maybe twenty different indicators that come under the category of oscillators, and they duplicate each other. I pretty much stick to RSI and stochastics. We have two classes of indicators: moving averages, which are good in a trending market, and oscillators, which are good in a sideways market. I like MACD, which was developed by Gerald Appel, because it combines both: It's a moving-average system, which gives us good signals, but it also tells us when the market has gone too far up or too far down. If I had to choose just one indicator, that would probably be the one.

PRECHTER: The least reliable indicators are oscillators, moving averages, deviation percentages, and other direct derivatives of price, which almost everyone uses. That is not to say they're not useful; they're just less useful. The most reliable indicators are the hardest to use, such as waves, patterns, cycles, sentiment indicators, and comprehensive momentum indicators. The latter include tick, Trader's Index (TRIN), and the A/D (advance/decline) line, for indicating divergence, although the latter two have been compromised in recent years. The change to decimal pricing has destroyed the value and history of the A/D line. The stock funds, bond funds, and preferreds listed on the NYSE have hurt that and TRIN, too. As for one quasi-technical indicator, Standard & Poor's changed its definition of earnings around 2001, so the P/E ratio no longer has a seventy-five-year history.

RASCHKE: The most useful indicators are the momentum functions, no doubt about that. I'm looking for something to tell me that there's a supply-and-demand imbalance, period. And I want to trade in that direction, because that's what created the edge. So I'm looking for anything that measures that there is an impulse, momentum, or range extension, and I try to put that in a structure that supports that framework.

What are the least useful indicators? I don't know. *Indicator* is a pretty broad, vague word. For me, an indicator is anything that I can quantify. I have to be able to run an indicator on multiple markets and multiple time frames and still see a similar profile in the results I get and in the tendencies I get. If you've been up for two days, what are the odds that the next day is going to be down, or if you have two days that trade from low to high, what are the odds that the next day is going to trade from low to high? I don't know if you would call these indicators, but those are the types of things I look at.

I like looking at an ADX (average directional index). That's an easy way for the eye to see that you've had a lot of price bar overlap—in other words, consolidation, accumulation, or distribution—and that the market has wound down to an equilibrium point. When the market winds down to an equilibrium point and then gets out of line again, you have a supply imbalance or demand imbalance, and the market moves to the new level. Then it has to do the testing back and forth, until it winds down to an equilibrium point again. At some point, the market comes back into equilibrium at a new level. At that point, you see the ranges contract, you see the volume and the volatility contract; everybody is happy. But when the market moves out of that level, you're either going to have the buyers on the wrong side, or the sellers on the wrong side. Then you hit these short-term positive feedback loops, where you have new buyers coming in and stops being triggered, etc., where new buying attracts even more buying. That's 100 percent of the model I use. It's pure price; there is no volume, no relative strength, no sentiment—nothing but price.

Do you also look at classic continuation and reversal chart patterns, such as, for example, the head-and-shoulders pattern?

I do, but I look at them in a different way. If you looked for a classic head-and-shoulders pattern, which is probably my least favorite out there, you could take a ruler and draw a sideways line, and you would see that it goes through numerous price bars. So really you have a long sideways line—they use that term in point and figure charts—where you have the price trading at the same level numerous times, back and forth around that level for a long period. That could show up as a head and shoulders, a rectangle, or a wedge. Eventually, that right shoulder will end up at an equilibrium level on my data. My indicators are going to show that contraction in volatility and that loss of momentum, at which point you'll eventually have a breakout from a chart formation. The main difference between the two types of patterns is that the reversal patterns tend to be much longer, and take longer to unfold than continuation patterns, which are short and quick. Probably, continuation patterns offer the best risk/reward ratio for a trader.

TABELL: As a means of looking at individual stocks, I would feel very uncomfortable without having point and figure charts. This was for fifty years my preferred way of looking at individual stocks. Reliability is hard to measure, because you cannot do standard statistical testing on a point and figure chart; you can only evaluate the reliability of the opinion that arises from looking at that chart. But this would be the most reliable method of looking at individual stocks, more reliable than bar charts or candlestick charts. Among the least reliable are the Gann angles. I have not been as infatuated with the Elliott wave principle as many people are, though I still look at it.

What do you think of the classic continuation and reversal patterns, such as, for example, the head-and-shoulders pattern?

All of the standard patterns apply to point and figure analysis. To put it in the simplest terms, if you're looking at the point and figure chart or any kind of a chart for that matter, there are three kinds of patterns: a base, which takes place prior to the time the stock goes up; a top, which takes place prior to the time the stock goes down; and the third would be "I don't have a slightest idea as to what the stock is going to do." Now we have a base, which is a precursor to the stock going up, and a subspecies of that base is a head-and-shoulders bottom. I've always been suspicious about trying to put too much nomenclature on it. This was something the early technicians did. They were probably trying for more precision than they had the equipment to achieve. If you want to simplify things and say that this is one of a number of patterns that tends to make the stock go up or down, you tend to stick a name to it. So, sometimes you have to turn things around. In the words of our friend Mike Epstein, "There is nothing more bullish than a failed head and shoulders."

WEINSTEIN: That's a very tough call. I wouldn't pick any one indicator. I break down my indicators on the market into three groupings. The momentum indicators, or, as I call them, the "here-and-now indicators," are the most reliable. Here we're talking about advance/declines, divergences, the A/D versus the Dow, about the things that are here and now, and the things that deal with trend. The second level belongs to the sentiment indicators, and they are a little less reliable. They're still helpful; believe me, I look at them. But I always take what I call my "weight of the evidence approach," which I developed years ago, and that is, I listen to the majority of indicators. For example, if you look at the VIX, which is the volatility indicator, that would say the market is dangerous. If you look at the percentage of bullish market advisers, that would say the market is too complacent. I respect those, but I will override them if the majority of my indicators, especially in the momentum area, stay bullish. Finally, the third grouping is the monetary indicators—things like the net free reserves. They're important too; I wouldn't use them if they didn't matter. I use all three of them, but I think the momentum indicators are the most important, the sentiment indicators a little less important, while the monetary ones have some relevance, but are not as important as the other two.

◈ How do you test patterns or indicators before you start using them with real money? Do you ask for other people's opinion when you're making such decisions?

ACAMPORA: I've never back-tested them, and I'm not saying that's good. I've used patterns for many years, and my experience has been very good as a result. The same is true for those who preceded me. They started using these techniques forty or fifty years ago. They worked then, and it's amazing how they still work today. The tenets of technical analysis are rooted in the laws of supply and demand. Going forward, quantitative documentation of pattern recognition will enhance the status of technical analysis.

BIRINYI: The difference between what we do and a lot of research that's done on Wall Street lies in the fact that Wall Street research begins with a conclusion. They want to prove that something works, so they find those data points that support their idea. We get all the data, work through it, and end up with a conclusion. We start from ground zero. But more and more, because the market has changed so much, because we have hedge funds, exchange-traded funds, electronic communication networks, we find that there is no precedent. In terms of electronic trading, one of the things we look at is what's happening in the foreign markets, because those markets were doing electronic trading before we were. It's disappointing to find out that the Securities and Exchange Commission has not done enough of that sort of research to find out what does happen with the electronic markets. For us it's almost like an academic exercise: we get all the information, see what has happened in the past, and move forward.

DESMOND: Yes, we do. And we found that there are some indicators that used to be very useful, but because of the evolution of the market, they're not useful any more. People used to look at odd-lot trading, which refers to purchases or sales of fewer than one hundred shares. That was considered to be an indication of what the small investor was doing. It was supposed to be a reverse indicator. In other words, when odd-lot buying became very active, it was an indicator that the market was probably ready to turn back down again. But the amount of odd-lot activity has dramatically diminished, and it was used heavily by traders who were trying to get around the rules of selling short. They would put an order for ninety or ninety-five shares, rather than one hundred shares, where they had to short on an uptick. That way they would get around the rules. The data became unimportant, and the indicator has just disappeared.

Practically all technical indicators are based on practical studies of historical data. If you were to run fundamental data in real time against the stock market, you'd find some dramatic weaknesses in the fundamental story. So, the fundamental data is, I think, much more irrational than technical analysis indicators are. If you look at earnings trends during 1929–1933, the stock market was down and the Dow was cut in half before earnings stopped going up. The same was true in 1973–1974. Corporate earnings improved almost all the way through 1973–74, while the market was dropping dramatically. And yet, fundamental analysis would typically tell you not to worry about what the stock market is doing—just buy based on fundamentals. That's just not always based on the factual evidence.

FARRELL: I don't go though rigorous mathematical testing, though we have done that on some things when we were using our internal data, like on margin account buying and selling or on internal short selling. We found that when you put parameters on indicators— saying this level is bullish or that level is bearish—the levels tend to change over time. I have always been an adviser, and I do not run money other than my own. Therefore, when I started using technical indicators with real money, it was my own money and I was pretty cautious. As you might guess, I'm a pretty cautious person. There are certain patterns that I pay attention to. In the early stages, a market goes up little steps at a time, but when the market is in the late stages, it often goes up in a straight line or in big, unsustainable increments. That's the blowoff stage, something you would describe as the final panicky buying stage. You can see that on a chart. Lots of times, that's the best time to own a stock; that is, you make the most money in the shortest time in late-stage blowoffs. For example, Internet stocks in the late 1990s were doubling and tripling in a matter of weeks, yet that was also the period when the greatest risks were developing. I know what patterns will influence me. One of the mistakes I made was being early in recognizing extremes in crowd psychology. In the technology boom, I thought in 1998 and 1999 that it was getting excessive, but it kept going up. So there is this fine line between being early and being wrong. It's one of the trickiest parts of the business, but you should be able to recognize when your risks are really rising even when you're making a lot of money.

MURPHY: I guess it's trial and error. I've never gone back and done a historical study. It's very hard to do quantitative analysis of chart patterns, because they're somewhat subjective. You can teach a computer to do all kinds of wonderful things. For example, if you're using a dual moving average system, a computer can tell you when one goes over the other—that's a buy signal. A computer is very good at that. But chart patterns are somewhat subjective. It's very hard to teach a computer to read a chart pattern. But having worked for more than thirty-five years now, I am comfortable with some patterns. I've thrown out most of them—things like diamonds, flags, pennants (which are very short-term patterns), rounding tops and bottoms. They're just not that common. There are only a few that I really pay attention to—things like head and shoulders, double tops and bottoms, triangles. Those are the things that I see quite often, and I have quite a lot of confidence in them. Rectangle tops and bottoms I would probably classify as good, reliable patterns. With the trading analysis software called MetaStock, we've developed a chart pattern recognition package, which has actually worked quite well, but we've limited ourselves just to head and shoulders, triple tops, double tops, and triangles (and their inverse or bottom counterparts). That's all we did. We decided that those were the only ones that were relevant.

How do you test some of the more readily quantifiable indicators?

Again, it's largely by trial and error. One of the reasons it's hard to test indicators is that the indicators are really very secondary. There are so many other factors to consider. If you're in a trending environment, for example, many of the indicators will work beautifully. Let's take an indicator such as stochastics. I've seen people writing articles, proving that stochastics doesn't work. The problem is these articles are often written by analysts who don't know how to use the indicators they're writing about. Stochastics is just an overbought/oversold oscillator: when the number goes above 80, you might want to sell; when it goes under 20, you might want to buy. But that's a very crude description. Nobody really uses it like that. If you're in an uptrend or a bull market, you wait until it goes under 20 and then you buy it. You're not really worried about the selling part, because you're in an uptrend. If you're in a downtrend, it's just the opposite. You're looking to sell the rallies, and you're looking to buy the dips. I've seen people look at a major downtrend and say that someone who bought it every time it went under 20 wouldn't have made money. Yes, but no one uses it that way. If they do, they're very bad analysts. That's the problem with testing indicators.

Another example is the moving average indicator. It works very well in a trending environment, but it does not work well in a trading-range environment, so you have to know which environment you're in. Now we have indicators that tell us whether we're in a trending or in a trading environment. Indicators often depend on other indicators, so you have to know which indicators depend on which. Furthermore, there are times to be aggressive, and there are times to be cautious. There are times to buy breakouts, and there are times not to buy breakouts. Everything fits together.

RASCHKE: The way I use indicators is very broad. For instance, I might use a pattern recognition algorithm off of a two-period rate of change, which is superior to a simple one-period rate of change (here we are back to the notion of the signal-to-noise ratio). I'll use that to give me my bias. For example, I know that today has an 80 percent chance of trading from low to high, and a certain percent chance that it's going to close up. So it will just give me a bias. In terms of framing the trade, I use basic price structure. I ask myself, am I going to try to buy a test of the support area? Am I going to put a buy stop if it takes out this certain level? How am I going to frame that bias in terms of risk and reward? How am I going to know where to put my risk point? In terms of framing the actual trade, it's always going to be off of price, off of the short-term support and resistance level, or off of some price function that's going to pull me into the trade if the price moves out of a certain level.

SHAW: It's very easy for me to validate the usefulness of pattern identification. For instance, consider a head-and-shoulders top or bottom. This is funny terminology, isn't it, because it makes people think of a shampoo. Now, a head-and-shoulders top simply captures the ending of an uptrend and the beginning of a downtrend. The forces of supply and demand are creating that pattern as it unfolds, shifting a pattern of demand into a pattern of supply. It's that simple. Let's take an ascending triangle. Why do we perceive that this pattern may resolve itself to the upside? First of all, we have to understand that price patterns have their place within a stock's progression. There are *reversal* patterns, and there are *continuation* patterns. Head and shoulders is usually a reversal pattern; that is, it indicates that the trend is reversing from up to down or from down to up. Ascending, descending, and symmetrical triangles are continuation patterns, and you'll find them more often *within* a trend. Now, an ascending triangle shows you a pattern of supply being essentially neutral, but underneath this neutral supply there is an aggressive demand, as manifested in the higher and higher lows. Because we see the aggressive demand and the neutral supply, we assume that this pattern will resolve to the upside. There is some simple logic behind the interpretations. Each of these patterns is a pattern of supply and demand. If you get into the concept of an ascending triangle and understand that in that case the demand is more aggressive than the supply, you'll immediately understand why it's reasonable to expect that pattern to resolve itself to the upside. And you can test patterns like that simply if you take the time to go back and find them in historical data.

◈ Have you encountered patterns or indicators that generally work well but become misleading under certain market conditions?

ACAMPORA: To understand a secular and a cyclical market and the ways in which they can coexist, you have to go back in time. This generation is going through a painful lesson of trying to adapt to a changing time. We're no longer in a secular bull market; we're in a secular bear market. I grew up in such an environment. I came into the business in mid-'60s, which was the time of a secular bear market. The first sixteen years of my career consisted of getting beaten up in the market, but it was probably the best thing that ever happened to me, because it was a difficult time and it was very instructive. People who did well in those days were those who were less market oriented and more sector, group, and stock specific. The long term for them was not a matter of decades, as some people say today. The long term for them was measured in months, maybe a year or two. In a cyclical bull market, like we're in now, you're apt to get a lot of false moves in technical analysis. I know that happened to me in the '70s. You get breakouts that don't work, patterns that don't fulfill themselves. You just have to be flexible. People are probably going to be upset with technical analysis in the next few years, because they're going to see a lot of false moves, but we're prepared for that. One must use and interpret indicators differently during different market periods. In a cyclical market, some of the trending tools, some of the moving averages, might not look as good.

You have to be a little careful with those, and, at times, when looking for climactic market lows, one might find that important bottoms develop less dramatically.

BIRINYI: The market changes constantly, and so does a great majority of indicators. Things like the NYSE specialist purchase/sales ratio or mutual fund cash no longer play the role they once did. In the past people believed that foreign buying was reflected in the first half hour [of trading], but that's not the case anymore, because so many stocks trade more often. There used to be a time when if you went to a Wall Street desk, no one could give you a clue as to where the Nikkei closed. The attitude was, "That's Japan. What does that have to do with our market?"

Many indicators are not keeping up with the market as the market changes. Things like options expiration can give you a distorted reading for a day. Excluding hugely exogenous events like 9/11, markets tend to be changing in a gradual way. The whole idea of hedge funds and day-trading has been an evolution. So certain indicators over time have become less useful.

What people don't want to recognize is that the '50s and '60s probably were good times for technicians, because a chart reflected what happened. In the '50s and '60s, if a stock opened up half a point, the chances were that by the end of the day it would be up a quarter or three quarters. Now a stock can open up 2, trade down 3, go up 4 in the afternoon, and close unchanged. On a chart, you'll see that there is no change; yet there was this tremendous amount of movement during the day, all this intraday activity, because you have so many more types of noise.

In 1974, we had three economic indicators that we looked at (including the consumer price index and the producer price index), whereas now we have every Fed report. It's very frustrating when at eight thirty something like consumer sentiment comes out and it's good, then at nine thirty something else comes out and it's bad, and at ten o'clock a third indicator comes out and it's bad. You have to decide which one is most important, which one is the market focusing on. You have indicators such as consumer confidence, which is a very iffy poll. I don't think it's a scientific sample at all, and yet people hang their hats on it because they have an incredibly short-term focus.

DESMOND: The market generally moves in one of two patterns, either in a trending mode or a trading mode. If you can't distinguish between the two, you have a problem, because many indicators that work well in a trending market don't work at all in a trading market. So a major consideration in using any indicator is what kind of market you're in. And many investors think that indicators ought to be good at both tops and bottoms. That's just not true. A set of indicators you use to see market tops and a set you use to see market bottoms are almost entirely opposite.

DUDACK: In the last five or so years there have been many patterns in the indexes, such as head and shoulders, tops or bottoms, or wedges, that haven't worked very well. Traditionally these are excellent patterns. There are two things to say here. First, patterns that get a lot of attention, like the ones I'm talking about, are patterns in indexes, or composites. People don't realize that a pattern is only effective if you can see the same pattern in the majority of the components within the index. If you see a head-and-shoulders top in the Dow, but not in the thirty components of the Dow, the odds of that pattern working out are slim to none. One should look at the components of the index; most people don't. That is the mistake. I think patterns tend to work pretty well with individual stocks, but less well with composite indexes. I've also studied patterns in the bond market, since the bond market is a psychological trigger for stocks. I'm frustrated with that right now, because I find that some patterns that work well with stocks do not work when applied elsewhere. For example, there is a four-year downtrend line that has been broken in the bond market. This is followed by a triangular pattern, but there is a whipsaw on the way down, and now it looks like there is a whipsaw on the way up. It appears to be a real pattern, but it's very frustrating to me as a technician because I'm convinced that if the same pattern had occurred in a stock, it would have resolved itself and done beautifully already. This mammoth global Treasury bond market is different because the pattern has not "worked." I would relate this to the fact that Treasury bonds are affected by a variety of political factors. It's not just pure supply and demand. It's supply and demand plus political ramifications, cross-border investment flows, the dollar, etc. In other words, you can analyze patterns, but sometimes something bigger is at work. Right now Iraq, global politics, and the presidential election are bigger than the markets. All of this creates tremendous uncertainty, leading to a lack of follow-through on many trends. Few investors—be they the public, the hedge funds, or mutual funds—are willing to take a defined stand for very long. The hedge funds will take a stand, but only for a day. That is what's different about this market. The public makes a decision and tends to stick with it for months or years. The hedge funds stick with it for an hour. It has been a frustrating year and that is part of the reason.

MURPHY: Yes. This is another thing about chart patterns that people often don't understand. For example, let's take a head-and-shoulders bottom or an inverse head and shoulders. You may look at the chart of a certain stock, and you may see a perfect inverse head-and-shoulders bottom. Everything may look absolutely perfect, but it doesn't work. People say to me, "It was perfect; why didn't it work?" and I ask them if they looked at the industry group it was in. For example, it has been estimated that as much as half of the stock's direction is determined by the industry. If you're looking at a retail stock, and it's forming a bottom, but the retail group is in a downtrend, then the odds are very much against you. What about the stock market? If the stock market is going up, and you find a good inverse head-and-shoulders pattern, it will probably work pretty well, especially if it's in a good sector. But if you see the same head-and-shoulders bottom when the market is in a bear market, it's just not going to work. People say, "We've got a breakout in a certain stock, so I bought the stock, but it went down. What happened?" And I'll point out that the market went down by 500 points that day. You have to consider the sector that something is in, and you have to consider whether the stock market is going up or down or not. Patterns will work in the right environment, and you just have to make sure that you're in the right environment. That's where skill and experience come in. The odds of a buy signal working are much better if you're in a bull market, as opposed to a bear market.

Could you give me an example of a pattern or an indicator that is particularly sensitive to such changes in the environment?

It's going to happen to any pattern. The pattern is only as good as the industry group that it's in and the stock market. This may be a little bit off the subject, but until 2000, we had a lot of people who were day-trading. They were making a fortune. I remember giving a lot of seminars to these people. Then we went into a big downtrend in stocks, and they all went broke. I remember a lot of them saying to me, "Mr. Murphy, these signals did not work anymore." Of course, they didn't work. All they were doing was buying. The short-term buy signals that you get are legitimate if the market is going up. If the market is going down, those little buy signals don't work. You have to look at the environment! So it's not so much the signal; it's the environment.

PRECHTER: Yes, but only if you expect all market environments to be the same. Some people construct "boundaries" that indicators supposedly respect, but they behave utterly differently in a range market versus a mania or crash. The real answer is no, as long as you have a basis upon which to judge the market environment and adjust your expectations for indicators accordingly. The wave principle provides a context in which this is possible. Accomplished cycle analysts can do it, too.

RASCHKE: Many people would select momentum indicators as their number one choice indicators: some type of oscillator, and it doesn't matter if it's a stochastic or a moving-average oscillator. But a directional indicator like that is going to work best in a normal trading market. It's not going to work in a very low-volatility environment, where there are no swings to measure. And it's not going to work in an extremely high-volatility environment, unless you still have a trend intact, in which case it will work very well, in terms of the momentum function preceding price. And when momentum precedes price, that's probably your strongest edge in the market. But after you've had a buy climax or a sell climax, if you're using the directional indicators, the first signal will be a false one. For example, you don't want to make the mistake of buying the pullback after a buy climax. Or in a sell climax, where you have a sharp spike down and a sharp reaction up, you get at least a spike reversal. It's the highest volatility that you've had in the market. Any directional oscillator is going to fail you at that point.

SHAW: It comes down to interpretation. For instance, I can show you a lot of periods when the market was overbought. You'll see, when you look at the price trend, that that was a bull market. So some people might look at that overbought condition and think of it as a bearish notation, whereas in our view, this was a condition of the bull market. This was proof that a bull market was in place. I can't really pinpoint or identify any indicator that has been misleading in terms of the market trend that was in place, because we always try to understand the overriding trend.

For example, the number of issues listed on the NYSE continues to increase. The impact of the Nasdaq has grown in recent years because of the way technology has evolved. We take that into account as we look at the different indicators. We might be supporting our Nasdaq call with the work that we do on technology groups and stocks. Or we might support our Dow Jones call with the work we do on basic material stocks. Our work is really dictated by outsiders. For instance, when there is a substitution in the makeup of the Dow Jones average, our interpretation of that average and the indicators we use with it have to change. If a higher-priced stock or a lower-priced stock is added to the average, that immediately has an impact on our analysis, because we know it's a price-weighted average. In the 1940s, they took IBM out of the average and replaced it with AT&T. The Dow Jones would have gone through 1,000 many years earlier if they hadn't taken that stock out. Similarly, the changes in the makeup of the groups may lead us to change the way we analyze the groups.

TABELL: Yes, all my life. That's part of the challenge of technical analysis. Markets remain the same and they change. For the first twenty or thirty years of my career, one of the most accurate examples of a market top indicator that I know of was the measurement of total volume and upside volume. Invariably, starting in the 1930s and through, I think, the 1970s, all markets topped down in exactly the same way—by volume declining, and that volume decline would be totally caused by a decline in upside volume, and all this took place with something like a six-month lead time. This happened with every major top my father and I could recall throughout the early stages of our careers. Then it stopped. It didn't work anymore. It doesn't work to this day. The markets now top on increasing volume, not on decreasing volume. This is where you get into all that art and science fun.

❖ Is the number of indicators you follow greater when the amount of money involved is larger?

ACAMPORA: No. It's always pretty much the same. What I've been using for the last twenty years is basically what I'm using now. From time to time, I'll bring in a couple of new indicators, or I'll create something new if need be.

MURPHY: Because I do a lot of sector work, my job is more and more trying to determine if a given sector is moving up or down, and if it's outperforming the market. To do that, I use a lot of relative-strength analysis, I look at the volume, etc. It's not so much looking at a lot of different indicators; it's just having a handful of indicators that make sense. For example, we use moving averages, and we won't buy anything that's under its 200-day moving average, because that means we are in a bear market. That's just a very simple rule. If we're trading a certain sector, the 50-day moving average is very important for short and intermediate term. We generally don't like to buy anything if it's below its 50-day moving average. The moving average rules act like filtering devices. If we're looking for buying opportunities and we want to put money into the market, for example, we follow a simple rule: we find out which sectors are trading above their 50-day moving averages, or which ones are moving up through their 50-day moving averages, because those are the ones that are leading the market higher, and that's what we concentrate on. If a group goes under its 50-day moving average, we may sell that group. It's a very simple indicator, but it works very well. So the moral of this is, whereas many of the younger people in our business seem to gravitate toward the very fancy indicators— exponentially smoothed averages and all this—the old-timers are using some of the simpler ones. I have come to believe that the simpler indicators actually work better. They're simple, they're easily understood, and, surprisingly enough, not as many people look at them. Taking a Nasdaq market as an example, we did a study going back thirty to forty years comparing the buy-and-hold strategy to a strategy of buying it whenever it's selling above its 50-day moving average. The results were staggering. Just a simple little thing like that would have kept you out of most of the bear market of 2000. The 200-day moving average would be used in basically the same way: you hold the market, unless it's below its 200-day moving average. An economist would laugh at that, but it keeps you out of every single bear market. It's that simple. It's a discipline.

TABELL: The number of indicators grows over time. I was following more indicators at the end of my career than I had conceived possibly could exist. And the single factor that came into the picture was the computer. Think about a moving average. You kept up a moving average by counting back, punching the numbers into a calculator, and keeping up the results in a notebook. You should go sometime to the Market Technicians Association library and look at what people like Richard Russell and some of the old-timers were doing to keep up their indicators. You'll find it unbelievable. You couldn't keep more than a few dozen indicators; there were not enough hours in a day.

References

Alexander, S. 1961. Price movements in speculative markets: Trends or random walks. *Industrial Management Review* 2:7–26.

Alexander, S. 1964. Price movements in speculative markets: Trends or random walks, no. 2. In *The random character of stock market prices,* ed. P. Cootner. Cambridge, MA: MIT Press.

Allen, F., and R. Karjalainen. 1999. Using genetic algorithms to find technical trading rules. *Journal of Financial Economics* 51:245–271.

Blume, L., D. Easley, and M. O'Hara. 1994. Market statistics and technical analysis: The role of volume. *Journal of Finance* 49:153–181.

Brock, W., J. Lakonishok, and B. LeBaron. 1992. Simple technical trading rules and the stochastic properties of stock returns. *Journal of Finance* 47:1731–1764.

Brown, D., and R. Jennings. 1989. On technical analysis. *Review of Financial Studies* 2:527–551.

Chang, K., and C. Osler. 1994. Evaluating chart-based technical analysis: The head-and-shoulders pattern in foreign exchange markets. Working paper, Federal Reserve Bank of New York.

Clyde, W., and C. Osler. 1997. Charting: Chaos theory in disguise? *Journal of Futures Markets* 17:489–514.

Cootner, P. 1962. Stock prices: Random vs. systematic changes. *Industrial Management Review* 3 (Spring):24–45.

Cowles, A. 1960. A revision of previous conclusions regarding stock price behavior. *Econometrica* 28:909–915.

Cowles, A., and H. Jones. 1937. Some a posteriori probabilities in stock market action. *Econometrica* 5:280–294.

References

Fama, E. 1965. The behavior of stock market prices. *Journal of Business* 38: 34–105.

Fama, E., and M. Blume. 1966. Filter rules and stock market trading profits. *Journal of Business* 39:226–241.

Granger, C., and O. Morgenstern. 1963. Spectral analysis of New York stock market prices. *Kyklos* 16:1–27.

Grundy, B., and M. McNichols. 1989. Trade and revelation of information through prices and direct disclosure. *Review of Financial Studies* 2: 495–526.

Kendall, M. 1953. The analysis of economic time series–Part I: Prices. *Journal of the Royal Statistical Society* 96:11–25.

Larson, A. 1960. Measurement of a random process in futures prices. *Food Research Institute* 1:313–324.

Lo, A., and C. MacKinlay. 1988. Stock market prices do not follow random walks: Evidence from a simple specification test. *Review of Financial Studies* 1:41–66.

Lo, A., and C. MacKinlay. 1999. *A non-random walk down Wall Street*. Princeton, NJ: Princeton University Press.

Lo, A., H. Mamaysky, and J. Wang. 2000. Foundations of technical analysis: Computational algorithms. *Journal of Finance* 55:1705–1765.

Mandelbrot, B. 1963. The variation of certain speculative prices. *Journal of Business* 36:394–419.

Neely, C., P. Weller, and R. Dittmar. 1997. Is technical analysis in the foreign exchange market profitable? A genetic programming approach. *Journal of Financial and Quantitative Analysis* 32:405–426.

Neely, C., and P. Weller. 1999. Technical trading rules in the European monetary system. *Journal of International Money and Finance* 18 (3): 429–458.

Neftci, S. 1991. Naive trading rules in financial markets and Wiener-Kolmogorov prediction theory: A study of "technical analysis." *Journal of Business* 64:549–571.

Niederhoffer, V. 1997. *Education of a speculator*. New York: John Wiley & Sons.

Osborne, M. 1959. Brownian motion in the stock market. *Operations Research* 7:145–173.

References

Osborne, M. 1962. Periodic structure in the Brownian motion of stock prices. *Operations Research* 10:345–379.

Osler, C., and K. Chang. 1995. Head and shoulders: Not just a flaky pattern. Staff Report No. 4, Federal Reserve Bank of New York.

Pau, L. 1991. Technical analysis for portfolio trading by syntactic pattern recognition. *Journal of Economic Dynamics and Control* 15:715–730.

Pruitt, S., and R. White. 1988. The CRISMA trading system: Who says technical analysis can't beat the market? *Journal of Portfolio Management* 14:55–58.

Roberts, H. 1959. Stock-market "patterns" and financial analysis: Methodological suggestions. *Journal of Finance* 14:1–10.

Roberts, H. 1967. Statistical versus clinical prediction of the stock market. Unpublished manuscript, Center for Research in Security Prices, University of Chicago.

Taylor, S. 1994. Trading futures using a channel rule: A study of the predictive power of technical analysis with currency examples. *Journal of Futures Markets* 14:215–235.

Treynor, J., and R. Ferguson. 1985. In defense of technical analysis. *Journal of Finance* 40:757–773.

Tversky, A., and D. Kahneman. 1974. Judgment under uncertainty: Heuristics and biases. *Science* 185:1124–1131.

Weingarten, H. 1996. *Investing by the stars: Using astrology in the financial markets*. Boston, MA: Harvard Business School Press.

Working, H. 1960. Note on the correlation of first differences of averages in a random chain. *Econometrica* 28:916–918.

Index

Index

Index

Index

Index

Index

Janis, Irving, 78
"Japan vs. U.S." (Shaw), 95
Jiler, William, 67, 131
Johnson & Johnson, 21
Jones, H., xiv
Journal of Behavioral Finance, 75

Kahneman, D., xxii
Kaufman, Perry, 87, 148
Kidder Peabody, 1
Kindleberger, Charles, 127
Knight Equity Markets, 1
Krondratieff cycle, 179

Landfield, Sandy, 48–49
LBR Asset Management, 81
LBRGroup, 81
Leading Indicators for the 1990s (Moore), 147
LeBaron, Dean, 25, 27
Lindsay, George, 153
Lo, Andrew, xiv–xvi, xviii
London School of Economics, 75
Long-Term Capital Management, 158
losing money
    Acampora on, 126, 199–200
    Birinyi on, 19, 126, 200
    Deemer on, 126, 200
    Desmond on, 127, 200
    Dudack on, 127, 200–201
    Farrell on, 128, 201
    McAvity on, 128
    Murphy on, 128–129, 201–202
    Prechter on, 129, 202
    Raschke on, 129, 202
    Shaw on, 129, 202
    Weinstein on, 129–130
Louise Yamada Technical Research
    Advisors, 91
Lowry, L. M., 31–33
Lowry Research Corporation, 31
luck
    Birinyi on, 167
    Deemer on, 168
    Desmond on, 167, 168
    Dudack on, 168
    Farrell on, 169
    McAvity on, 169–170
    Murphy on, 170
    Prechter on, 170–171
    Raschke on, 171
    Shaw on, 171
    Tabell on, 171
    Weinstein on, 171
Lynch, Peter, 25

MacKinlay, C., xiv–xvi
Magazine of Wall Street, 100
Magee, John, 66, 67, 106, 108, 131–132, 217
Mahar, Maggie, 39
Maloney, Bill, 167
Mamaysky, H., xviii
Managed Futures Association, 81
Manhattan College, 47
Manhattan Fund, 25, 29
Manias, Panics, and Crashes (Kindleberger), 127
"Market Breadth" (Birinyi), 228
Market Cycles II (Birinyi), 229–230

Market Technicians Association (MTA), 67, 144
    annual award, 65, 92
    board of directors, 81, 99
    Chartered Market Technician (CMT)
        Program, xx–xxi, 224
    Educational Foundation, 143
    founders, 1, 3–4, 25, 47, 49, 91, 99
    library, 143, 248
    presidents, 1, 4, 25, 31, 39, 49, 76, 99
McAvity, Ian, xx
    on astrology, 174–176, 181
    on balancing career and personal life, 62–63
    bio, 57
    career advice from, 223–224
    on career start, 58
    on computers/technology, 159, 219–220
    Deliberations on World Markets, 57, 59, 60, 63
    on Elliott wave theory, 169, 170, 180–181, 189
    on emotions, 204
    on evolution of technical analysis, 159
    favorite patterns and indicators, 232
    on Gann analysis, 169, 181
    on innovative process, 60–61
    on intuition, 60
    on losing money, 128
    on luck, 169–170
    on mistakes, 59
    on outside influences on decision making,
        174–176, 181
    on personality traits for success, 223–224
    on random noise versus early signal
        detection, 60
    on reputation/perceptions of technical
        analysis, 123
    on sharing/teaching, 62
    on stress, 62
    on style of technical analysis, 57
    on talent/skill/success, 59–60, 189
    on tools of the trade, 59–61, 159, 169–170,
        180–181, 219–220, 232
    on validity of technical analysis, 115, 117–
        118, 123, 128, 131, 134–135
    on workday, 63
McLuhan, Marshall, 191
Merrill Lynch, 3, 4, 25, 47–51, 54–55, 65, 66, 71,
    76, 124, 128, 139, 182
MetaStock, 239
Midwood Securities, 39
Mississippi Review, 12
mistakes
    Acampora on his, 4, 5
    Birinyi on his, 15–16, 19–20
    Desmond on his, 35
    Dudack on her, 41, 42
    Farrell on his, 51, 52
    McAvity on his, 59
    Murphy on his, 68–70
    Prechter on his, 77–78
    Raschke on her, 85–86
    Tabell on his, 103
    Weinstein on his, 107–108
MIT, 17, 24, 75, 143, 144, 212
Mitchell Hutchins, 11
Money, 143
Money Game, The (Smith), 23
Moore, Geoffrey, 147
Moore, Steve, 83

Index

Index

Index

Index

Index

About the Authors

ANDREW W. LO is the Harris & Harris Group Professor of Finance at the MIT Sloan School of Management and the director of MIT's Laboratory for Financial Engineering. His previous books include *The Econometrics of Financial Markets, A Non-Random Walk Down Wall Street,* and *Hedge Funds: An Analytic Perspective.* He is also the founder and chief scientific officer of AlphaSimplex Group, LLC, a quantitative investment management company based in Cambridge, Massachusetts.

JASMINA HASANHODZIC is a research scientist at AlphaSimplex Group, LLC, where she develops quantitative investment strategies and benchmarks. She received her PhD from MIT's Department of Electrical Engineering and Computer Science. Her work has proposed new methods for automating technical analysis and replicating hedge fund betas and has appeared in the *Journal Of Investment Management* and Institutional Investor's *Alpha* magazine.

About Bloomberg

BLOOMBERG L.P., founded in 1981, is a global information services, news, and media company. Headquartered in New York, Bloomberg has sales and news operations worldwide.

Serving customers on six continents, Bloomberg, through its wholly-owned subsidiary Bloomberg Finance L.P., holds a unique position within the financial services industry by providing an unparalleled range of features in a single package known as the Bloomberg Professional® service. By addressing the demand for investment performance and efficiency through an exceptional combination of information, analytic, electronic trading, and straight-through-processing tools, Bloomberg has built a worldwide customer base of corporations, issuers, financial intermediaries, and institutional investors.

Bloomberg News, founded in 1990, provides stories and columns on business, general news, politics, and sports to leading newspapers and magazines throughout the world. Bloomberg Television, a 24-hour business and financial news network, is produced and distributed globally in seven languages. Bloomberg Radio is an international radio network anchored by flagship station Bloomberg 1130 (WBBR-AM) in New York.

In addition to the Bloomberg Press line of books, Bloomberg publishes *Bloomberg Markets* magazine.

To learn more about Bloomberg, call a sales representative at:

London: +44-20-7330-7500
New York: +1-212-318-2000
Tokyo: +81-3-3201-8900